Jesus Wars

*How Four Patriarchs, Three Queens, and
Two Emperors Decided What Christians
Would Believe for the Next 1,500 Years*

—

Philip Jenkins

HarperOne
An Imprint of HarperCollinsPublishers

HarperOne

Italics in scriptures are author's emphasis.

FIRST HARPERCOLLINS PAPERBACK EDITION PUBLISHED IN 2011
Designed by Level C

Library of Congress Cataloging-in-Publication Data is available.

ISBN 978–0–06–176893–4

11 12 13 14 15 RRD(H) 10 9 8 7 6 5 4 3

Contents

Acknowledgments

I want to thank all my friends and colleagues at Baylor University's Institute for Studies of Religion for their help and support, particularly Byron Johnson, Tommy Kidd and Rodney Stark.

At Penn State, special thanks to Christian Brady, Baruch Halpern, Paul Harvey, Kit Hume, Gary Knoppers, and Gregg Roeber.

Thanks to Roger Freet, my editor at HarperOne, and to Elyse Cheney, my agent.

Thanks above all others to my wife, Liz Jenkins.

Introduction

Who Do You Say That I Am?

Jesus once asked his disciples, "Who do people say that I am?" They answered that all sorts of stories were circulating—that he was a prophet, perhaps Elijah or John the Baptist come back to earth. "But," he asked, "Who do *you* say that I am?"[1] Over the past two thousand years, Christians have formulated many different answers to this question. Yes, most believe Jesus was a human being, but at the same time he was also God, one of the three persons of the Trinity. He was both God and man.

But when we have said that, we have raised more questions than we have answered, as the basic belief in Jesus Christ demands combining two utterly different categories of being. Such a transgression of boundaries puzzles and shocks believers of other faiths, especially strict monotheists such as Muslims and Jews. But even those Christians who accept the basic concept probably could not explain it with anything like the precision demanded by early church councils. By those rigorous standards, virtually all modern nonspecialists (including many clergy) would soon lapse into grave heresy.[2]

The Bible is anything but clear on the relationship between Christ's human and divine natures, and arguably, it is just not possible to reconcile its various statements on this matter. In the New Testament, Jesus says quite explicitly that he is identical with God: "I and the Father are one," he declares. "Anyone who has seen me has seen the Father."[3] John's gospel reports Jesus' telling the crowd, "You are from below; I am from above: you are of this world; I am not of this world." He goes on, "Before Abraham was, I am." His listeners are appalled, and not just because this seems to be an outrageous boast of extreme old age. The words that Jesus uses for "I am"—in Greek, *ego eimi*—recall the declaration that God made to Moses from the burning bush. We might better translate it as I AM. Jesus appears to be saying that he is the same eternal God who brought Israel out of Egypt, not to mention creating the world. Not surprisingly, the crowd tries to stone him for blasphemy. For later readers of the Gospels, then, Father and Son must be one and the same.[4]

But just as we are absorbing that amazing fact, we read on to find Jesus stating that he is distinct from God the Father. "The Father is greater than I," he says. When Jesus foretells the end of the world, he admits that the exact timing is unknown either to the Son or to the angels, and only the Father knows precisely. If the Son knows less than the Father, the two must be different.[5]

What does it mean to say that Christ was at once God and man? Certainly the Jesus of the Gospels seems utterly human—he bleeds, he loves, he gets angry, he dies in grotesque agony. Yet somehow we have to reconcile that fact with the doctrine of the Incarnation. The opening words of the gospel of John identify Christ with the Logos, God's Reason or creative Word:

In the beginning was the Word [*Logos*], and the Word was with God, and the Word was God. The same was in the beginning with God. . . . And the Word became flesh, and dwelt among us.[6]

The Word was made flesh, God became man. But how does that Word relate to the man called Jesus? What does the letter to the Colossians mean when it proclaims that all the fullness of God lives in Christ, in bodily form?[7]

Problems and paradoxes abound. When Jesus arrived in Bethany to find that his friend Lazarus has died, he mourned: he groaned in the spirit, we are told, and he was troubled. Jesus suffered all-too-human grief, and, as is reported in one of the most famous verses of the whole Bible, "Jesus wept."[8] Incidentally, the source of that verse is John's gospel, the same text that reports Jesus' speaking the hair-raising language of I AM. But think that text through. Jesus wept, so Christ the anointed wept—and, therefore, are we to believe that God, the creator and source of all being, really wept? More sensationally, how, in fact, had Christ suffered on the cross—had *God* really died? These paradoxes were not concocted by later Christian theologians, working long after the supposedly straightforward beliefs of the apostolic age. As early as 110, while the New Testament was still under construction, the great martyr-bishop Ignatius of Antioch proclaimed Christ as "God come in the flesh." Ignatius addressed believers, whose hearts were kindled in "the blood of God." God weeping is one thing, but *bleeding*? Even faithful Catholics who accept that the communion wafer is Corpus Christi, the Body of Christ, dare not make the leap that would proclaim it the Body of God. God and Christ are different.[9]

Through the first four centuries of Christianity, believers tried many ways of resolving these problems of Scripture and logic. Different churches—leading thinkers and scholars—varied in the stress they placed on Jesus' humanity or his divinity, and without exercising too much ingenuity or text twisting, they found biblical passages that supported all these opinions.[10] Some early Christians thought that Christ was so possessed by Godhood that his human nature was eclipsed. In that sense, we should think of Christ as a manifestation of God walking the earth, clothed in human form as a convenient disguise. The Word took on flesh as I might put on an overcoat. So, are we to believe that Christ's sufferings, all the tears and blood, were a kind of playacting or illusion? Others saw Jesus as a great man overwhelmed by God-consciousness. Somehow, the Spirit of God had descended on him, with his baptism in the Jordan as the likely moment of transformation—but the two natures always remained separate. Christ, from that perspective, remained chiefly human. Some thought the two natures were merged, indissolubly and eternally; others thought the connection was only partial or temporary.

So was Jesus a Man-bearing God, or a God-bearing man? Between those extreme poles lay any number of other answers, which competed furiously through the first Christian centuries. By 400, most Christians agreed that Jesus Christ was in some sense divine, and that he had both a human nature (Greek, *physis*) and a divine nature. But that belief allowed for a wide variety of interpretations, and if events had developed differently—if great councils had decided other than they actually did—any one of these various approaches might have established itself as orthodoxy. In the context of the time, cultural and political pressures were pushing strongly toward the idea of Christ-as-God, so that only with real difficulty could the memory of the human Jesus be maintained. Historically, it is very remarkable that mainstream orthodoxy came out so strongly in favor of asserting Christ's full humanity.

And yet it did just that. When most modern churches explain their understanding of Christ's identity—their Christology—they turn to a common body of ready-made interpretations, an ancient collection of texts laid down in the fifth century. At a great council held in 451 at Chalcedon (near modern Istanbul), the church formulated the statement that eventually became the official theology of the Roman Empire. This acknowledges Christ in two natures, which joined together in one person. Two natures existed, "without confusion, without change, without division, without separation; the distinction of natures being in no way annulled by the union, but rather the characteristics of each nature being preserved and coming together to form one person."[11]

We cannot speak of Christ without declaring his full human nature, which was not even slightly diluted or abolished by the presence of divinity. That *Chalcedonian* definition today stands as the official formula for the vast majority of Christians, whether they are Protestant, Catholic, or Orthodox—although how many of those believers could explain the definition clearly is open to debate. But as we are told, Chalcedon settled any controversy about the identity of Christ, so that henceforward any troublesome passages in the Bible or early tradition had to be read in the spirit of those powerful words. For over 1,500 years now, Chalcedon has provided the answer to Jesus' great question.

But Chalcedon was not the only possible solution, nor was it an obvious or, perhaps, a logical one. Only the political victory of Chalcedon's supporters allowed that council's ideas to become the inevitable lens through which later generations interpret the Christian message. It remains quite possible to read the New Testament and find very different Christologies, which by definition arose from churches very close to Jesus' time, and to his thought world. In particular, we easily find passages that suggest that the man Jesus achieved Godhood at a specific moment during his life, or indeed after his earthly death.

In political terms, the most important critics of Chalcedon were those who stressed Christ's one divine nature, and from the Greek words for "one nature," we call them *Monophysites*. Not only were Monophysites numerous and influential, but they dominated much of the Christian world and the Roman Empire long after Chalcedon had done its work, and they were only defeated after decades of bloody struggle. Centuries after Chalcedon, Monophysites continued to prevail in the most ancient regions of Christianity, such as Syria, Palestine, and Egypt. The heirs of the very oldest churches, the ones with the most direct and authentic ties to the apostolic age, found their distinctive interpretation of Christ ruled as heretical. Pedigree counted for little in these struggles.

Each side persecuted its rivals when it had the opportunity to do so, and tens of thousands—at least—perished. Christ's nature was a cause for which people were prepared to kill and to die, to persecute or to suffer martyrdom. Modern Christians rarely feel much sympathy for either side in such bygone religious wars. Did the issues at stake really matter enough to justify bloodshed? Yet obviously, people at the time had no such qualms and cared passionately about

how believers were supposed to understand the Christ they worshipped. Failing to understand Christ's natures properly made nonsense of everything Christians treasured: the content of salvation
and redemption, the character of liturgy and Eucharist, the figure
of the Virgin Mary. Each side had its absolute truth, faith in which
was essential to salvation.

Horror stories about Christian violence abound in other eras,
with the Crusades and Inquisition as prime exhibits; but the intra-
Christian violence of the fifth- and sixth-century debates was on a
far larger and more systematic scale than anything produced by the
Inquisition and occurred at a much earlier stage of church history.
When Edward Gibbon wrote his classic account of the *Decline and
Fall of the Roman Empire,* he reported countless examples of Christian violence and fanaticism. This is his account of the immediate
aftermath of Chalcedon:

> Jerusalem was occupied by an army of [Monophysite] monks;
> in the name of the one incarnate Nature, they pillaged, they
> burnt, they murdered; the sepulchre of Christ was defiled with
> blood. . . . On the third day before the festival of Easter, the
> [Alexandrian] patriarch was besieged in the cathedral, and
> murdered in the baptistery. The remains of his mangled corpse
> were delivered to the flames, and his ashes to the wind; and the
> deed was inspired by the vision of a pretended angel. . . . This
> deadly superstition was inflamed, on either side, by the princi-
> ple and the practice of retaliation: in the pursuit of a meta-
> physical quarrel, many thousands were slain.[12]

Chalcedonians behaved at least as badly in their campaigns to enforce their particular orthodoxy. In the eastern city of Amida, a
Chalcedonian bishop dragooned dissidents, to the point of burning
them alive. His most diabolical scheme involving taking lepers,
"hands festering and dripping with blood and pus," and billeting
them on the Monophysite faithful until they saw reason.[13]

Even the Eucharist became a vital component of religious terror. Throughout the long religious wars, people were regularly (and frequently) reading others out of the church, declaring formal anathemas, and the sign for this was admitting or not admitting people to communion. In extreme episodes, communion was enforced by physical violence, so that the Eucharist, which is based upon ideas of self-giving and self-sacrifice, became an instrument of oppression. A sixth-century historian records how the forces of Constantinople's Chalcedonian patriarch struck at Monophysite religious houses in the capital. Furnished with supplies of consecrated bread, the patriarch's clergy were armed and dangerous. They "dragged and pulled [the nuns] by main force to make them receive the communion at their hands. And they all fled like birds before the hawk, and cowered down in corners, wailing and saying, 'We cannot communicate with the synod of Chalcedon, which divides Christ our God into two Natures after the union, and teaches a Quaternity instead of the Holy Trinity.'" But their protests were useless. "They were dragged up to communicate; and when they held their hands above their heads, in spite of their screams their hands were seized, and they were dragged along, uttering shrieks of lamentation, and sobs, and loud cries, and struggling to escape. And so the sacrament was thrust by force into the mouths of some, in spite of their screams, while others threw themselves on their faces upon the ground, and cursed every one who required them to communicate by force."[14] They might take the Eucharist kicking and screaming—literally—but once they had eaten, they were officially in communion with Chalcedon and with the church that preached that doctrine.

Battles over Christ's nature raged far beyond the confines of the church itself, and vicious civil wars still reverberated two hundred years after Chalcedon. So vital did this question appear, so central to the character of faith and the future of Christianity, that partisans on either side were prepared to divide and weaken the church and empire and risk revolutions and civil wars. In the long term, these schisms led directly to the collapse of Roman power in the eastern world, to the rise of Islam, and to the destruction of Christianity through much of Asia and Africa. Apart from Islam, the greatest winner in the conflict was European Christianity, or rather the fact that Christianity, for better or worse, found its firmest bastion in Europe. So much of the religious character of the world we know was shaped by this conflict over the nature of Christ. The mainstream church kept its belief that Jesus was fully human—but at the cost of losing half the world.

If religion shaped the political world, then politics forged the character of religion. When we look at what became the church's orthodoxy, so many of those core beliefs gained the status they did as a result of what appears to be historical accident, of the workings of raw chance. In the controversies of the fifth and sixth centuries, the outcome was shaped not by obviously religious dimensions but by factors that seem quite extraneous. This was not a case of one side producing better arguments in its cause, of a deeper familiarity with Scripture or patristic texts: all sides had excellent justifications for their positions. All, equally, produced men and women who practiced heroic asceticism and who demonstrated obvious sanctity. What mattered were the interests and obsessions of rival emperors and queens, the role of competing ecclesiastical princes and their churches, and the empire's military successes or failures against particular barbarian nations. To oversimplify, the fate of Christian doctrine was deeply influenced by just how well or badly the empire was doing fighting Attila the Hun.

In the long term, the christological debate was settled by one straightforward issue: which side gained and held supremacy within the Christian Roman Empire and was therefore able to establish its particular view as orthodoxy. And that was a political matter, shaped by geographical accident and military success. Just because one view became orthodoxy does not mean that it was always and inevitably destined to do so: the Roman Church became right because it survived. It was all mere chance and accident—unless, of course, we follow a tradition common to Christians, Jews, and Muslims of seeing God's hand in the apparently shapeless course of worldly history.

However remote these conflicts may appear, they involved all the vital themes that would so often rend the Christian world in later eras, from the Reformation through the Victorian conflicts between faith and learning, and on to our own day. Great councils like Chalcedon were debating such core issues as the quest for authority in religion, the relationship between church and state, the proper ways of reading and interpreting Scripture, the ethics and conduct demanded of Christians, and the means of salvation.

Pivotal to these ancient Jesus Wars were the four great questions that, to different degrees, have shaped all subsequent debates within Christianity. Foremost is the deceptively simple question posed by Jesus himself: "Who do you say that I am?" And building on this are the three follow-ups: What is the church? By what authority do you do this? And, what must I do to be saved? More perhaps than in any subsequent conflict within Christianity, these debates over Christ's nature involved the most fundamental realities of faith and practice.

Terms and Definitions

In approaching the conflicts that rent the Christian world in the fifth century, we should from the start be familiar with the basic terms—and I should explain why I am cautious about using some words.

Much of the religious conflict involved *Monophysite* opposition to what became the empire's official theology, but the word raises some problems. Some enemies of Chalcedon were true Monophysites in believing Christ had a single divine nature, but others held a more moderate position. While they agreed that the incarnate Christ had one nature, they held that this was made up of both divine and human components. The technical name for this group is *Miaphysites*, and their views were once widespread. Miaphysite bodies today include Egypt's great Coptic Church, and the so-called Oriental Orthodox churches of Syria, Ethiopia, and Armenia. These churches reject charges that they are Monophysite, although that is the label by which most historians know them.

At least in terms of their technical theology, Chalcedonians and Miaphysites can find some common ground, and the modern heirs of both schools have reached broad agreement on their theological statements. But matters were very different during the savage religious struggles of the fifth and sixth centuries, when differences were much more extreme, and when pure Monophysite ideas really were commonplace. The popularity of the Monophysite label also owes something to rhetorical practice, as each side framed the debate in ways that made its enemies look as bizarre and outrageous as possible. Today, for instance, an American conservative might condemn a liberal as a communist; the liberal in turn might call his conservative foe a fascist. In ancient times, Chalcedonians insultingly called their Miaphysite opponents "Monophysites," and that name has stuck.

Even historians who thoroughly understand the theological issues still refer to the anti-Chalcedonian opposition in Egypt, Syria, and elsewhere as Monophysite, although they recognize that this term is less than accurate. The great W. H. C. Frend, one of the finest historians who studied that era, published a valuable study of *The Rise of the Monophysite Movement.* In this book, I have tried to avoid the term *Miaphysite* because it is unknown outside the realm of academic theology. Following Frend's precedent, I use *Monophysite,* especially for the distinct churches that emerged in the sixth century. But as I suggest here, I am aware of the limitations.

The Chalcedonians also pose problems of description. When historians look back at that era, they sometimes describe those views as *Orthodox,* but that term is slanted. Literally, it means "right teaching," and, of course, everyone believes that his or her particular views are correct. The main reason we call these opinions orthodox is that they were held by the Roman Church and the papacy, and over time, that church survived the political disasters that overwhelmed other once-great centers like Antioch and Alexandria. In the great debates over Christ's nature, anti-Chalcedonians also called themselves Orthodox, and if matters had worked out differently, perhaps that faction would have won out. At least in their own minds, everyone is always "orthodox." English bishop William Warburton explained the difference frankly: orthodoxy is my doxy; heterodoxy is another man's doxy.

So what word can we use? *Chalcedonian* is time-specific: we can't really use it for people who held those views before Chalcedon. With some reluctance, then, I will on occasion use the word *Orthodox* or *Orthodox/Catholic* as the counterpart of Monophysite. In order not to burden the text with distracting quotation marks and phrases like *so-called*, I will use these terms without the caveats and qualifications they deserve.

Hoping to avoid simple retroactive judgments, I will also, throughout this book, use the terms *One Nature* and *Two Nature* belief as statements of broad religious orientation. In doing this, I hope to describe where people stood in terms of the conflicts of the day without necessarily pinning them down to particular factions or movements.

Less critical, but still important, is the language we use for the great churches that dominated the Christian world and the popes and patriarchs who headed them. From earliest times, church leaders became known as bishops, and some gained more exalted titles. The bishop of Rome became the pope, but that title could also be used for other bishops, especially the head of the Alexandrian church. In this book, the word *pope* used without further qualification refers to the pope of Rome.

From the end of the fifth century, the church within the Roman Empire was organized around five great patriarchates, namely Rome, Constantinople, Alexandria, Antioch, and Jerusalem. Although this structure was formalized only in 451, the idea of great sees having patriarchal authority dates back at least to the late fourth century. With a little anachronism, I will on occasion use the word *patriarch* to refer to the bishops who held authority under this earlier arrangement.

Since all the events described in this book occurred in the Christian Era, I have not felt the need to specify that they occurred "A.D." or "C.E." Thus I refer to the year 431, rather than A.D. 431

The Near Eastern Christian World

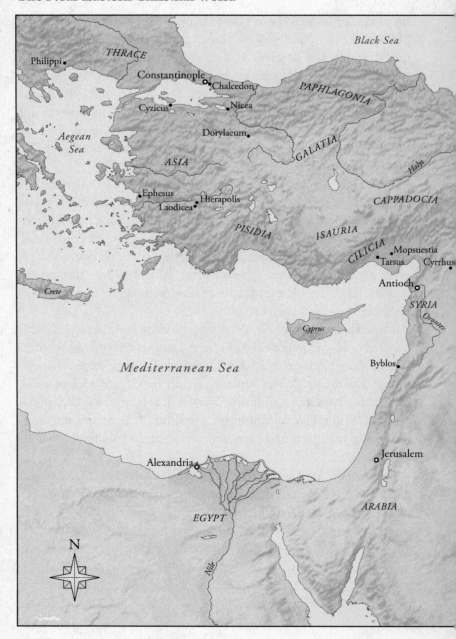

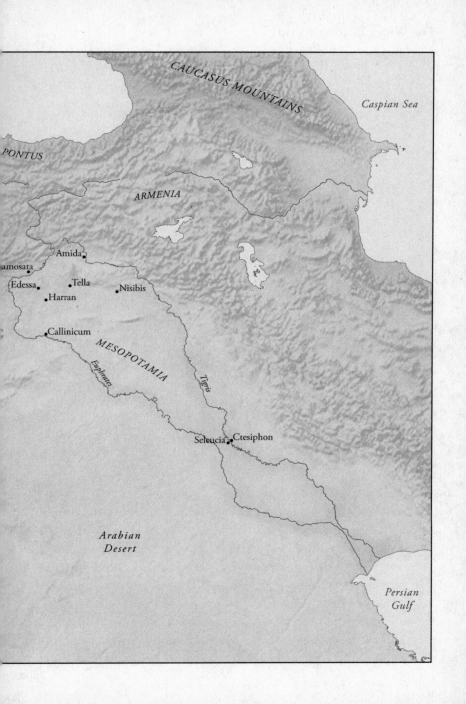

The Wider Roman World

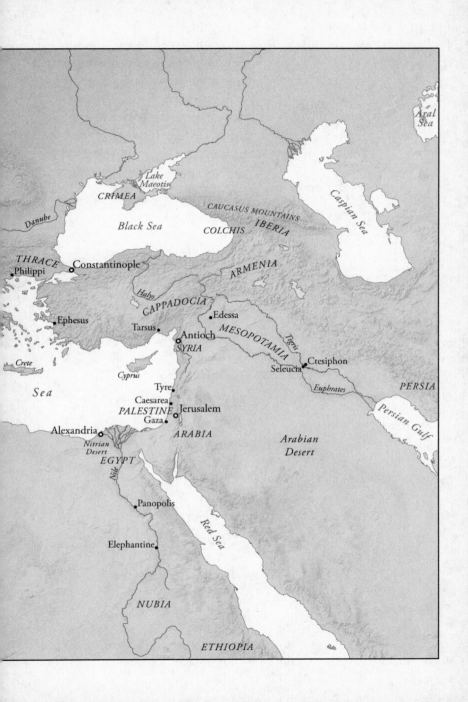

1

The Heart of the Matter

May those who divide Christ be divided with the sword, may they be hewn in pieces, may they be burned alive!
Second Council of Ephesus, 449

In 449, the leading Fathers of the Christian church met in Ephesus, in Asia Minor, to debate pressing theological issues. At a critical moment, a band of monks and soldiers took control of the meeting hall, forcing bishops to sign a blank paper on which the winning side later filled in its own favored statement. The document targeted the patriarch of Constantinople, Flavian, one of the three or four greatest clerics in the Christian world. Yelling "Slaughter him!" a mob of monks attacked Flavian, beating him so badly that he died a few days later. So outrageous was the intimidation that the ultimate winners in the conflict invalidated this whole council. They repudiated it as a *Latrocinium*—loosely, a Gangster Synod.[1]

From later history, we know of many episodes when Christians would resort to violence, especially against members of other faiths, but in this instance, the different sides agreed on so much. Both factions accepted the same Scriptures and the same view of the church and the hierarchy, and both agreed that Jesus Christ was God incarnate, the Second Person of the Holy Trinity. Where they disagreed so violently was over the nature of Christ. Flavian's enemies, and their monkish militia, believed that Christ existed in a single nature in which the divine dominated. They felt that by failing to proclaim this truth, by advocating a Christ in Two Natures, Flavian's party had betrayed the core of Christianity. Literally, they thought, Flavian had divided Christ.[2]

From a modern point of view, we are baffled to see such extraordinary violence unleashed over what might appear to be a trivial philosophical row. Surely, we might think, these debates involved overfine distinctions quite as trivial as the proverbial disputes over the number of angels who could sit on the head of a pin. Just what could have caused such bitter hatred? In fact, the conflict involves a paradox that is quite central to the Christian faith. Christians must believe that God is wholly human and wholly divine, but it is easy for a believer to stray too far in one direction or the other. Either we might think of Christ purely as God, in which case he is no longer human, has no share in our human experience, and becomes a divinity in the sky like Zeus or Thor; or else, in contrast, we focus so much on his humanity that we underplay the divine element and deny the Incarnation. We would preach a Christ of two natures and two minds, literally a schizophrenic being. According to his enemies—unfairly and inaccurately—that was Flavian's sin, and brutal violence was the only appropriate response to his gross insult to the Son of God.

The violence was unforgivable, and so were all the acts of persecution and forced conformity. But in one sense, ancient Christians were exactly right to be so passionate about their causes, if not the means by which they pursued them. Far from being philosophical niceties, the central themes in the religious debates really were critical to the definition of Christianity and to the ways in which the faith would develop over the coming centuries. The Christ controversies did, and do, have immense consequences, for culture and politics as much as for religion.[3]

Jesus Wars

In the early centuries of Christianity, very strong forces were pulling Christ Godward and heavenward. Across the religious spectrum, early prophets and founders usually are exalted over time. In his last words, the Buddha commanded his followers to rely on no external savior, but within centuries, Buddha had himself become a divine transworldly being whose worldly relics were cherished and all but worshipped in their own right. Within Christianity, too, the persistent temptation has always been to make Christ a divine figure free of any human element. Whenever Christianity has been a confident faith that dominated empires, believers have commonly imagined a fearsome heavenly judge or cosmic ruler, the *pantokrator* or All-Ruler who glared down from the dome of a mighty basilica and whose human status was hard to accept.

In more recent times, fictional portrayals of a too-human Christ ignite furious responses from those reluctant to imagine a figure too involved in worldly concerns. In the 1980s, the image of a Jesus married with a family stirred worldwide cries of blasphemy against the film *The Last Temptation of Christ*. So many bristled at any suggestion that the founder of the faith might have experienced any human passions or weaknesses, any doubts or qualms about his mission. Human sexuality apparently represents a stain that can in no way be associated with a purely divine being. Christ moves among humanity like a divine tourist.[4]

And yet, through the centuries, other Christians have fought to preserve the human face of Jesus, placing him firmly on earthly soil and in human society. Partly, the idea arises from the common human need for an accessible divinity, a figure who shares our experience and can hear our prayers. Even the societies that pushed

Christ so far from human reach created a substitute in the form of the loving Mary, virgin and mother. But the concept of a human Jesus is vividly present in the New Testament. Believers have never forgotten the image of the Galilean who suffered physical agony, who knew doubt and temptation, who was the brother and exemplar of suffering humans. They knew that Jesus wept.[5]

Over the last two thousand years, Christians have repeatedly struggled to resolve this perpetual tension between Christologies from above and from below, yet never was the debate more central to Christianity than during the councils of the fifth century. For some decades it seemed almost inevitable that the church might all but abandon its belief in the human nature of Christ and describe him overwhelmingly as a divine being.[6]

The main outline of the story is quickly told. Underlying all the intellectual debates were profound rivalries between the church's great patriarchates, with Alexandria on the one hand and Antioch on the other, and with Constantinople as the primary battlefield. Antioch stressed the reality of Christ's human nature; Alexandria fought any statement that would separate human and divine. During the 420s, the monk Nestorius brought his Antiochene teachings with him when he was appointed archbishop of Constantinople, and disaster followed. At the First Council of Ephesus in 431, Nestorius was condemned for teaching a doctrine of Two Natures, of separating the divine and human.[7] (See appendix to this chapter: The Church's General Councils.)

Once Nestorius was crushed, believers in One Nature pushed ever harder to establish their teachings, supported by the juggernaut power of the patriarchs of Alexandria. In 449, the One Nature party managed an effective coup at the Second Council of Ephesus—the Gangster Synod—proclaiming their own doctrine and all but breaking links with the papacy in Rome. Over the next two years, the Orthodox/Catholic made a dazzling comeback. They organized around one text above all, the letter of Pope Leo that became known as the Tome. Their political resurrection culminated in the Council of Chalcedon in 451, which accepted the Tome as the definitive guide to Christology. Very gradually—over the next century or so—Chalcedon became the touchstone of imperial orthodoxy.[8]

Some decades after the council, a writer in the Latin West summarized Chalcedon's conclusions in a series of theological propositions, with an unnerving conclusion. After listing Chalcedon's edicts in agonizing detail, the so-called Athanasian Creed (which actually had nothing to do with the venerated saint Athanasius) proclaims that "This is the catholic faith, which, except a man believe faithfully, he cannot be saved." Quite literally, your eternal salvation depends on holding a precisely correct faith, which meant the definition laid down in 451.[9] (See Table 1.)

TABLE 1
THE ATHANASIAN CREED

Furthermore, it is necessary to everlasting salvation that he also believe rightly the incarnation of our Lord Jesus Christ.

For the right faith is that we believe and confess that our Lord Jesus Christ, the Son of God, is God and man.

God of the substance of the Father, begotten before the worlds; and man of substance of His mother, born in the world.

Perfect God and perfect man, of a reasonable soul and human flesh subsisting.

Equal to the Father as touching His Godhead, and inferior to the Father as touching His manhood.

Who, although He is God and man, yet He is not two, but one Christ.

One, not by conversion of the Godhead into flesh, but by taking of that manhood into God.

One altogether, not by confusion of substance, but by unity of person.

> For as the reasonable soul and flesh is one man, so God
> and man is one Christ;
>   . . . This is the catholic faith, which, except a man believe
> faithfully, he cannot be saved.

SOURCE: J. N. D. Kelly, *The Athanasian Creed* (New York: Harper and Row, 1964).

Between them, First Ephesus and Chalcedon shaped Christian theology right up to the present day, teaching that no complete vision of Christ could omit either the divine or human aspects. Christ did not just come *from* two natures; he existed *in* two natures. As Pope Leo wrote, it was clearly human to be hungry and thirsty, to be weary, and to sleep; but Christ was just as evidently divine when he fed the five thousand, walked on the water, and ordered the storm to cease. The human Jesus mourned his friend Lazarus; the divine Christ spoke words that raised that same friend from the dead. Leo concluded, "For His manhood, which is less than the Father, comes from our side: His Godhead, which is equal to the Father, comes from the Father." We are so used to the triumph of Chalcedon that the phrasing of the Tome seems like a straightforward and even anodyne expression of Christian belief. Yet for all its apparent striving to be fair and balanced, the Tome met fierce opposition throughout the oldest centers of Christian faith.[10]

What If God Was One of Us?

The battle of the Natures shapes one's fundamental views of the world. Someone who thinks of Christ as wholly divine is hard-pressed to see any goodness in the material world and tends to set a wholly good spiritual world against a totally depraved material creation. In contrast, those who believe in a human Christ are more likely to accept the potential goodness of the material world. Although (they hold) that world may now be plunged into sin, then at least it can be redeemed. Belief in the Incarnation leads to a sacramental vision. For Leo, denying the Two Natures led to even worse theological errors: "their blindness leads them into such an abyss that they have no sure footing in the reality either of the Lord's Passion or His Resurrection. Both are discredited in the Savior, if our fleshly nature is not believed in Him." Material acts redeemed a material world.[11]

Ultimately, the fifth-century controversies focused on the issue of atonement, and without that idea, Christianity would have developed quite differently. Christian believers have long argued over the meaning of Christ's death, but whatever their disagreements, most churches preach that Christ shared humanity, and that fact allowed him to redeem humanity through his sacrificial death. In order for redemptive doctrine to make any sense, Christ would have to be fully human, in the sense of having a body made of flesh, but also of having a human will and mind. As church father Gregory Nazianzus wrote, "If anyone has put his trust in Christ as a Man without a human mind, *he* is really bereft of mind, and quite unworthy of salvation. For that which Christ has not assumed, He has not healed."[12]

Yet this association with humanity was precisely what troubled the believers in One Nature. Unless Christ were fully divine, they argued, his death could not save us. Christ, moreover, had come to offer not just salvation, but deification, which remains a potent idea in some Eastern churches, including the Orthodox. As the great Alexandrian bishop Athanasius declared in the fourth century, the Son of God became man so that we might become God, and only a truly divine Christ could offer his followers that divinity. That was a heady promise.[13]

The quality of Christ's humanity also affected the ethical lessons that believers took from his life and suffering. At one extreme, a One Nature believer like Apollinarius presented Christ as a kind of automaton controlled by a Logos from above, so that he could not in any real sense face temptation: he could not wrestle with moral dilemmas or overcome the seductions of evil. *Of course*, implies

Apollinarius, God can withstand temptation and resist sin, but what good is that to us? If Apollinarius was right, we can respond only by worshipping the divine superhero who came to rescue us from the dark forces holding the world in bondage. But authentic Two Nature adherents, like the third-century Christian Paul of Samosata, had a very different message. They taught that the man Jesus became Christ when the Spirit of God descended on him, so that the purity and sanctity of his life was a major factor in letting him become divine. Paul taught that ordinary believers could and must emulate Jesus.[14]

This ethical component was strongly marked in theologians of the school of Antioch, who would be on the front lines of the Jesus Wars. Although they rejected any crude ideas of the separation of the natures, they fought to retain the notion of a human will in Christ. In their view, Christ actively resisted temptations and did good until he atoned for sin both through his death and by the example of his good works. By so doing, he showed ordinary people the way of salvation and offered the potential for human nature to be raised to the level of the divine. To use the title of one of the most famous Christian texts ever written, the *Imitation of Christ* is not just possible but demanded. When modern liberal theologians protest that the exalted divine image of Jesus places his ethical teachings beyond attainable reach, they are reviving one of the oldest debates in Christendom.[15]

Theology apart, the debates had powerful outcomes for what we term the real world—although theologians of the time would undoubtedly have argued that such a title could only be applied to the heavenly realm and not this transient life. The memory of a human Jesus has throughout Western history repeatedly driven men and women to imitate him, through social activism and political reform, not to mention the mystical quest and the arts. In recent times, liberation theologies have portrayed a Jesus who so utterly empties himself of his divine privileges and honor that he walks the earth as one of the very poorest and most marginalized. He is at once an exemplar for the poor and their leader in struggles for justice. As Charles Sheldon famously argued in his 1897 novel of sweeping urban reform, *In His Steps*, Christians must always ask, "What would Jesus do?" Of course, myriad blunders in the history of the churches prove they have not always asked that question, or produced an appropriate answer. But at least the aspiration never died.

To raise another ethical issue, how do we know how much weight to attach to the words of Christ recorded in the New Testament? Just who do we hear speaking? Assume for the sake of argument that the scriptural text accurately records Jesus' sayings, which, of course, it may not always do. When Jesus tells a parable or utters a pronouncement, do those words come directly and literally from the mind of God, or are they the thoughts of an individual bound by the constraints of his time and place? To take a specific example, if Jesus really was speaking with divine authority, then believers need to take very seriously the radical division that he proclaims between light and darkness, together with a literal belief in the devil and demons. To assert Christ's humanity is not to undervalue or ignore his teachings, but it must make later believers think more carefully about the authority those words carry and how they can be applied to modern circumstances.

Christ the divine, or Christ as divine-and-human? The best way of understanding the two approaches is to think what each side thought it would lose if its opponents triumphed. For each, the central idea of the faith was the title Emmanuel, *God with us*. Each in its way feared any theology that would impair human access to the fullness of the divine, but each viewed the solution in quite different ways. For Antiochenes, a One Nature creed that made Christ thoroughly divine uprooted him from humanity and removed him from any sense of human identification. Such a statement also raised the monstrous absurdity of God the Creator suffering and dying, of being "passible," in theological terms. One Nature believers, in contrast, wanted to guarantee the intimate solidarity linking God to humanity. This linkage must be a total union, rather than just a conjunction or association. They feared weakening the image of Christ so that he became anything less than a manifestation of God within us. Aspiring to the same goal, the two sides chose very different roads.[16]

Living Christ

In other ways, too, preserving the human aspects of Christ prevented the divine withdrawing to an alien and unimaginable supernatural realm. If Christ was the human Jesus, he was born in a specific time and place and was a Jew. Even Leo, who so despised Jews and Judaism, stressed that Jesus was absolutely rooted in his Hebrew ancestry and in the world of the Old Testament. The genealogies quoted in the Gospels, those long lists of begats that send modern readers to sleep, decisively proclaimed Christ's human status. Chalcedon wrecks any attempt to de-Judaize Jesus.

Each side, likewise, offered a different way of reading the Bible. Alexandrians worked from a Greek philosophical tradition and used the scriptural text to illustrate their conclusions. Every word and line of the Bible became an allegory bearing a spiritual truth, which might or might not have any connection with actual historical events in first-century Palestine. Nestorius, in contrast, had his roots in Antioch, which read the scriptural text in terms of historical events, to be expounded and commented upon. When you read the Gospels in that way, it is hard to avoid the idea of a human Christ, the man who wept. The definitions of Chalcedon reasserted the real rather than symbolic nature of biblical truth.[17]

Just as central to the story is the struggle to preserve the feminine face of the divine. Driving much of the fifth-century controversy was the astonishing rise of the cult of the Virgin Mary and the boast that she was literally Mother of God. Pagans mocked these claims to create a new goddess, but many Christians, too, were offended. Some thought that the concept of Mother of God was absurd—as Nestorius asked, shockingly, was God really present in the world as a two-month-old infant?—while others rejected any attempt to undercut the deity of Christ at any stage of his earthly life. On this point at least, One Nature believers agreed wholeheartedly with the Orthodox/Catholic church, and Marian devotions flourished. Egyptians especially had a potent devotion to the Mother of God, who is the subject of a magnificent tradition in early art, and the Coptic Monophysite church has had a long love affair with Mary.[18]

Stressing the human Jesus also permitted the development and growth of Christian visual art, and thereby of much of Western culture. We easily forget just what an extraordinary phenomenon this visual tradition was. Monotheistic religions are often deeply suspicious of visual art, whether of sacred figures or of the human form as such. Partly, this reflects a fear of idolatry, but it also shows reluctance even to attempt to reproduce holy forms. Although that restraint is not universal—at various times in history, both devout Muslims and Jews happily painted human beings—it is widespread. Christianity could certainly have followed a similar path, and various movements through the centuries have practiced iconoclasm, the smashing of images. Yet Christian visual art survived, with the overwhelmingly rich depictions of Christ's humanity, all the images of the child with his mother, of the teacher, and of the crucified victim.

Losing Half the World

The way these councils are remembered tells us a great deal about how Christian history is written and, by extension, the history of other great causes or movements. We often hear the complaint that winners write history, but the situation is in fact worse than that. In practice, historians write retroactively from the point of view of those who would win at some later point, even if that victory was nowhere in sight at the time they are describing. That is certainly what happens when we identify Chalcedon as the final triumph of orthodoxy.[19]

Accounts of early Christianity make the year 451 a decisive break, a vital transition from the ancient origins of the faith to its medieval millennium. But such an account ignores the century or so after Chalcedon when that particular school of thought might easily have been reversed. Between 451 and the 540s, Chalcedonians and their enemies rose and fell in their power at the Roman court, and there were periods of several decades when Monophysites controlled not just the empire but most of the main bishoprics and patriarchates. Focusing on 451 misses the long centuries after Chalcedon had secured recognition as the empire's official creed, but when in many lands—in Egypt, Syria, and Palestine—Chalcedonians were at best a suspect minority. Debates over the nature(s) of Christ were still vividly active in 650 or 800. And in much of the world, those battles ended in crushing victory for Chalcedon's foes. The result wasn't even close.

Despite the theological slogans of the time, Christ was not divided; but the Christian world certainly was, irreparably. Now, Christian divisions as such were not new. At least since the apostles left Jerusalem, at no point in Christian history has one single church plausibly claimed the loyalty of all believers to the exclusion of rival institutions. In the mid-fourth century, perhaps half of all Christians belonged to some group that the Great Church regarded as heretical or schismatic, and new splits continued to form.[20] Viewed historically, a denominationally divided world is not an exceptional circumstance for Christians, but the conventional norm. Dilemmas of interchurch conflict and cooperation go back literally to the foundation of the faith.

But post-Chalcedonian splits were on an unprecedented scale. Sustained resistance to official doctrine spawned two vast and enduring movements that the winning party would call heretical, respectively the Nestorians and Monophysites, and each has left remnants up to the present day. In terms of historical tradition and continuity, those churches have a far better claim to a connection with the ancient sources of the faith—in terms of geography, culture, and language, not to mention ethnicity—than do the upstart communities headquartered in Rome and Constantinople.[21] Within a century or so after Chalcedon, the Christian world fragmented into several great transcontinental divisions—Orthodox/Catholic, Monophysite, Nestorian, and Arian. Although each church agreed fully with its neighbors in essentials, each declared itself to be the one and only true church and did not acknowledge the credentials of other bodies or share communion with them. Already by 550, Christendom was quite as divided as it would be during the great early-modern split between Catholics, Protestants, and Orthodox.

Back to the Catacombs

The history of these dissident Eastern churches makes us rethink what we assume about the political trajectory of Christianity. According to a familiar cliché, Christianity changed utterly after it made its great alliance with the Roman Empire under Constantine, the devil's bargain in which the church sacrificed principles for earthly power and wealth. But in fact, Chalcedon forced the historic mainstream core of the church to forsake that Roman alliance, and it rapidly reverted to the antistate opposition that is perhaps the natural state of Christianity. After the twin shocks of 431 and 451, much of the most advanced and sophisticated Christian thought and culture in the East went underground politically.

Egypt illustrates this story. Alexandria—and the realm of Egypt beyond it—had an excellent claim to a dominant role in Christian life and thought, as the source of much of the faith's intellectual strength and growth. It would be quite feasible to write an Egypt-centered history of the first five or six hundred years of Christianity. Christians there lived under a hostile state apparatus from apostolic times until the grant of toleration in the fourth century, and they shared state power from 312 until the 450s. But the Monophysite majority coexisted peacefully with Roman regimes only sporadically over the next century or so, and imperial Christian forces often persecuted them. Those Christians who followed Chalcedon were slightingly dismissed as Melkites or Emperor's Men, apostates and time-servers. And although Egypt's churches enjoyed peace from the seventh century, that was only within the constraints of a Muslim-dominated state. At no point over the last fourteen centuries has Egypt's Coptic Church enjoyed much more than grudging toleration.[22]

Looking back at its long history, Egypt's Christians only knew state favor for a fleeting interval, and a similar story could be told of Syria, that other ancient center of the faith. From 542 to 578, the greatest leader of the Monophysite church was Jacobus Baradaeus, whose nickname refers to the rags he wore to escape the attention of imperial authorities constantly on the watch for this notorious dissident. Translating his name as "Hobo Jake" would not be far off the mark. Instead of living in a bishop's palace, he remained ever on the move, wandering from city to city. He roamed between Egypt and Persia, ordaining bishops and priests for the swelling underground church. His career, in other words, looked far more like that of an early apostle than a medieval prelate, and there were many others like him. Numerically, Jake won far more converts than Paul of Tarsus, and he covered more ground. The heart of the Christian church never left the catacombs, or if it did, it was not for long.[23]

That story tells us a great deal about the nature of Christian loyalties in the centuries after the Roman Empire's conversion. If your emperor or king was formally Christian, then self-preservation alone dictated following his lead, so that we need not think that church members actually had any high degree of knowledge or belief in the new faith. But if the church was itself in deadly opposition to the state, and faced actual persecution, then people had no vested interest whatever in belonging to it—quite the contrary. Why risk your life by following Hobo Jake? Through most of the Middle

East, and for long centuries after Constantine's time, then, people followed these dissident churches for exactly the same reasons that their ancestors would have adhered to the beliefs of the earliest Christian communities. They followed because they thought they would obtain healing in this world and salvation in the next; because they wanted signs and wonders; and because the ascetic lives of church leaders gave these figures a potent aura of holiness and charisma. Ordinary Christians followed not because they were told, but because they believed.

Winning New Worlds

Besides its religious significance, the fifth-century crisis changed the shape of global political history. Chalcedon gave an enormous boost to the power and prestige of those growing parts of the church in new and emerging areas—roughly speaking, in Europe— at the cost of the older heartlands of faith. A new emerging Christian world broke away from an older Christendom, the two separated by what critics saw as troubling theological innovations. Modern observers might draw parallels to the contemporary movement of the Christian center of gravity from Europe and North America to the global South.

The ancient geographical shift dramatically increased the power and prestige of the popes of Rome, slowing efforts to raise other centers to equal or greater status. Chalcedon and its aftermath consecrated the power of the Roman church, crippling potential rivals elsewhere, above all at Alexandria. Chalcedon, in fact, marks the real beginning of the medieval papacy.

The political victory of faith made-in-Rome meant that Europe's emerging Christianity would develop in intimate alliance with the Roman Empire and with the Western successor states, rather than (as in the East) returning to the catacombs. In consequence, Europe's churches kept alive the vision of a Christian empire, an intimate church-state alliance. This would be a political manifestation of the City of God, which they repeatedly tried to recreate in practice. So wedded were Westerners to the vision of a Christian empire that, when the real Roman Empire lost influence, the popes invented a whole new structure in the form of Charlemagne's Frankish regime. Europeans had to live with the consequences of that decision for a thousand years.[24]

The split within ancient Christianity prepared the way for outside powers who would exploit intra-Christian divisions—first the Persians, and eventually the Muslims. Without the great split, the rise of Islam would have been unthinkable. Without the religious crisis, Islam could not have stormed into the political near-vacuum it found in the seventh century, into an empire where most Eastern subjects—Monophysite and Nestorian—rejected their Orthodox/ Catholic emperors. So alienated were the Christian dissidents that few were prepared to resist Muslim invaders, who promised (and practiced) tolerance for the diverse Christian sects. In its earliest phases, the new faith offered a clean break from the historic cycle of violence and persecution that had so disfigured late-antique Christianity. Islam, in contrast, offered toleration, peace, and an enviable separation of church and state.[25]

A modern observer might see in this process a warning about the dangers of mixing church and state. The Christian world could only know peace when government was definitively removed from the business of making and enforcing religious orthodoxy, after which competing churches could coexist happily under a regime that despised its subjects impartially. Yet dissident churches ultimately paid a catastrophically high price for their freedom from Orthodox Christian control. Whatever dissident Christians thought initially, the new Muslim power had its own very different values and objectives and worked effectively to implement them.

Although the process took centuries, Christianity ultimately faded in the lands that fell under Muslim power. To illustrate the scale of the ruin that overcame the ancient churches, we recall that the fifth-century struggles involved a war for dominance between the sees of

Rome, Alexandria, Antioch, and Constantinople, and that war had clear winners and losers. Yet today the last three of those cities are now in countries overwhelmingly Muslim in population and tradition, with Christian minorities barely hanging on. Ephesus itself now stands in the western portion of the Muslim land we call Turkey, which is almost Christian free. Chalcedon and its aftermath so divided the Christian East that its ruin was inevitable.[26]

Modern believers should take from this historical experience quite different lessons, and certainly not simplistic alarms about the supposed threat from Islam. Communities should not become so obsessively focused on their internal feuds that they forget what they have in common and fall prey to far more substantial external dangers that they have been too blinkered to notice.

Imagining Other Worlds

What ultimately became accepted as Christian orthodoxy was hammered out in a process that was painfully slow, gradual, and often bloody. This conflict was marked by repeated struggles, coups, and open warfare spread over centuries. It is easy to imagine another outcome in which the so-called Orthodox would have been scorned as heretics, with incalculable consequences for mainstream political history, not to mention all later Christian thought and devotion.

We might even say that the later history of Christianity depended not just on any one person, but on one horse, the one that stumbled in 450, causing the death of the pro-Monophysite emperor Theodosius II. Only forty-nine at the time of his death, he could easily have reigned for another twenty years. That "might have been" is intriguing because, had he lived, the history of the world would have been quite different. If Theodosius had not died, there would have been no Chalcedon, and in that case, the Western, European, Catholic part of the empire might have been the one to slide into secession over the following century. That was the direction in which events so often seemed to be moving.[27]

We can imagine a counterfactual universe in which the schism between Rome and the East occurred in the fifth century, not the eleventh, and papal Rome never recovered from subjection to successive waves of barbarian occupiers. By 450, much of the old Western empire was under the political control of barbarian warlords who were overwhelmingly Arian Christians, rather than Catholics. Perhaps the papacy might have survived in the face of Arian persecution and cultural pressure, perhaps not. In the East, meanwhile, the Monophysite Roman Empire would have held on to its rock-solid foundations in a faithfully united Eastern realm that stretched from Egypt to the Caucasus, from Syria to the Balkans. This solid Christendom would have struggled mightily against Muslim newcomers, and conceivably, they would have held the frontiers.

Later Christian scholars would know the fundamental languages of the faith—Greek, Coptic, and Syriac—and they would have free access to the vast treasures surviving in each of those tongues. Latin works, however, would be available only to a handful of daring researchers willing to explore that marginal language with its puzzling alphabet. Only those bold Latinists would recall such marginal figures of Christian antiquity as Saints Augustine and Patrick. In contrast, every educated person would know those champions of the mainstream Christian story, Severus of Antioch and Egypt's Aba Shenoute.[28] In this alternate world, the decisive turning point in church history would have been not Chalcedon, but Second Ephesus, which we today remember as the Gangster Synod, the Council That Never Was. And the One Nature would have triumphed over the noxious errors of the Dyophysites, the Two Nature heretics.

If only because of the other paths that could so easily have been taken, these debates give the mid-fifth century an excellent claim to be counted as the most formative period in the whole history of Christianity. Much recent writing stresses the earlier Council of Nicea (325) as the critical moment in defining the beliefs of that faith, the critical dividing line between early and medieval Christianity. In reality, the struggle even to define core beliefs raged for centuries beyond this time and involved several other great gatherings, any one of which could have turned out very differently.

In many modern accounts, too, the church's history is portrayed as a steady move toward the otherworldly aspects of faith, toward seeing Christ as a heavenly redeemer rather than a prophet or a mystically minded social teacher. For Elaine Pagels, for instance, part of this process involved replacing the cryptic gospel of Thomas with the incarnational text of John ("In the beginning"). Thomas, she suggests, is for seekers and mystical inquirers, while John is for the devoutly unquestioning faithful. Meanwhile, some think, the canon of the New Testament became more rigidly defined in order to support Jesus' steady ascent to Godhood. In this scholarly vision, the democratic, egalitarian, and Spirit-filled Jesus movement of the earliest times atrophied into the repressive, bureaucratic Catholic Church of the Middle Ages: Christ *pantokrator* overwhelmed the human Jesus. For many writers, Nicea marks the tragic end of a glorious phase in the history of Christianity and the commencement of something grimmer.[29]

The more we look at the two hundred years or so *after* Nicea, though, the shakier this perception must become. Arguably, fourth-century councils like Nicea marked the point *When Jesus Became God*, to quote scholar Richard Rubenstein—but that was the easy part. The fifth and sixth centuries had to tackle the far more stressful task of preventing Jesus from becoming entirely God. Many lives would be lost in the process, and at least one empire.[30]

By What Authority?

The Jesus Wars tell us much about how Christianity has developed over time and, by extension, how other world religions evolve as they confront new circumstances. Many of the issues are perennial, not least the enduring question of how churches determine the acceptable limits of Christian belief.

Assuming that people disagree over matters that seem essential, just how do they decide which side is right, which is closer to the mind of God? How does the church make up its own, all-too-human mind? Societies change, circumstances change, ideologies change, especially within a global church that contains so many separate cultures and political traditions and which is in daily contact with other faiths. It's natural for a church living in a particular society to accept the standards prevailing in the wider community, whether these involve issues of gender and sexuality, property and slavery, war and peace, religious tolerance or bigotry. Christian teaching in one part of the world evolves according to the standards of the wider society, while believers elsewhere fear that the faith is being compromised beyond recognition. Over time, churches in different nations and continents inevitably draw apart.

So how does a church ensure conformity, at least to the extent that each regional entity acknowledges the full Christian credentials of its counterparts elsewhere? This kind of question remains very much alive in modern-day disputes over gender and sexuality within various denominations, in the global Anglican Communion, but also among Catholics, Lutherans, Methodists, and Presbyterians.

For a modern audience, used to centuries of religious diversity and toleration, the stress on maintaining conformity seems unnecessary. Today it seems obvious that when different sides are thoroughly estranged, they should agree on an amicable separation. They should form their own denominations, agreeing to differ peaceably, and live in mutual respect. Yet that option was just not available in the early church, and not simply because Christians then were in any sense morally inferior to their descendants. Central to Christian thought—Catholic, Monophysite, or Nestorian—was the concept of the church as the undivided body of Christ. If a body was not united, then it was deformed, mutilated, and imperfect, and such terms surely could not be applied to the body of Christ.

The Eucharist was the material symbol or sacrament of this united body. However much worship practices differed around the world—and the differences were spectacular—one could only share communion with fellow Christians who held a correct view of

Christ and the core of theological truth. If colleagues deviated from that, then they suffered anathema or condemnation, followed by excommunication. The word *anathema* was very potent, and it even had violent implications. Greek translations of the Old Testament use this term to describe the total condemnation or annihilation of a city, such as Jericho, where God commands the Israelites to massacre "everything that breathes." A person under anathema was equally cut off from both the church and civil society.

To be "in communion" meant sharing a basic core of assumptions that drew the line between being a true member of the body of Christ, and *not* being. This issue resurfaces regularly today, when many liberal Christians see no problem in taking communion in other churches as a sign of good will and fellowship but are dismayed by the rigidity of some churches. This kind of restriction is a running source of grievance at Catholic funerals, where liberal priests will invite all comers to participate fully in communion, to the horror of more orthodox believers. But in this matter, it is the harder-line churches who reflect the views of the ancient church, with their exalted view of communion as the symbol of belonging and unity. You are who you eat bread with.[31]

The Church's Mind

Pressures toward uniformity grew after the empire officially accepted Christianity in the fourth century. Just as all limbs and organs formed one human body, so there must be one organic church, one hierarchy, with its different regions operating in harmony and sharing communion—or so ran the theory. Over time, though, disputes and new questions arose within the Great Church, and doctrine needed to develop and advance in such a way that different factions did not condemn one another for forsaking the faith.

No one individual or group had the power to settle such disagreements: no single church leader or patriarch held universal authority. Conflicts rending large sections of the Christian community had to be resolved by general statements of the whole body of the church, in the form of councils, an idea that first appears in the Jerusalem gathering of the apostles described in the book of Acts. If the church was a body, then these councils served, however imperfectly, as its rational mind.

Through the early Christian centuries, local councils met regularly at diocesan and regional levels, but by the fourth century we see the first gatherings that sought to be universal or ecumenical. The idea presented many challenges. In the very earliest days of the church, it might just have been possible to gather all Christian believers together in one setting to decide an issue, but that option was simply not feasible when Christians ran into the millions. Instead, there had to be an assembly of some broadly representative gathering of bishops and higher clergy, drawn from as wide a sampling of the Christian world as was feasible. That has something in common with the principle of a modern opinion poll or survey, although with a supernatural justification. Councils represented the voice of the church as guided by the Holy Spirit, and once an assembly had spoken definitively on given issues, its pronouncements claimed absolute authority.[32]

In reality, councils rarely bore much resemblance to the intended pattern of collective holiness and usually looked more like the very worst of American political-party conventions. In studying the church councils of this era, certain themes come to mind, including Christian charity; restraint; common human decency; a willingness to forgive old injuries, to turn the other cheek. None of these featured in any of the main debates. Instead, the councils were marked by name-calling and backstabbing (both figurative and literal), by ruthless plotting and backstairs cabals, and by a pervasive threat of intimidation.[33]

Human sinfulness apart, several specific reasons ensured that the councils would be so messy, so violent, and, ultimately, so divisive. One structural problem was that no commonly accepted principle determined who should or should not appear at councils, no guideline that gave a right of attendance to Bishop X or Bishop Y. Even if such a plan existed, it would have been made almost useless by the infrequency with which councils met and the rapidly changing circumstances within the empire that made some areas more or less powerful over time. Between 325 and 680, only six councils were acknowledged as ecumenical, or possessing worldwide authority, far too few and infrequent for any individual or group to develop any kind of institutional memory.[34]

A council should be large in the sense of at least some hundreds of participants—318 bishops reputedly attended Nicea—but no written constitution specified a minimum number of participants, or how they should be chosen. Nobody even knew how many bishops held power at any given time. A common guesstimate in the 440s was that the Roman Empire contained 1,200 bishops, a number that usually surfaced rhetorically in a sentence such as, "How dare you, one man, set yourself against 1,200?" But as some regions, particularly North Africa, massively overproduced bishops in terms of the overall population, that rough figure was an underestimate. Nor did it include bishops from beyond the Roman realms, for instance from Ethiopia or Persia. So was a council legitimate if it had 200 members? 150? What about 50? No official quorum existed. Did the council have to include representation from every region of the Christian world, or just those for whom travel was geographically feasible? That last factor really mattered in an age when the roads and sea routes were playgrounds for barbarian raiders, for Huns, Vandals, and Goths.

Nor did any established plan explain just how the Holy Spirit would make his or her intentions known through the voices of the gathered bishops. The idea of voting and claiming a majority was as familiar an idea in the fifth century as it is today, but voting commonly took the form of acclamation. Groups of participants shouted for particular causes, probably with slogans and chants prearranged in caucuses. No definite lines separated a church council from a street demonstration. Moreover, it was never clear whether Christology was to be settled on the basis of a simple majority or some kind of supermajority. Even after a decisive vote was taken, the council still had to seek ratification from the emperor, which introduced splendid new opportunities for lobbying and influence peddling.

This infuriating lack of precision explains the generally chaotic nature of proceedings, when respective parties mobilized large numbers of their own followers, while disqualifying rival delegations. Even if a council voted in a particular way, dissidents were quite capable of establishing a rival minority council of their own, voting as they thought fit, and sending that decision to the emperor for approval. Decisions generally involved condemning rivals or subjecting them to anathemas, and after some councils—especially First Ephesus—an observer needed flash cards to trace who exactly had excommunicated or deposed whom.

That process—or rather, lack of process—gave quite as much power to the imperial family and to imperial officials as to patriarchs or bishops. Any account of the Jesus Wars would begin with the great patriarchs, with pivotal church figures such as Leo of Rome or Cyril of Alexandria and their counterparts at Antioch and Constantinople; but making the final decisions were the emperors, Theodosius II and Marcian. And besides them, at least as important would be the empresses and princesses of the day. This meant, above all, the empress Pulcheria, whose alliance with a succession of barbarian generals gave her effective control of the Eastern Empire for thirty years, while Galla Placidia long dominated the West. Hardly less significant was Eudocia, a poet and rhetorical genius in her own right and the sponsor of the Monophysite movement after its defeat at Chalcedon. Without these and other royal women, neither side could have long existed or competed. Pulcheria, above all, was vital to defining what became Christian orthodoxy. Without her personal and constant intervention, the struggles at First Ephesus and Chalcedon would certainly have taken different courses. The church was giving her no more than her due when it proclaimed her a saint. On the other side, the freestanding Monophysite church could not have survived without the patronage of the sixth-century empress Theodora.[35]

All the theological rows had immense political consequences. All the great councils involved a confrontation between the great patriarchal sees, each represented by a prelate who went on to become either a great saint and father of the church, or a condemned heretic. Several of these church leaders, also, represented a particular tradition of political power, and indeed of monarchy. As the Roman Empire crumbled, older patterns reasserted themselves, so that Alexandrian patriarchs like Cyril thought of themselves and acted like—literally—ancient pharaohs or Ptolemaic god-kings. Leo and the Roman popes saw themselves as successors of the ancient Roman emperors, the patriarchs of Constantinople as leaders of a Christian theocracy. The theological rows make no sense except in terms of this clash of self-images, as the shades of monarchies past and future tried to secure their supremacy as the legitimate successors of a fading regime. Ephesus and Chalcedon were battles for the political future as much as a war for eternal truth.

Violent Faith

Bishops debated theological points in the incense-filled back rooms of the councils, but their decisions had a deadly impact in the streets and villages, where ordinary laypeople were convinced that the essential core of Christian belief was at stake. What might to us seem like philosophical niceties drove ordinary people to the point of wishing to kill, torture, or expel their neighbors. The potential for violence and persecution existed at a far earlier stage of Christian development than many believe, certainly in the time of the early church rather than the Middle Ages. The councils led to outrageous violence in many parts of the empire—to popular risings and coups 'd'état, to massacres and persecutions. Only with difficulty did imperial forces maintain their hold on whole regions of the empire, especially such prosperous but disaffected territories as Egypt and Syria.[36]

Nor was violence confined to intra-Christian struggles. Historians have often commented on the growth of intolerance in the church after it achieved official status within the empire, how it became ever more hostile toward heretics, pagans, and Jews. But it is especially in the years of the great councils, between 410 and 460, that the level of intolerance rises frighteningly. This story is both a direct outcome of the theological debates, and its natural outcome. Pulcheria, who saved orthodoxy in 451, was also the driving force in a violent campaign against Jews, which foreshadows the anti-Semitic persecutions of the European Middle Ages. Adding to the "medieval" feel of some of these events—the religious violence and bigotry, the anti-Semitism and fanaticism—the ruling dynasty through the era of Ephesus and Chalcedon, including Pulcheria herself, was of Spanish origin. While no one would suggest any kind of ethnic determinism, it is curiously appropriate that the Christian world of the fifth century looks so much like the time of Torquemada, the notorious Grand Inquisitor.[37]

When historian Edward Gibbon described the turbulent response to the Council of Chalcedon, he expressed astonishment that such savagery could erupt "in the pursuit of a metaphysical quarrel." But powerfully justifying violence was a factor that moderns often ignore and which goes far beyond mere metaphysics. It also makes nonsense of attempts to distinguish religious from nonreligious motivations. The vast majority of people at this time, educated and ignorant, believed in providential views of the world. They believed that wrong conduct or heretical belief stirred God to anger, and that such anger would be expressed in highly material terms, in earthquake and fire, invasion and military defeat, famine and pestilence. Unless evildoers or wrong-believers were suppressed, society might perish altogether. In order to destroy those malevolent groups, activists took steps that look worldly, political, and cynical, but we can never truly separate those political acts from their compelling underlying motivation, which was supernatural. However historians may use the term, no "secular world" existed independent of church and religion, and the Roman state, pagan or Christian, never was secular in any recognizable modern sense. Nor was there any such thing as "just politics."

The Monopoly of Violence

But even if religious believers are outraged by some deviant creed, then or now, that does not of itself mean that violence will ensue. Rather, violence occurs when the state has neither the will nor the ability to restrain highly motivated private groups. This condition might arise from extreme state weakness and the breakdown of public institutions, but state agencies might consciously decide to ally with private groups. In either case, the state loses what sociologist Max Weber famously described as its monopoly of violence, and the consequences for political stability can be dreadful. Violence breeds violence, without any external forces to bring it to an end.

This is what happened in the fifth century, when the forces of church and empire were still unsure about the appropriate limits of each other's power. Yes, the empire was Christian, and church leaders should be accorded all due prestige and favor. But where exactly did their power end in terms of suppressing paganism or fighting religious rivals? By 400, emperors gave very mixed signals about just how far they were prepared to let church authorities go in terms of serving as agencies of government, with the powers of coercion and enforcement that this involved. However hard dedicated civil officials tried to keep the peace at councils, they faced a losing battle when the imperial court failed to back their decisions.[38]

Meanwhile, radical new religious currents transformed ideas of the basis of power, giving vast authority to charismatic religious leaders. In the new Christian vision, the rejection of sexuality and the material world led God to grant amazing supernatural power to his chosen followers, and these gifts were best manifested in visions and healing miracles. Potentially, this strength outmatched any amount of force that the secular world could deploy against it. The thousands who abandoned worldly society—the monks and hermits—became the heroes and role models for those who could not bear to make the full sacrifice. And far from challenging this alternative world of spiritual power, with its parallel hierarchies, worldly leaders sought rather to imitate it. Even the imperial family now aspired to goals of world rejection and celibacy, and they listened carefully to the pronouncements of saints and visionaries.

By the fifth century, bishops and other Christian leaders could mobilize an impressive amount of muscle to promote their causes, making them powerful independent political actors. The church became not so much a state within a state, as a parallel state mechanism. Bishops commanded the absolute loyalty of their faithful clergy and other followers, much as secular lords and patricians could rely on their clients. Monks especially served as private militias, holy head-breakers whom charismatic bishops could turn out at will to sack pagan temples, rough up or kill opponents, and overawe rival theologians. These were not rogue monks or clergy gone bad, but faithful followers of the church, doing exactly what was expected of them over and above their disciplines of prayer, meditation, and healing. When cities or regions divided along lines of theology or faith, rival bishops and monks literally fought for domination in the hills and on the streets.[39]

Driving extremism was the concept of honor. Throughout the centuries, ideas of honor have often served as an underappreciated component of religious conflict, and not just within Christianity. Looking at the conduct of some church institutions in these years, it is tempting to draw half-joking parallels to modern criminal or terrorist organizations—at times, the patriarchate of Alexandria did behave like the Sopranos. But such a comparison is more plausible than it may appear, in that both in ancient and modern times, Mediterranean societies were cemented together by certain cultural themes: clientage and patronage, honor and revenge, devotion to family and clan. Honor and family dominated social relations in different regions of the Roman Empire, and in extreme circumstances these had to be defended by force. Much of everyday life revolved around a constant series of honor challenges, ripostes, and one-upmanship. People struggled to assert the honor of their group and, hardly less important, inflict shame upon rivals. If we do not understand the ritualized forms of blood feud and vendetta, we stand no chance of comprehending Mediterranean and Near Eastern societies, whether in the fifth century or the twenty-first.

Although monks and clergy pledged to renounce those ideas of personal honor as meaningless vanity, they easily transferred these loyalties to institutions. This might mean a new loyalty to the church as a whole, or to a particular see or monastery, and clergy fought for that church or religious house with all the zeal they might earlier have applied to defending the honor of a city or a clan. Defeated rivals had to be shamed formally, with all the ritual symbolism of degradation and submission available to church and empire. We can hardly comprehend the astonishing venom that marked the long battle between the great churches of Antioch and Alexandria unless we realize that we are dealing here with a quite literal blood feud that spanned a century or more. In later eras, the idea of satisfying aggrieved honor even became central to Western theology. Around 1100, the monk Anselm depicted Christ as the only sacrifice meritorious enough to pay the debt of honor to God, which he did through his death on the cross. This theory of the atonement became standard for both Catholic and Protestant churches.[40]

Lay people, too, joined in the battles through mobs and organized gangs, as religion served as a cultural badge in struggles for political power. As a later parallel, we might compare the religious factions with the gang structures of nineteenth-century urban America, as commemorated by Martin Scorsese's film *Gangs of New York*. Constantinople—New Rome—worked in very similar ways. Street gangs mobilized the masses, but not just for mindless intertribal violence. These gangs overlapped with political factions and government, and the keenest struggles raged over official influence and patronage. Regional rivalries also featured, as ordinary people came to identify particular leaders, particular schools of thought, with their own cities and homelands.[41]

Religious passions even extended to the two great sports factions in the Hippodrome, adopting the flag of the Orthodox (Blue) or Monophysite (Green). To imagine a modern parallel, we would have to suppose that current debates within the Anglican Communion were fought out at international soccer matches, between tens of thousands of football hooligans, representing the churches of (for instance) England and Nigeria. Each side would be heavily armed with knives and Molotov cocktails; each would have its distinctive colors, slogans, and banners—placards, for instance, bearing the likeness of England's Rowan Williams on one side, of Nigerian primate Peter Akinola on the other. Nigerian mobs would yell for scriptural inerrancy, the English for interpreting the Bible in the light of reason and evolving standards of decency. At the end of the day, each side would tally its dead and maimed.

Christianity and Islam

Out-of-control clergy, religious demagogues with their consecrated militias, religious parties usurping the functions of the state . . . It all sounds like the worst stereotypes of contemporary radical Islam, in Iran and Somalia, Iraq and Lebanon. And then, as now, the problem lay not in any characteristics of the religion itself, of its doctrines or Scriptures, but in the state's inability to control private violence. Just a century after the conversion of the Roman empire, Christian churches were acting precisely on the lines of the most extreme Islamic mullahs today. This in itself suggests that none of the violence or intolerance commonly seen in modern-day Islam is, so to speak, in the DNA of that religion but just reflects particular social and political circumstances.

An event that occurred in Constantinople around the year 511 suggests the parallels. The church of the day had a beloved hymn, the Trisagion or Thrice Holy, which praised, "Holy God, Holy and Mighty, Holy Immortal" (Orthodox churches sing it to this day). But the emperor, Anastasius, wanted to revise it in the Monophysite fashion, by lauding this God "Who was crucified for our sakes." The new formula proclaimed that it was God alone who walked the soil of Palestine in the first century and suffered on the cross, a view that ignores the human reality of Jesus. So angry were the capital's residents that they launched a bloody riot:

> Persons of rank and station were brought into extreme danger, and many principal parts of the city were set on fire. In the house of Marinus the Syrian, the populace found a monk from the country. They cut off his head, saying that the clause had been added at his instigation; and having fixed it upon a pole, jeeringly exclaimed: "See the plotter against the Trinity!"[42]

We can imagine the response if, in the twenty-first century, a Muslim mob beheaded a dissident theologian and paraded the grisly trophy around the streets. Not only would the crime be (properly) denounced, but Westerners would assume that such behavior was part of the fundamental character of that religion—a bloodthirsty, warlike intolerance that could be traced back to the sternest passages of the Quran. The beheading would be seen as a trademark of Islamic fanaticism. Surely, we would say, Christians would never act like that. But they assuredly did.

While it is tempting to dismiss the religious politics of the fifth century as just a matter of faction and conventional partisanship, we also need to recall the special concepts of authority driving religious politics. Charismatic hierarchs claim guardianship of holy truths; prophets and visionaries seek to redirect history according to the personal instructions of the divine; religious orders bypass the secular state in order to create theocracy; and a cult of martyrdom sustains an escalating cycle of violence. Again, the better we understand the contemporary politics of the Islamic Middle East, the more intelligible becomes the Christian past; and vice versa. Constantinople or Alexandria then; Baghdad and Mogadishu today. Although the kind of weaponry involved is different, the ancient armies of obstreperous monks can easily be compared to the Shi'ite forces supporting Muqtada al-Sadr in contemporary Baghdad and Basra. The Christ Army predated the Mahdi Army by some 1,600 years.[43]

Watching how church factions in the age of the councils appropriated spiritual authority so often recalls the modern Muslim world. For centuries, Muslim *fatwas* or religious decrees were issued only by accredited institutions of scholars and lawyers, and these texts carried real weight around the Islamic world. During the twentieth century, though, different factions and even individuals arrogated to themselves the right to issue such fatwas, generally with the goal of justifying extremist or violent actions. Today, as in the fifth century, radical clerics not only denounce more moderate enemies, but officially read them out of the faith. A fatwa might declare that however X describes himself in religious terms, he is in fact no longer a member of the Muslim community and is thus a suitable target for violence. In other words, they subject them to anathemas, just as Christians did in the fifth century. Radical Islamists even have a direct modern equivalent of the Christian anathema, in the form of *takfir*, the act of declaring a Muslim person or even a state to be *kaffir*, or infidel. The notion of *takfir* is fundamental to the extremist Islam that produced Osama bin Laden.

Other analogies also unite ancient and modern extremists. As in late Roman times, a providential view of the world drives political action today. Islamist radicals believe that only by purifying the faith can the Muslim world regain God's favor and reverse its long modern history of defeats and disasters. And ideas of honor still stir violence in societies shaped by notions of personal and family pride. Just as early Christian monks fought for the honor of their church, so modern Islamic protesters defend the honor of the

Prophet, most passionately when his image is demeaned in cartoons or novels. The concept of blasphemy is meaningless except in the context of ideas of honor and shame.

When we think of the history of Christianity, we picture certain key individuals and objects. We think of medieval cathedrals, of superb paintings and sculptures of the crucifixion or the Madonna, and generally, of some of the glories of European culture—together, of course, with some of the nightmare aspects of that story, the intolerance and fanaticism. But we think above all of a Christianity rooted in Europe and one unafraid to explore the image of the human face of Christ. We know a medieval Christian world with its spiritual and intellectual cores in Rome and Paris, not Alexandria and Antioch. At every stage, then, we are thinking of a world shaped by the outcome of those almost forgotten struggles of the fifth century, which occurred in a world of empires and states that have all faded into ruin. But these conflicts left an impact that survives into the present day. The gatherings at Ephesus and Chalcedon remade a faith.

Appendix to Chapter One:
The Church's General Councils

Through the centuries, the church called many councils and gatherings at regional and local levels, but a few great events were recognized as having special authority for the whole Christian world. These were general or universal (ecumenical) in nature. Catholic, Orthodox, and Protestant churches agree on accepting the first seven of these general councils as authoritative. Although these councils dealt with many miscellaneous items of belief and practice, each focused chiefly on an issue or debate that was particularly divisive at the time. Each council proclaimed a set of views that became established orthodoxy for much of the church, although in each case, the defeated party did not simply cease to exist overnight.

The first seven councils were:

I. *First Council of Nicea (325)* The church was divided over Christ's divinity. Followers of Arius believed that, as a created being, Christ was inferior to God the Father. Their opponents, led by Athanasius of Alexandria, taught that all three persons of the Trinity—Father, Son, and Holy Spirit—were fully equal. The Council of Nicea resulted in a decisive victory for the Trinitarian party over the Arians. Athanasius went on to become bishop of Alexandria.

II. *First Council of Constantinople (381)* The emperor Theodosius I called this council mainly to settle continuing debates concerning the Trinity. Arianism remained powerful long after the Council of Nicea, while some groups denied the full divinity of the Holy Spirit. The Council of Constantinople tried to resolve these issues, and it defined the role of the Holy Spirit within the Trinity. This council created an expanded version of the creed originally declared at Nicea, and when later generations use the so-called Nicene Creed, they are in fact using the form accepted at Constantinople in 381.

III. *Council of Ephesus (431)* With Trinitarian issues largely settled, the main focus of debate now turned to Christology, that is, the proper understanding of the character of Christ and the relationship between his human and divine natures. Nestorius, patriarch of Constantinople, was accused of dividing the two natures in a way that made the Virgin Mary the mother of Christ, but not of God. His leading opponent, the patriarch Cyril of Alexandria, taught the full unity of Christ's natures. Cyril's views triumphed, with the support of the Roman pope, and the Nestorian party was condemned. It remains open to debate whether Nestorius did in fact hold the views attributed to him.

[Second Council of Ephesus (449) Although later generations refused to recognize the credentials of this council, it was called in much the same way as its predecessors. The church of Constantinople was deeply split, with a strong party emphasizing Christ's single divine nature. Constantinople's bishop Flavian condemned these views as extreme and heretical. Under pressure from the Alexandrian patriarch Dioscuros, a council met to investigate and condemn Flavian and to support One Nature teachings. The council degenerated into a mob scene, in which Flavian suffered mortal wounds. This gathering was subsequently rejected as a "Gangster Synod" and not a true council.]

IV. *Council of Chalcedon (451)* The fourth council was called to reverse the disastrous results of the recent Gangster Synod. The council condemned the actions of Dioscuros of Alexandria and his allies. After intense debate, it also formulated a definition of Christ's being that presented him as both fully divine and fully human. This historic Chalcedonian definition owed much to the thought of the Roman pope Leo I.

V. *Second Council of Constantinople (553)* In the century following Chalcedon, the church continued to be severely split over christological issues, with many regions continuing to stress Christ's One Nature (the Monophysite movement). Partly in order to reconcile these dissidents, the emperor Justinian called a council that would condemn the writings of some long-dead theologians whom the Monophysites regarded as gravely heretical. The Second Council of Constantinople did condemn the controversial writings—the so-called Three Chapters—but at the cost of creating new disagreements. Only after some years as a prisoner of the empire could the Roman pope Vigilius be bullied into accepting the council's decisions.

VI. *Third Council of Constantinople (680–81)* In a last-ditch attempt to settle the christological wars, the Byzantine emperors had tried to establish that, whatever people thought about Christ's natures, at least they could all agree that he had a single will. Unfortunately the compromise pleased nobody, and many attacked this imperial policy as a Monothelete (One Will) heresy. The Third Council condemned Monotheletism, proclaiming instead the belief that Christ was of two wills as well as of two natures.

VII. *Second Council of Nicea (787)* From the 720s, the Byzantine Empire split violently over the question of icons and images, with some activists arguing that such pictures should be prohibited as idolatrous. The Second Council of Nicea declared that such images were legitimate, provided they were venerated as opposed to being worshipped in their own right.

Part 1

—

God and Caesar

I will treat of the origin and progress and destinies of the two cities, the earthly and the heavenly, which are in this present world commingled and, as it were, entangled together.

Augustine of Hippo

2

The War of Two Natures

The mystery of the humanity of Christ, that He sunk Himself into our flesh, is beyond all human understanding.
Martin Luther

Even if it were desirable, replied the Good Fairy, angelic or spiritual carnality is not easy, and in any case the offspring would be severely handicapped by being half flesh and half spirit, a very baffling and neutralizing assortment of fractions since the two elements are forever at variance.
Flann O'Brien

In 428, Nestorius, the new patriarch of the imperial capital of Constantinople, denounced what he thought was a worrying trend in popular devotion. Christians might well venerate the Virgin Mary, he thought, but they should not call her *Theotokos*, God-Bearer or Mother of God. Far better to call her *Christotokos*, Mother of Christ, which did not raise such alarming theological questions.

Yet this attempt to avoid dangerous innovations was itself seen as a rash challenge to received doctrine, and Nestorius's intervention began a series of conflicts that tore apart both church and empire. The process was extraordinarily rapid. Within just three years from his appointment, he had become associated with a heresy and stirred up opposition that had divided the church in Constantinople and throughout much of the Eastern world. He had suffered a devastating counterattack, culminating in a general council that came close to causing a schism throughout the Christian world; and he had been denounced, deposed, and utterly defeated. Three years. That time frame indicates the amazingly rapid communications still prevailing within the empire and the easy cultural transmission permitted by the Greek language. The Christian world might stretch from the Atlantic to Persia, but it could still look like a small village.

But the speed with which the crisis evolved suggests that the issues were anything but new. Rather, they were present in the cultural background, just awaiting the correct spark to set them alight, and the fast-moving story suggests the tinderbox atmosphere of church politics in this era. The Nestorian furor was yet another phase in a battle that had been raging for centuries. Participants had long wrestled with the idea of the Word made flesh and developed a whole world of specialized terms and concepts: being and nature, person and substance. But how, in fact, had Christology become so brutally divisive and, ultimately, an empire killer?[1]

1. Comprehending Christ: c.30–300

GOD AND MAN?

The Gospels allow for many interpretations concerning the nature and identity of Christ. How explicitly did Jesus claim to be one with God? If you take your main picture of Jesus Christ from the gospel of John, then you are more likely to focus on a divine figure. Reading the synoptic Gospels (Matthew, Mark, and Luke) demands that we pay more attention to the human reality.[2]

Undoubtedly, the idea of Christ as both God and man is ancient in the church. Early in the second century, Ignatius of Antioch wrote in terms that would be quite familiar to later believers right up to the present day. As he wrote, "Jesus Christ Our Lord" was:

> Of the flesh and of the spirit,
> Born and unborn,
> God come in the flesh . . . from both Mary and God.

But other interpretations were possible, and indeed common. Since apostolic times, many groups had formed their own particular interpretations of the relationship between human and divine. Lists of ancient heresies include many groups holding diverse views on Christology. Of course, the fact that we regard them as heresies and isms means only that they ultimately lost out in the struggle of ideas and became byways of belief rather than the mainstream.[3] (See appendix to this chapter: Some Early Interpretations of Christ.)

Some early followers of Jesus saw him as prophet or messiah, but not as a divine figure or an incarnate God. These Jewish-Christian groups were usually termed *Ebionites,* and it is an open question whether they represented a fossil of the very earliest Jesus movement. As tensions grew between Jews and Christians, the church condemned any views that seemed too close to Judaism. This Jewish issue would often resurface in later theological debates, as thinkers who over-emphasized Christ's human nature were charged with Jewish sympathies.[4]

Two Natures? The Adopted Son

Other widely held theologies imagined two separate natures, human and divine, but spoke of the divine nature, the Logos, invading and overwhelming the human. *Adoptionist* teachings proclaimed that

Jesus was altogether human, but upon him had descended a divine power who granted him his anointing, his Christship. He acquired Sonship at a specific moment, through a process of divine adoption.[5] And however far removed these ideas are from later Christian orthodoxy, they do follow quite logically from reading some parts of the New Testament.

Assuming that Christ became God, when and how was he Godded? Modern Christians see little difficulty in the question, so familiar are they with the doctrine of the virgin birth. This idea is reinforced by stories and paintings of the annunciation to Mary, together with centuries of accumulated Christmas lore, the events surrounding the birth of Emmanuel. Of course, we think, that was self-evidently the moment at which a divine being appeared in the world in human form. But a wide range of early thinkers read the story very differently, and they had good scriptural grounds for their beliefs.

The idea of the virgin birth is unquestionably present in the gospels of Matthew and Luke, but elsewhere in the New Testament the idea leaves not a trace. Among Paul's epistles, Galatians speaks of God sending his Son, "born of a woman," but neither here nor elsewhere does Paul suggest anything unusual about Jesus' conception or birth. Although Paul could have written explicitly "of a virgin," instead he uses the word for woman, *gyne/gynaikos*. Two of the gospels, Mark and John, make no reference to a birth story for Jesus, and neither did the hypothetical lost gospel Q. Nor do early alternative gospels like Thomas. Even in Matthew and Luke, the virgin birth idea never reappears after the initial chapters: it is not mentioned in Luke's sequel to his gospel, the book of Acts. And although some would argue that Revelation refers to Mary and her child, the text is open to debate, and in any case, it does not speak of a virgin birth. In the New Testament, at least, no apostle or Christian preacher ever tries to convince an audience by stories of Jesus's miraculous conception or birth, or of a manger surrounded by angels or kings. Ignatius definitely believes in the virgin birth, but otherwise the idea makes little impact on the so-called apostolic fathers, the Christian thinkers from the period between about 90 and 140.

Reading Mark, John, or Q, in the absence of the Christmas stories, we would assuredly think of Jesus' baptism, rather than his birth, as the moment when he acquired divinity. Let us for instance read the account of Mark that is, according to scholarly consensus, the oldest surviving full gospel; but imagine that we come to this without the assumptions that we have from any previous reading. The text begins with the theme of preparing the Way, the term that the first Jesus followers used for their new faith. We hear of the mission of John the Baptist, and then Jesus himself appears to be baptized, without any description of his antecedents or any suggestion that they were at all out of the ordinary. At that point, the Spirit descends on him like a dove, and then he flees into the wilderness, presumably to confront the astonishing new reality he has encountered. John's gospel offers a very similar sequence. The difference there, of course, is that the text begins with the famous prologue describing the Incarnation, the Word becoming flesh. We are used to reading this as a Christmas story, of the Word being born in a Bethlehem manger, and that is a perfectly possible interpretation— but not the only one. Someone could even understand the "word becoming flesh" in terms of a divine figure materializing in the Judean wilderness in the guise of a thirty-year-old man, ready to begin a spiritual mission; and that is roughly how early Gnostic Christian believers did take it. Or else, we could read the prologue as describing what is about to happen to Jesus when he emerges from the Jordan.

For many early Christians, Jesus was a good or holy man, but only at the moment of his baptism in the Jordan was he suddenly overwhelmed by the power of divinity, the Logos or Holy Spirit. Early in the second century, the influential Gnostic thinker Cerinthus popularized this idea of Jesus' being possessed by a divine force at his baptism. The crucifixion would then have marked the moment that the power of Christ abandoned the man Jesus. According to the second-century gospel of Peter, Christ on the cross cried out "My Power, my Power, why have you forsaken me?" According to the orthodox church father Irenaeus, writing around 180, Cerinthus

> represented Jesus as having not been born of a virgin, but as being the son of Joseph and Mary according to the ordinary course of human generation, while he nevertheless was more righteous, prudent, and wise than other men. Moreover, after his baptism, Christ descended upon him in the form of a dove from the Supreme Ruler, and that then he proclaimed the unknown Father, and performed miracles. But at last Christ departed from Jesus, and that then Jesus suffered and rose again, while Christ remained impassible, inasmuch as he was a spiritual being.

Irenaeus further explained that, according to the Gnostic view,

> This Christ passed through Mary just as water flows through a tube; and there descended upon him in the form of a dove at the time of his baptism, that Savior who belonged to the *Pleroma* [the Fullness of divinity].

Other New Testament passages also support views of Christ that fall well short of what became standard orthodoxy, although they point to the Resurrection, rather than the baptism, as the moment when Jesus acquired Godhood.[6]

We can even argue that the mainstream church kept alive this ancient fascination with Christ's baptism long after its official theology rejected the idea that this marked the moment at which he became divine. Although the idea is speculative, what we know as the date of Christmas may preserve memories of a time when some Christians made a special celebration of the baptism of Christ—rather than his birth—as the key moment in his life.

When we look at church calendars, it is puzzling that modern Christians celebrate Christmas in midwinter, whereas the early church located Christ's birth in May. (No sane Judean shepherd would have been out on the hills watching his flocks in December.) But other possible explanations exist for this winter celebration. Late in the second century, we know that Egyptian Gnostic followers of Basilides commemorated Jesus' baptism as especially holy, and they celebrated it on January 6. Over the centuries, the Orthodox churches used the midwinter date to commemorate the birth of Jesus rather than his baptism, and January 6 marks the feast of the Epiphany. For Western churches, this is the day on which the Magi reputedly visited Jesus in the stable, proclaiming the manifestation of Christ's glory as a newborn child. Over the centuries, though, other Christian cultures combined the celebration of Christ's birth with a remembrance of his baptism in the Jordan. Eastern Orthodox churches celebrate Epiphany as the festival of Christ's baptism. In the ancient church of Ethiopia, Jesus' baptism is the focus of the feast of *Timqat* or Epiphany, which is still one of the greatest festivals of the liturgical year. *Timqat* is the local Amharic word for "baptism."[7]

Adoptionist doctrines survived through the third century, and they revived powerfully in the 260s through the influence of Paul of Samosata, bishop of Antioch. Paul held that Mary was the mother of the man Jesus, on whom the Logos descended at his baptism.

> Having been anointed by the Holy Spirit he received the title of the anointed [*Christos*], suffering in accordance with his nature, working wonders in accordance with grace. For in fixity and resoluteness of character he likened himself to God; and having kept himself free from sin was united with God, and was empowered to grasp as it were the power and authority of wonders.

At the time, the view was denounced as Ebionite and Jewish, because it put so much emphasis on Jesus' human nature. It matters for later debates because Paul became the ancestor of Two Nature theories about Christ.[8] And while the church of Antioch rejected Adoptionism, its theologians always insisted on emphasizing the human reality of Christ, in addition to the divine.

ONE NATURE? CHRIST AS GOD ALONE

Other early believers stressed Christ's divinity to the point of all but denying his humanity: Christ had one nature, and it was God's. And these Christians, too, could find support in Scripture and in ancient tradition. In one version of this view, Christ only took human form as a guise in which to visit the world, and his appearance and sufferings were a matter of illusion—hence the name *Docetists*, from the Greek word *dokein* meaning "to seem." Already in the New Testament era, the Epistles of John condemned those who denied that Christ had come in the flesh. Some Docetists turned for scriptural support to the hymn recorded in Philippians 2, in which Christ takes the form or shape (*morphe*) of a slave, and was born in human *form*, in human *likeness*. That hymn is so ancient that already by 60 or so, Paul seems to be quoting it as a well-known text. It predates any of the four Gospels as we have them.

That belief in Christ as illusion had massive implications for church practice and devotion—if Christ was immaterial, for instance, then believers could receive only a symbolic benefit from the Eucharist. That belief set Docetists apart from the emerging church and was one of the main grounds on which Ignatius of Antioch denounced them early in the second century: he called them "atheists and infidels." But similar ideas enjoyed a long history in Syria and the East, where they were consecrated through their inclusion in many alternative gospels. This theology also became part of the new religion founded by Mani, who preached a radical conflict between light and darkness, spirit and matter. From that antimaterial point of view, it was monstrous to suggest that Christ had a bodily form, or (as Mani mockingly said) that he was "born of blood and flesh and women's ill-smelling effluent!" In the West, one of the strongest advocates of Christ's real, material nature was the African Tertullian, writing around 200. In his work *De Carne Christi* ("Of the Flesh of Christ"), he argued that none of the doctrines of Christianity made sense unless we accepted the real physical nature of the Incarnation: "God must have flesh, in order to have a real death and real resurrection." Although he never used the exact phrase, his work is best remembered for the justification he offers for his faith in the Incarnation: I believe it because it is absurd![9]

Mainstream churches fought repeatedly against One Nature beliefs through the second and third centuries. From about 200, the main controversy involved the view that Christ had a human body but no identity or personality separate from that of the one united God. Father, Son, and Spirit were just modes of one reality, three names for one substance, and it made no sense to speak of a Trinity. This was the theory proposed around 220 by one Sabellius, although his ideas were so controversial that we have virtually no record of his actual words. According to this view, Christ was one with the Father, to the extent that it was the Father who suffered on the cross. In terms of later theories about the identity of Christ, this represented an extreme version of One Nature belief. The *Sabellian* idea appealed to Christians who retained the Jewish horror of any departure from strict monotheism and who worried about making Christ a second and distinct God.[10]

KEEPING CHRIST HUMAN

Memories of these debates were very much alive in Nestorius's time. The names and labels served as convenient code words to stigmatize enemies. If someone emphasized the single nature of Christ too strongly, his critics would denounce him (outrageously) as a Sabellian. Someone who veered too far the other way, overstressing the two separate natures, ran the risk of being labeled a follower of Cerinthus or Paul of Samosata. By the late third century, the Western church had evolved a formula designed to avoid both extremes. In Latin terms, Jesus Christ was one *persona* (person) in whom are the two *substantiae*, substances, of divinity and humanity.[11]

In light of later assumptions about the course of Christian doctrine, it is worth stressing just what the different sides were assuming about the divinity of Christ. For many modern readers, claims about Christ's divinity represent a later distortion of his original claims. According to this view, the earliest church saw Jesus as a man, and only later and retroactively was he promoted to Godhood. This elevation was associated especially with the Roman Empire's conversion to Christianity and events like the Council of Nicea in 325. Dan Brown's novel *The Da Vinci Code* argues that Nicea was the moment at which Jesus *became* God, as a result of power plays in the empire and church: he owed his Godhood to majority vote.

But for at least a century before that, the reality of Christ's divinity was scarcely at issue, and certainty in this belief grew with the increasing dominance of the canonical four Gospels. The more popular Matthew and Luke became as standard accounts of Jesus' life, the harder it was to get over the powerful stories of his miraculous conception and birth. Memories of these accounts permeated the minds of readers approaching Mark and John to the point where they assumed that these works, too, must have had some kind of birth story. Battles erupted not over the divinity of Jesus Christ, but rather involved questions of what, if any, human elements remained within him. Already by 200, those Jewish-Christian movements that had seen Jesus as a purely human figure were becoming rare and isolated. The real struggle involved a very different issue: how could Christ be kept human?

2. *The Fourth Century*

NICEA'S NEW WARS

The question of how fully Christ was united with God the Father provoked the so-called Arian crisis. Arius was a priest who agreed that Christ was an immensely powerful and holy figure of supernatural dimensions, but as the Father had created him at a specific moment, we could not regard him as equally divine. Others, led by the Egyptian Athanasius, believed just as passionately that Christ was fully equal with the Father, entirely part of a God who was Three-in-One, and he had always held that status. The orthodox position was neatly summarized in a slogan that roughly translates as "There never was a was when He wasn't."[12] As so often occurs in such philosophical battles, the differences between the two sides were actually not huge. Arians and Athanasians both held that Christ was intimately close to the Father and existed before the created universe. Athanasians believed that Christ was the same being (*homoousios*) with the Father; Arians thought that he was "of like being" (*homoiousios*)—similar, just not the same. The one letter made all the difference.

Athanasius scored a massive victory in this conflict, but in so doing, he also opened the door to One Nature understandings of Christ. In 325, the Council of Nicea condemned the Arian view as heretical. The council asserted its belief in

> one Lord Jesus Christ, only-begotten Son of God, begotten from the Father, that is from the substance [*ousia*] of the Father, God from God, light from light, true God from true God, begotten not made, of the same being or substance [*homoousios*] with the Father, through whom all things came to be, both those in heaven and those in earth; for us humans and for our salvation he came down and became incarnate [enfleshed, *sarkothenta*], became human [was "manned," *enanthropesanta*].[13]

The Council of Nicea became one of the legendary moments in the church's history, marking the triumph of a newly declared orthodoxy. And although enforcing this view over the whole church took centuries (Arian Goths and Lombards still ruled large portions of western Europe in the sixth century), Athanasian doctrines eventually prevailed. Even today, hundreds of millions who attend liturgically oriented churches echo the doctrine every week when they recite a creed declaring, in whatever language, that Christ is of one being with the Father. But far from ending theological debate, Nicea actually opened whole new battlefronts. By the end of the fourth century, the mainstream church had reached fair agreement on the nature of God and the Trinity, but debate now shifted to the nature of Christ. Those christological debates dominated the fifth century.[14]

The Nicene definition itself posed real problems for ideas of Christ's humanity. The text does indeed assert a belief in the human Christ. Not only did Jesus become incarnate, but he also became human, *anthropos*. But people might disagree over what those terms might mean, and this debate opened a gulf between the churches of Alexandria and Antioch. John's gospel talked about the Logos "becoming flesh" (*sarx*), and later thinkers viewed the Logos as the principle guiding Christ's flesh or body. This *Logos-sarx* (Word-flesh) approach appealed to Alexandrian thinkers like Athanasius. But it would be possible to understand this as seeing God inhabiting a human body without any real identity of its own: Jesus in that sense would just be a generic representative of the human species. Antiochenes on the other hand worried that this approach underplayed Jesus' full humanity. He was not just a body; he was a real individual man with a particular background and life story, with the human mind, will, and desires that this implied—he wept. Antioch's thinkers accordingly put more emphasis on the human Christ, the *anthropos*, so that we speak of a *Logos-anthropos* (Word-man) view. Taking humanity, becoming *anthropos*, had to imply fully human status.[15]

And then there was that loaded word *homoousios,* which now gained almost scriptural status in its own right as a concept that could not be safely challenged. But it could very easily be used to support One Nature theories. If in fact Christ shared a common substance with the Father, what then became of the man Jesus? Significantly, the Nicene Creed says literally nothing about what Jesus did between his incarnation and his crucifixion under Pontius Pilate. We hear not a word about his miracles or parables, his sermons or teachings, or anything at all in his earthly human life: it is almost as if none of his intervening life or career mattered in the slightest. However hard he tried, even Athanasius could not make a convincing case for the human nature of his Christ. In fact, critics of Nicea had solid grounds for claiming that the great council had just reinstated the old Sabellian doctrines in a new guise, the idea that Christ was just a form or mode of one divine being. Ironically, the same church gathering that had denounced Paul of Samosata back in 268 had explicitly condemned the term *homoousios,* which that earlier council had regarded as one of Paul's heretical innovations. In 268, the church dismissed the word as heretical nonsense; sixty years later, it was the watchword for unifying orthodoxy.[16]

APOLLINARIUS

In its drift to One Nature theories, the church was dabbling with dangerous ideas. If Christ was really one with God, that would mean that God himself was carried in the Virgin's womb, was born, was destined to suffer and die. Historian Edward Gibbon rightly suggests the consequences of Nicea for doctrine: "The faith of the Catholics trembled on the edge of a precipice where it was impossible to recede, dangerous to stand, dreadful to fall."[17] It was left to one of Athanasius's closest disciples to carry his logic to its natural conclusion. As a fierce enemy of Arianism, Apollinarius of Laodicea in Syria wanted to stress the divine nature of Christ, and he did so in a brilliant series of essays and letters in the 360s and 370s. But in reacting against the Arians, who underplayed the divinity of Christ, he went so far in the opposite direction that he all but removed the human nature, in an extreme form of Word/flesh Christology. He became the ancestor of all later One Nature or Monophysite theologies.

Apollinarius rejected any suggestion that Christ could have a human mind. Like most thinkers of his age, he followed Plato in seeing human beings as possessing a body (*soma*), soul (*psyche*), and mind (*nous*). The *psyche* controlled animal functions, but the *nous* was the rational higher mind that made us human. Apollinarius argued like this: if Christ was of the same nature (*homoousios*) as God the Father, he was therefore divine. But surely a divine being could not so debase itself as to share human nature, and so could not have a human mind, *nous*, "a mind changeable and enslaved to filthy thoughts." If Christ had a human mind, that would have meant that he possessed a dual personality, what we would today call schizophrenia—literally, a split mind.[18]

Although the Incarnation involved a merger of human and divine elements, Apollinarius thought that the divine so dominated as to leave virtually nothing of the human in Christ except *soma* and *psyche*—the fleshly body, and the animal soul. Christ, said Apollinarius, contained no human mind (*nous*) or rational soul (*psyche logike*), but the divine Word supplied this role. "The Word of God has not descended upon a holy man, a thing which happened in the case of the prophets, but the Word himself has become flesh without having assumed a human mind . . . but existing as a divine mind immutable and heavenly." Christ shared human nature, but in no sense could he be a human individual. In Christ, Apollinarius argued, the divine nature so prevailed that he became "God born of a woman," a "flesh-bearing God." "There is no distinction in Holy Scripture between the word and his flesh: he is one nature, one energy, one person, one *hypostasis*, at once wholly God and wholly man."[19]

However logical his argument, Apollinarius attracted massive criticism. If he was right, and Christ had no human mind, what exactly was salvation all about? Had Christ come to save and redeem just the flesh? As the nineteenth-century commentator Philip Schaff wrote, "the rational spirit of man requires salvation as much as the body." At worst, Apollinarius seemed to be denying the real humanity of Jesus and reverting to a kind of Docetism. Several synods denounced his ideas, which were definitively condemned at the Council of Constantinople in 381, the so-called Second Ecumenical Council (Nicea was the first). Pope Damasus concurred: "If any one speaks of Christ as having had less of manhood or of Godhead, he is full of devils' spirits, and proclaims himself a child of hell."[20] The Roman church anathematized "all who maintain that the Word of God moved in human flesh instead of a reasonable soul. For this Word of God Himself was not in His own body instead of a reasonable and intellectual soul, but assumed and saved our soul, both reasonable and intellectual, without sin."[21]

But taking Apollinarius's own work off the table did not solve the dilemmas concerning the Natures, or end argument. If he was wrong, and the One Nature idea was false, did that now mean that the Two Nature theory was correct? So was Cerinthus the Gnostic right after all? The Apollinarian affair launched the long wars that erupted into open conflict at Ephesus and Chalcedon, and beyond.

THE NEW LANGUAGE OF GOD

The Apollinarian crisis also showed how much of the controversy in the church arose from disputes over shades of language. By the end of the fourth century, theologians drew subtle yet critical differences between a number of words that earlier had been thrown around in far vaguer terms. The most significant thinkers were the so-called Cappadocian Fathers: Basil of Caesarea, Gregory Nazianzus, and Gregory of Nyssa. Through their work, the church developed a whole new Christian philosophical system, complete with a terminology that would allow for greater precision in argument. This allowed Christology to be discussed in terms of levels or degrees of

union, in a way that avoided a simple equation of *Christ = God.* The
vocabulary they created shapes all the controversies of the fifth
century.[22]

The most important of these terms are *ousia, physis, hypostasis,* and
prosopon. (See Table 2.)

TABLE 2
SOME KEY TERMS IN
THE CHRISTOLOGICAL DEBATES

Greek:	*ousia*	*physis*	*hypostasis*	*prosopon*
Latin:	*essentia*	*natura*	*substantia*	*persona*
English:	being	nature	individual reality	personality

Physis meant nature, in the sense of "one's true nature." *Hypostasis* is
a complex word but can be translated as "individual reality." The
word suggests "underlying" and could have an architectural sense,
implying the foundations of a house. *Prosopon* implied personality.
The word originally implies mask, as in a theatrical performance,
and the Latin equivalent would be persona. In terms of modern
psychology, it is fitting to think that what we call our "person" or
personality is in fact a mask that we show to the outside world; but
in a theological sense, it had no such sense of deception or illusion.[23]

The distinctions are important. In terms of the Trinity, the Cap-
padocians imagined three individual beings—Father, Son, and
Spirit—each with its own identity, *hypostasis,* but sharing a common
being or *ousia.* God the Son is indeed of the same being, *ousia,* with
the Father, as Nicea had declared, but that does not take us back to
the Sabellian debates. As a human being, I share a common *ousia*
with other humans, so we are of the same sort, but that does not
mean that we are all identical. I have my individual identity, which
differs from that of John Smith or Mary Jones. Christ could thus be
homoousios with God without being identical to God.[24]

But other key questions proliferated. If Christ had both a human and a divine nature (*physis*), what was their relationship? At what stage did they come together? Did this happen from the conception of Christ, from his birth, or from some other time? And what happened to the human nature after that union? Did the human nature survive the Incarnation? Did it exist after the Resurrection? Just how human was the Christ who walked in Galilee was a knotty question.

What did Christ know, and when did he know it? Presumably Christ had knowledge that fell short of that of God the Father, but how constrained was he? We might agree that the infant Jesus in the manger did not have total awareness of the inner workings of the universe, but did the adult man? Jesus' degree of knowledge might in theory have developed gradually, as the man grew, matured, and suffered. But could we identify a specific point at which Jesus gained awareness of his divine identity, rather than a gradual realization?

3. Declaring the Jesus Wars: The Fifth Century

ALEXANDRIA

Much of the debate leading up to Chalcedon involved a decades-long war between two major intellectual centers, the twin hearts of Christianity: Alexandria and Antioch. Each was among the most ancient centers of the faith, with an overwhelming sense of continuity and tradition. Both cities grew mightily in power and prestige as the fifth century went on. The harder the barbarians struck in the west, against Gaul and Spain and Africa, the more the shrunken empire came to rely politically and economically on Syria and Egypt—that is, on Antioch and Alexandria. Each city, also, came to represent a particular interpretation of the Natures controversy, with Alexandria holding firmly to One Nature doctrine, and Antioch being open to Two Nature ideas. Nestorius himself was very much a product of Antioch, and the Alexandrians were his deadliest enemies.

Alexandria's distinctive heritage can be traced to the early-third-century scholar Origen, who was the source of many of the theories and much of the vocabulary—including *ousia* and *hypostasis*—that would shape Christology. Origen also pushed Alexandrian theology in highly philosophical directions, and he pioneered the symbolic, spiritualizing approach to Scripture that so often marked Egyptian thinkers. In the decades following Nicea, Alexandria's heroic representative was the bishop Athanasius. He had insisted absolutely on the divinity of Christ, on the doctrine of homoousios, and fought any attempt to undermine the divine nature within Christ. This tradition was kept alive by a series of Alexandrian successors. The greatest was Cyril, who was at once a brilliant thinker and—let it be said—an obnoxious bully. Cyril struggled mightily against any concession to Two Nature doctrine. He rejected the suggestion that the Word became man through a kind of joining based merely on will or pleasure. The union had to lie deeper than that.[25]

Cyril's greatest contribution to doctrine was the formula that he devised in opposition to Nestorius, that of the hypostatic union. According to this view, which the Council of Chalcedon consecrated as official doctrine, two different natures came together in a "union according to hypostasis" (*henosis kath' hypostasin*), a dynamic unity, "and from both arose one Christ, one Son."

The Word, having united to himself hypostatically in an ineffable and inconceivable manner flesh animated by a rational soul, became man and was called son of man. . . .While the natures that were brought together in true union are different, yet from them both is the one Christ and Son . . . the Godhead and the Manhood, by their ineffable and indescribable coming together into unity, perfected for us the one Lord and Christ and Son.

Mary was the Mother of God because she bore flesh that was indissolubly united to the divine Logos. "So we shall acknowledge one Christ and one Lord, not worshipping a man together with the Word . . . but worshipping him as One and the same."[26]

Also vital in terms of later Christian practice was Cyril's proclamation of eucharistic doctrine. If Christ was God incarnate, then believers could access that divine life through the body and blood of the Eucharist. Although we have not yet quite arrived at the medieval Western idea of the Mass as an act of transubstantiation, Cyril forcefully expresses the idea that the bread and wine are utterly transformed. We receive the Eucharist, he writes, "not as the flesh of a man sanctified and associated with the Word by a unity of dignity, or as having God dwelling in him, but as Life-giving of a truth and the very own flesh of the Word himself. For being, as God, life by nature, when he became one with his own flesh, he made that flesh life-giving." As for many other thinkers, Cyril's very high interpretation of Christ led to an exalted view of the sacraments and the clergy who dispensed them.[27]

The problem in all this was that Cyril was drawing much more heavily than he realized on extreme One Nature doctrines, and these systematically influenced his work. In forming his ideas, he was entranced by a phrase that he believed had been written by his solidly orthodox predecessor, Athanasius, who had supposedly spoken of Christ as "one Nature (*mia physis*) of the Logos of God Incarnate." Through Cyril, this idea became the basis of emerging Christian orthodoxy. The problem was that the text in question was forged, and the idea actually came not from Athanasius, but from Apollinarius, the condemned heretic. Although Antiochene theologians tried to expose the forgery, few Christian leaders listened. Based on these spurious texts, the Alexandrian tradition became ever more committed to ideas of One Nature. Particularly hair-raising was Cyril's proposition that "the Word of God suffered in the flesh, and was crucified in the flesh, and tasted death in the flesh."

Nothing in that formulation would have surprised Apollinarius. Through Cyril's mishandling of a bogus text, the doctrines of Apollinarius left their stamp on mainstream Christology, pushing the image of Christ in much more exalted and divine directions than they might otherwise have done.[28]

ANTIOCH

The other intellectual center was Antioch, which yielded nothing to Alexandria in the depth of its Christian tradition.[29] Antioch's strong and distinctive intellectual tradition made its believers willing to explore daring interpretations of the Christian message. Paul of Samosata himself was bishop here before being deposed for alleged heresy; even Apollinarius lectured in Antioch. Long before the rise of Christianity, Antioch had flourishing schools of rhetoric and philosophy, and Christians drew on this pagan tradition, suitably modified. At the same time, they remained in dialogue with the substantial Jewish population. By the fourth century, too, Antioch was developing very differently from Alexandria in terms of its attitude toward reading and interpreting the Bible. The closer one read the Gospels as a historical text, putting passages in their context, the harder it was to get away from the presence of a very human Jesus. Hence the Antiochene taste for a Word/man Christology.[30]

These different influences shaped Antioch's role in the debates that followed Nicea. The founder of the great scholarly tradition was Diodore, from St. Paul's home city of Tarsus. Diodore attracted churchwide attention as a leading critic of Apollinarius, and in these debates he formulated his own Two Nature position.

Diodore's most important successor was Theodore of Mopsuestia (350–428), who held controversial views on many topics. Like Diodore, he was a universalist, believing that all would ultimately be saved, so that damnation was not eternal.[31] On the question of the natures, Theodore believed that human and divine were united in a single *prosopon,* a personality, but the union was like that of body and soul, or indeed of man and wife: although united, the two always remained recognizable. The presence of the Logos in Christ was like that of grace within the ordinary human being. While the Logos was an undoubted presence, it did not destroy the free will. The contact between the natures in Christ grew progressively as the man grew and matured. So willing was Theodore to stress the human component that he explicitly said that Christ must have been open to temptation as well as suffering. Long before Nestorius, he attacked the practice of calling Mary *Theotokos,* as that implied mingling and confusing the divine and human natures.[32]

Antioch's Christians held firmly to the distinctive ideas pioneered by Diodore and Theodore, however comprehensively these notions were denounced at successive councils. Even when Nestorius' name had become notorious, many Antiochenes were still reluctant to join in the required ritual condemnations. Well into the fifth century, Theodoret of Cyrrhus kept alive versions of Two Nature thought. Although he acknowledged a union of divinity and humanity, he still held that two natures existed after the Incarnation. Christ had one prosopon, but within that united personality, two natures remained.

Far from agreeing to disagree amiably, the two great churches of Antioch and Alexandria fought a generations-long war of attrition, seeking to destroy the evil ideologies of their opponents. When we realize that Nestorius was so closely associated with Antioch—that he had allegedly met Theodore shortly before taking up his bishopric at Constantinople—we appreciate just why every one of that school's many enemies had him in their sights. Not only was Nestorius destroyed politically, his name poisoned for all future eras, but the enemies of the Antiochene school were still pursuing its thinkers long after their deaths. Although Diodore died in 390, a council formally declared his Christology heretical over a century later, in 499. As late as the 550s, a fifth Ecumenical Council met with the goal of condemning Theodore of Mopsuestia (who died in 428), together with his Antiochene allies. This was not so much a theological war as a multigenerational vendetta.[33]

Slogans and Stereotypes

The debates that raged over Christ's nature involved highly technical distinctions. Surely ordinary believers, men and women in the street or the village, did not really appreciate the subtle differences between *ousia* and *hypostasis* or what such terminology implied for the shape of the church? Did the mobs baying for or against the Monophysite or Nestorian causes have the slightest idea of the theologies at stake? Some writers suggest they might have. In the 380s St. Gregory of Nyssa was appalled by the spread of theological discourse to every Constantinople shopkeeper:

> Every part of the city is filled with such talk; the alleys, the crossroads, the squares, the avenues. It comes from those who sell clothes, moneychangers, grocers. If you ask a money-changer what the exchange rate is, he will reply with a dissertation on the Begotten and Unbegotten. If you enquire about the quality and the price of bread, the baker will reply: "The Father is greatest and the Son subject to him." When you ask at the baths whether the water is ready, the manager will declare that "'the Son came forth from nothing."[34]

Popular enthusiasm was just as obvious in the mid-fifth century, although the substance of debate would have moved on from the Trinity to Christology.

People knew the slogans, but did they really understand them? Actually, an excellent case can be made that such distinctions were beyond the reach not just of ordinary believers but of many church leaders. And understanding how they responded to debate offers some depressing lessons about the character of religious argument in other faith traditions and in other historical periods, including our own.

Historian Ramsay MacMullen rightly says that the theological texts of the time are often marked by "complicated thought, strange vocabulary, drawn out proofs, the multiplication of provisos and conditions." To take an example almost at random, this passage is from the third letter of Cyril of Alexandria to Nestorius, a critical document in the controversy leading up to the First Council of Ephesus:

> Besides what the Gospels say our Savior said of himself, we do not divide between two *hypostases* or persons. For neither is he, the one and only Christ, to be thought of as double, although of two (*ek duo*) and they diverse, yet he has joined them in an indivisible union, just as everyone knows a man is not double although made up of soul and body, but is one of both. . . . Therefore all the words which are read in the Gospels are to be applied to One Person, to One hypostasis of the Word Incarnate.

This is dense stuff in translation, and it accurately conveys the convoluted structure of the Greek. That is anything but an extreme example of its kind. Such texts became a verbal minefield for contemporaries, who had to be desperately careful not to confound words with very similar meanings. Cities fell apart in violent conflicts over a single letter: was Christ of the same being with the Father, or of like being, homoousios or homoiousios? Was he from two natures (*ek duo*), or in two (*en duo*)?[35]

Such language is seriously off-putting for most modern readers, including many educated Christians. And it uses so many technical terms that almost seem to the uninitiated like secret codes. Person? Subsistence? Nature? A critic could be forgiven for comparing the straightforward words of Jesus, with all the everyday analogies and images—sheep and harvests, the sparrows and the lilies of the field, the erring brother and the widow's penny—to the arcane philosophical language used here. Jesus spoke of love; his church spoke in riddles. I may not be the only modern reader who hears the language of Chalcedon—two but not one—and finds his thoughts occasionally straying to the film *Monty Python and the Holy Grail*. A monk offers instructions for the Holy Hand Grenade of Antioch, in a deliberate parody of the Athanasian Creed:

> First shalt thou take out the Holy Pin, then shalt thou count to three, no more, no less. Three shalt be the number thou shalt count, and the number of the counting shall be three. Four shalt thou not count, nor either count thou two, excepting that thou then proceed to three. Five is right out.

Now, the fact that ancient christological ideas are complex does not mean that the authors were dealing in empty verbiage. Theologians at the time were trying to explore and express difficult and daring ideas as precisely as possible, avoiding possible ambiguity, and the results could be brilliantly concise and effective. But the writings were often inaccessible to lesser minds than Cyril's, which meant most of his contemporaries.

Worse, words shifted their meanings quite rapidly over time. A modern reader might feel abashed at not understanding a term as *hypostasis*, which was so readily thrown around in the fifth-century debates; but a hundred years earlier, even that weighty word had nothing of the same significance that it did in Cyril's time. In the religious struggles of the 320s, some informed scholars used the word *ousia* (being) interchangeably with *hypostasis*. By the 420s, such a confusion could at a minimum provoke fistfights between clergy and conceivably could attract an official persecution, at least in some parts of the world: the Latin West was much less sensitive to these nuances. St. Augustine himself claimed to see no real distinction between *ousia* and *hypostasis*.[36]

As theological debate continued, participants created and reinterpreted words for new purposes, to the utter confusion of the uninitiated. To use a modern parallel, Christian theological language was developing rather like cultural theory and postmodern literary criticism have in the last few decades, with the constant invention of puzzling new words like *othering* and *in-betweenness, phallocratic* and *scopophilic*. Bemused observers readily mock such PoMo-speak, especially when scholars invent or reshape words for their own idiosyncratic purposes; but that is close to what some of the greatest church fathers were doing in the christological debates.

Just as nonspecialists find such modern terms baffling, so many of those drawn into the religious wars of the fifth century had at best a shaky grip on the issues involved. That is worth stressing, as we might otherwise assume that Christians of this era operated at a stratospheric intellectual or philosophical level many leagues above what later generations might achieve. We need not be so pessimistic. Some of the fifth-century participants were authentically brilliant, and they boldly pursued the implications of their insights for church life and doctrine. Yet some of the best known champions on the various sides often found themselves out of their depth. Even friendly critics suggested that Nestorius himself had very little idea of the theological swamp he was entering when he first became engaged in christological controversy, and his later writings make it clear that he simply was not a "Nestorian" in the sense in which that term emerged. A far greater intellectual figure was Pope Leo the Great, whose Tome made him the primary shaper of Chalcedonian thought. Yet modern scholarship suggests that at the time of Chalcedon he was confused about what Nestorius had actually argued and that only some years afterward did he really grasp what the different sides were contending.[37]

If the bishops of Rome and Constantinople could go so wrong, what hope was there for ordinary clerics, and still less for humble believers? How could they judge the merits of the arguments put forward? Neither did such conflicts have any necessary ending in that all would ultimately agree that the church had arrived at a definitively correct answer. Theology is not and never has been a science in the sense that it forms testable hypotheses. Ancient audiences would have disagreed radically with that statement, as they believed that theological orientation had practical consequences for state and society. A state that practiced an incorrect form of Christianity would be punished in the form of invasion, plague, or famine. But if we do not accept that providential view, we really have no way of knowing which theological approach was closer to expressing and understanding the divine reality.

So if they did not understand the issues, how did people decide which side to support, which cause to see as God's? Issues of identity and culture played a major role. Egyptians (for instance) followed the kind of religious approach that was familiar and customary in their church, which found a face in successive patriarchs of Alexandria. Rather than thinking through the implications of the theology, they followed personalities and names: they were of Cyril's party, or Dioscuros's. Theological ideas were commonly presented in packages epitomized by simple phrases or slogans, and arguments revolved around such buzzwords. We will not divide Christ! God the Word died! Mary is the *Theotokos,* the God-Bearer! Christ is God! That, probably, was the level at which the baker and the money changer carried on their debates.

In the most literal sense, too, participants also operated in highly theatrical ways. Although Christians despised and feared drama and theater, they lived in a society thoroughly accustomed to the styles and conventions of the theater, which shaped their behavior. Bishops appealed to crowds through dramatic oratory, and supporters applauded or booed according to their sympathies. Significantly, the two great religious factions, the Blues and the Greens, traced their origins to rival theatrical cliques as well as circus fans. Church debates became a matter of dueling slogans, phrases shouted at councils and synods, or recited antiphonally in a precursor of modern rap, in order to drown out opponents. The church's battles continued through slogan, symbol, and stereotype rather than through any kind of convincing intellectual discourse.[38]

But if they did not fully understand the theology they believed, Christians knew passionately the kinds of religious thought that they loathed. They knew what they were against. Much of the debate at the time consisted of identifying sets of theological ideas and giving them the name of some unpopular leader, so that believers could unite against a despised and demonized ism. And once something was an ism, it presumably represented that person's twisted and peculiar view of church teaching, rather than the pure serene of authentic Christianity. Whatever he actually preached, Nestorius became the central figure in Nestorianism, a theological trend that supposedly divided Christ's natures. Once this stereotype was established, it could be used to taint any theological approach with which the speaker disagreed.

Theological debate became a game of guilt by association. Reading the denunciations of the time, we need to remember that each faction tended to caricature and exaggerate the positions of its enemies. After Chalcedon had issued its diplomatic and elaborately considered analysis of the divinity, some critics returned to their Palestinian homeland with the alarming news that the Nestorians had triumphed, so that now believers would be required to worship two Christs and two Sons. Furious listeners launched a bloody revolt against the triumph of the Two Nature heresy, Dyophysitism. On the other side of the contest, Christians knew that Apollinarius had taught the single nature in Christ, so that any later belief that erred too far in the direction of stressing the One Nature must be Apollinarian, however significant the distinctions with that older creed. The commonest reason to denounce doctrine X was that it could somehow be linked to doctrine Y.[39]

Understanding the war of isms also helps us trace the course of theological development through these centuries, as each great movement emerged as a reaction, and commonly an overreaction, to some earlier trend that had found itself dismissed as heresy. In the fourth century, the Arian movement preached a less than fully divine Christ, driving Apollinarius to stress Christ's absolute unity with the Father. Reacting against that idea led Nestorius to teach a separation of the natures. And angry rejection of Nestorius encouraged the belief in the dominance of one divine nature of Christ, a belief that others denounced as the Monophysite heresy. In each case, advocates were reacting as much to the stereotype of the enemy movement prevailing at the time rather than to any rational analysis of its teachings.

It would be cheering to think that all these struggling contraries culminated in a harmonious and balanced synthesis that we know as orthodoxy, which Chalcedon declared to the world. But Chalcedon itself became for millions of Christians a nightmare stereotype in its own right, a symbol of the enforcement of false and anti-Christian teaching by an evil secular regime.

Appendix to Chapter Two: Some Early Interpretations of Christ

During the first centuries of Christianity, various thinkers tried to explain the role of Christ and the relationship between his human and divine natures. Some leaned toward a One Nature approach, emphasizing his divinity. Others stressed that his humanity existed alongside his divinity: this view can be categorized as a Two Nature approach. Some key movements and thinkers included:

Adoptionists   A Two Nature approach that saw Christ as a man filled with the spirit of God, but that divinity descended on him only at a moment during or after his earthly lifetime. Human and divine natures existed separately.

Apollinarius   A fourth-century bishop, Apollinarius stressed Christ's divinity so absolutely that he denied the presence of any rational human soul in Christ. In his view, Christ had a single nature, and it was divine. The First Council of Constantinople (381) condemned his views as heretical.

Arians   Arians denied the full equality of God the Son with the Father and thus denied the Trinity.

Basilides   Gnostic Christian thinker of the second century, active in Egypt. He taught a complex mythology, in which Christ came to liberate the forces of light from the material realm of ignorance and evil. Christ was the Mind (*nous*) of God, who descended upon Jesus at his baptism.

Cerinthus   Gnostic Christian thinker (c.100) who argued that the spiritual being of Christ descended on the man Jesus during his baptism in the Jordan; this was an early (and radical) form of Two Nature Christology.

Chalcedonian   The position that became the orthodoxy of the mainstream church after the Council of Chalcedon (451). This approach holds that Two Natures are united in the one person of Christ, without confusion, change, division, or separation. Christ exists *in* two Natures.

Docetists   Early belief that Christ represented only an illusory shape taken by a purely divine being: he had no real human nature. Christ's sufferings on the cross were illusory.

Ebionites   Early Jewish-Christian movement following Christ as a human being, the son of Joseph and Mary; although he was the Messiah, he had no divine nature.

Eutyches   A Monophysite thinker active in the 440s, Eutyches saw Christ as a fusion of divine and human elements, but critics believed he left little room for Christ's human identity.

Gnostics   Gnostics saw Christ as a divine being come to redeem believers from the evil and contaminated material world. Christ's true identity or nature was always divine, and while on earth, he occupied a supernatural body quite distinct from humanity.

Manicheans   Originating in the third century, this movement became an independent world religion. Its founder, Mani, taught an absolute and eternal war between forces of light and darkness. Christ was a liberator come to redeem the elements of light trapped in the material world. He was thus a purely supernatural or divine being and any human or material elements must be illusory. This view overlaps closely with *Gnostic* and *Docetic* ideas.

Marcion   (c.85–160). Important early Christian thinker who argued for a radical distinction between the flawed God of the Old Testament and the true God of the New. Jesus Christ was the Son and representative of this greater God, who sent him to save the world from the old spiritual regime. Marcion was condemned for heresy.

Melkites   Originally an insulting term for those followers of Chalcedonian Orthodoxy who lived in regions dominated by Monophysites. As they followed the religion of the king or emperor, they were called "King's Men."

Miaphysites   A form of One Nature Christology associated particularly with Cyril of Alexandria and his successors. In this view, the incarnate Christ has one Nature, although that is made up of both a divine and a human Nature and still comprises all the features of both. Christ is *from* two Natures.

Modalists   See Sabellius.

Monophysites Believers in One Nature Christology. The term is often used generically to cover other less extreme approaches, including Miaphysitism.

Monotheletes In the seventh century, the Roman Empire tried to overcome the long war between One and Two Nature approaches to Christ. Instead, the empire and church leaders argued that Christ had a single Will. Critics called this view the Monothelete (One Will) heresy, and it was eventually condemned as such.

Nestorians Nestorius was accused of teaching that two Natures coexist within Christ but in a conjunction that falls short of a true union. Mary was thus the Mother of Christ, but could not be called Mother of God. Later scholarship tends to see Nestorius as much closer to mainstream orthodoxy than this description would suggest and not therefore a "Nestorian."

Paul of Samosata A third-century bishop of Antioch, Paul believed that the man Jesus became divine at the time of his baptism. This was condemned as a form of Two Nature heresy or Adoptionism.

Sabellius Sabellius taught in Rome in the early third century. He believed that Christ had a human body but was identical to God in his nature: he had no real human nature. In this view, Father, Son, and Spirit are not persons, but modes of one divine being. Christ was one with the Father to the extent that it was the Father who suffered on the cross. This was an extreme form of One Nature belief.

Valentinus	A second-century Egyptian thinker, Valentinus taught a classic form of Gnostic Christology in which the divine Christ came to redeem the evil world, but he had no true human nature, and his body was always supernatural rather than truly human.
Word/Flesh Christology	Theologians believed that God's Word, the *Logos*, became flesh (*Sarx*), so the Logos was the principle guiding Christ's flesh or body. This *Logos/Sarx* approach tended to see Christ as a representative of humanity rather than, necessarily, a fully developed individual in his own right.
Word/Man Christology	In this *Logos/Anthropos* approach, God's Word, the *Logos*, became human in the form of the man (*Anthropos*) Jesus Christ. Christ was not just a generic representative of humanity, but a fully individual human being.

3

Four Horsemen: The Church's Patriarchs

Alexandrians think the sun rises just for them.
Severus of Antioch

The story of church controversy in this era can be summarized in a line: Syria taught them, Constantinople consecrated them, and Alexandria tried to destroy them. In other words, Syrian schools taught the great church tradition of Antioch, and their graduates went on to hold high rank in Constantinople. But whether out of rivalry between the sees or suspicion of Antioch's theology, Alexandria's patriarchs promptly targeted them. And ultimately—in the long term—Rome benefited.

Underlying the religious struggles were other conflicts, between individuals, but also between different portions of an already vast Christian world. Patriarchs and bishops were fighting one another for supremacy within the church and for the place of the church within a rapidly evolving Christian empire. The conflict had a central political dimension.

Patriarchs and Popes

Through the successive councils, we see the activity of certain powerful individuals, usually patriarchs or popes of their particular sees, men such as Leo of Rome, Cyril and Dioscuros of Alexandria, Juvenal of Jerusalem. But when they participated in church debates, they were speaking not just for themselves, but for much wider and older interests, for multiple generations of predecessors. Each was surrounded by a cloud of witnesses.[1]

Of course, figures like Leo and Dioscuros had their personal interests and obsessions, but they also represented the much larger traditions of corporate entities, their sees or patriarchates. Each see developed its own sense of history, much as secular monarchies built on the traditions of their distinguished ancestors. In the see of Alexandria, Cyril was the great patriarch from 412 to 444. He in turn venerated such glorious predecessors as the early-fourth-century bishop Alexander and especially Athanasius, who dominated church politics through much of the mid-fourth century. Although sons did not succeed fathers as in pharaonic times, patriarchs did raise up and train their successors. Athanasius was "like a son" to Alexander and served as his secretary at the Council of Nicea. Cyril was nephew and secretary to his immediate precursor, Theophilus. Cyril's own secretary was Dioscuros, who in turn succeeded to Alexandria. Even without a direct biological or family link, patriarchates looked monarchical in their sense of continuity and pursued the long-term goals of something very like a dynasty.[2]

The great patriarchs were also long-lived, creating a sense of the permanence and inevitability of their regimes, all the more so in an age when ordinary life spans were so much shorter than they are today. Between 328 and 444, just three men—Athanasius (328–73), Theophilus (385–412) and Cyril (412–44)—held Alexandria's patriarchal throne for all but twelve years (including periods that Athanasius was in exile). By the time Cyril became patriarch at age 34, he probably never remembered a time when his uncle had not held the office.

Although Alexandria offers an unusually clear case of a dynasty, something similar can be traced in many centers. In Rome a clergyman rose through the ranks, serving as archdeacon or emissary for one pope before succeeding in his own right. Under Pope Celestine (422–32), the deacon Leo held important diplomatic posts before himself succeeding as pope in 440. Leo's archdeacon was Hilarius, who succeeded as pope in 461. As in Alexandria, some bishops had impressively long careers. Innocent I reigned as pope from 401 through 417 and endured all the disasters surrounding the Gothic sack of the city. Celestine held office for a full decade; Leo for twenty-one years. Through such connections, dioceses developed their sense of institutional memory and corporate loyalty.[3]

At least according to a powerful historical theory, this long continuity linked the contemporary church to apostolic times. When the Fathers assembled at Chalcedon in 451, they awarded high praise to Pope Leo's Tome, and they reportedly cried, "Peter has spoken thus through Leo!"[4] In saying this, they were not just flattering Leo by comparing him to the apostle but were acknowledging a theory that underlies the religious and political interactions of these years: bishops owed their authority to a direct spiritual inheritance from distinguished predecessors, some of whom had shed their blood for the faith. Indeed, the tombs and relics of these earlier figures served as a material source of mighty gifts and blessings available to the faithful. If somebody asked a bishop by what authority he spoke on a particular matter, he might reply that while he personally was a mere worm, he stood in an unbroken succession from these spiritual ancestors. Ultimately, this line of inheritance could be traced back to an apostle and thence to those who had personally heard Christ speak. The most important dioceses looked to apostolic founders, most famously in the case of Rome, which claimed as its founders both Peter and Paul.

Now, we have to be very careful about accepting such rhetorical claims, even if we do believe that the different apostles really did found the churches credited to them. The apostolic argument was not as ancient or universally accepted as Pope Leo's partisans liked to believe. It impressed Westerners much more powerfully than it did Easterners, who knew that the apostles had actually visited countless small and undistinguished centers. Also, a glance at the historical record shows that the power and prestige of churches supposedly founded by venerated apostles was anything but constant over time and had in fact changed dramatically according to political vagaries. During the fourth and fifth centuries, the leading churches were struggling both to expand their power and to find new legal and political justifications in which they could ground their claims, and the apostolic connection was one potent weapon in the spiritual arsenal. Rome especially was engaged in a furious process of invention and reinvention, from which emerged the titles and ideologies that would give the papacy hegemony over Western Europe for long centuries to come. The fifth-century councils provided the public setting—or rather, the theatrical stage—in which such claims were asserted and contested.

Rising and Falling Stars

Through most of the fifth century, four great churches held the greatest prestige throughout church and empire, and each played its role in the theological controversies. Three of these represented the Founding Triangle of early Christianity, namely, Antioch, Rome, and Alexandria; the fourth was Constantinople. All the councils witnessed the interplay of these four spiritual kingdoms.

By Constantine's time, certain sees occupied a special status through their place in Christian history but also from the prestige and wealth of the cities in which they were located. In 325, the Council of Nicea identified Rome, Alexandria, and Antioch as the preeminent churches. When the emperor Theodosius I established

Christianity as the official faith of the Roman realm in 381, he naturally had to specify which particular version of that religion was being approved, and he did so in terms of the belief held at Rome and Alexandria. Rome's Christianity was the religion laid down in the time of St. Peter, "and which is now professed by the [Roman] *pontifex* Damasus and by Peter, Bishop of Alexandria."[5]

Each great see presided over a wider region comprising several civil provinces, within which lesser bishops acknowledged the supremacy of the local bishop-of-bishops (The word "patriarch" evolved in the early fifth century). Each patriarchate constituted a kind of regional empire within the church, with boundaries that had to be defended against ambitious outsiders. That meant that established patriarchs were always likely to see up-and-coming bishoprics as potential rivals. In turn, rising contenders struggled against established incumbents, adding an element of instability to the ecclesiastical order. Any contemporary with the slightest knowledge of history knew that patriarchates could come and go and that centers could gain or lose prestige over time. There could, and probably would, be other popes. That fact contributed mightily to conflict between churches, however much those issues of power were disguised in theological terms.

A number of great churches could easily become candidates for patriarchal status in the future, joining or replacing existing centers. By all rights, Carthage should already have won this status at Nicea, and it would have done so if that church was not constantly tearing itself apart in bloody schisms. Milan was another promising candidate for future glory, while the Gaulish see of Arles had its aspirations. The Mesopotamian capital of Seleucia-Ctesiphon wanted to serve as the center of a great Eastern church beyond the Roman frontier, and that church's head actually did become patriarch of the East in 498.[6]

By far the most important addition to the patriarchal list was the city of Constantinople, New Rome, which was planned in 325 and consecrated in 330. It was developed as a doublet of Rome, with its own prefect and magistrates and a senate three hundred strong. Critically, its vast and superbly constructed walls—developed from 408—made it all but impregnable. Whatever other parts of the empire might slip away, Constantinople would for foreseeable ages serve as an indispensable bastion. The advantages of that position became obvious as the empire's military and political situation fell apart. Whatever happened to Rome or Antioch, Constantinople was there to stay—and it did remain a Christian center until 1453, when Turkish forces finally acquired heavy cannon.

As it became ever more clearly the capital of the Eastern empire—and ultimately, of the whole empire—the city naturally gained prestige within the church. In 381, the Council of Constantinople proclaimed that: "The Bishop of Constantinople shall have the primacy of honor after the Bishop of Rome, because it is New Rome." In fact, the city would often be referred to in later councils by the auspicious title of "Constantinople New Rome." This claim attracted opposition, and not just from the Roman popes, who refused to ratify the clause. After all, making Constantinople number two in the hierarchy destabilized an already fluid order. If acknowledged, the new status automatically demoted the other great sees— Alexandria to number three, and Antioch to four. And talking of New Rome implied an Old Rome—old, perhaps, in the sense of decrepit or obsolete.[7]

The balance of power between the great sees shaped church politics of the fifth century. Always in the background were the struggles between Alexandria and Antioch, but in addition, Constantinople was everyone's target. The upstart city could usually count on deadly opposition from Alexandria and, commonly, interference from Rome itself: Rome and Alexandria easily made common cause against Constantinople. The council of 381 marked the beginning of a three-sided war between those cities that culminated only at Chalcedon, in 451. On three occasions—in 404, 431, and 449—Alexandrian dabbling brought down bishops of Constantinople, in each case generating a whole-sale imperial crisis. In 458, Alexandrian-inspired discontent provoked the murder of a fourth patriarch of the imperial capital.

But other centers, too, had their distinctive agendas. Constantinople's rise was parlous news for Ephesus, supposedly the home of the apostle John and of the Virgin Mary herself. In the fourth century, these associations allowed Ephesus to hold senior ecclesiastical rank, with jurisdiction over most of western Asia Minor, a rich territory critical to the empire's survival. But if Constantinople was to be a great patriarchate, then its bishop needed to control his own set of provinces, and there was no way to develop such a power base except at the expense of Ephesus. At the start of the fifth century, Constantinople's archbishop John Chrysostom intervened freely in Ephesus, and it was only a matter of time before Ephesus fell entirely under the sway of the imperial city. That was, of course, unless Constantinople itself could be weakened as a nest of heretics. When Constantinople's Nestorius came under attack in 431, the fact that the great council called to settle the issues was held in Ephesus was a welcome gift to his enemies.[8]

Another controversial up-and-coming see was Jerusalem, which traced its glories back to the birth of the church. The Council of Nicea granted the city an honorary primacy, although keeping it for administrative purposes under the metropolitan of Caesarea. Jerusalem's later bishops fought to transform that honorary status into real power. The most important person in this story was Juvenal, who held the see from 422 through 458 and who repeatedly surfaced as a player in the intrigues surrounding the councils, always seeking the greater glory of his see. Carving out a suitable home territory meant detaching provinces from the patriarch of Antioch, who had to be weakened accordingly. This gave Juvenal a powerful motive for attacking Antioch's theology, as well as its alumni, like Nestorius. At the great council of Ephesus, then, Juvenal joined Memnon of Ephesus and the Alexandrians in opposition to Constantinople's bishop. Juvenal finally won patriarchal status for Jerusalem in 451, creating the system of five great patriarchates that endured for centuries.[9]

These regional interests could trump ideology. Although Juvenal was an extreme example of the type, he was not the only church leader to pursue power and office whatever official theology prevailed at any given time. Looking at some of the players in these struggles, British historians recall the fictional Vicar of Bray. The vicar is the antihero of an eighteenth-century song put in the mouth of a clergyman who has survived countless changes of regime and doctrine and has played along with all of them. Royalist? Republican? Presbyterian? The vicar will fly whatever flag he needs to. The ultimate pragmatist, his sole guiding principle is that of survival. The chorus boasts, "That whatsoever King may reign / I will be the Vicar of Bray, Sir!" The vicar had many predecessors in the fifth-century world. A contemporary wrote of one bishop that he "never abided by one opinion, being a double dealer, a waverer, and a time-server, now anathematizing the synod at Chalcedon, at another time recanting, and admitting it with entire assent."[10]

In the diverse Christianity of late antiquity, each patriarch in a sense lived in a different world, with a different political and geographical outlook, and a different perception of traditional allies and foes. Different patriarchs also enjoyed very different relationships with the empire. From the time of Constantine, the church was drawn ever more closely into the process of government, and at least two of the patriarchs—Rome and Alexandria—became so powerful over large regions as to appear almost royal in their own right. As they grew in power, spiritual and secular, older traditions reasserted themselves, traditions not just of apostolic succession but also of royal authority.

Rome's Imperator

Although we know in hindsight that Rome would be the great survivor, that fact was certainly not obvious at the time. Roman popes tried to act like emperors, and they inherited many of the attitudes and behaviors that in earlier years might have characterized an emperor rather than an early Christian bishop—but increasingly, they found themselves marginalized. Rome was stranded on an exposed and dangerous corner of the civilized world, cut off from the heart of cultural and intellectual life. Everything popes did in the various councils has to be seen in this context of vulnerability, the desperate need to cling to power and status within church and empire.

Although the papacy traced a lineal heritage from Peter and Paul, the institution had not always had the centralized structure it possessed in the fourth and fifth centuries. By the time of Nicea, the papacy was well established, with a prestige reinforced by a long succession of incumbents who had suffered persecution or martyrdom. But it was above all in the decades after 370 that the papacy emerged in anything like the awe-inspiring form that we know from later eras, with its famous titles and institutions, its rhetoric, and its claims to universal power. In 370, the bishop of Rome was a venerated cleric who mainly exercised power in Italy. By 460 the bishop was at least claiming a kind of universal headship and an immunity from the restraints of civil power. While at first the popes could do little actually to enforce their wishes in the secular world, later political events would give them enormous scope to expand their powers and aspirations. In terms of its later impact on European—and global—affairs, this ideological change constitutes a revolution of the first order. We are witnessing the creation of *the* key institution of medieval Europe.[11]

A series of brilliant papal entrepreneurs headed the Roman church between 370 and 430, creating the radical and expansive notions of church authority on which Leo and his successors could later build. Bishops of Rome named and claimed; these were the years in which they became popes, became heirs of Peter, became primates and pontiffs, exercised a principate, and ruled over the apostolic see (See Table 3). This was a church on the make.

TABLE 3
ROMAN POPES 366–468

366–84	Damasus I
384–99	Siricius
399–401	Anastasius I
401–17	Innocent I
417–18	Zosimus
418–22	Boniface I
422–32	Celestine I
432–40	Sixtus III
440–61	Leo I
461–68	Hilarius

Damasus I (366–84) has a fair claim to rank as the first great pope. He grounded Roman authority in the words of Christ himself: "Thou art Peter; and upon this rock I will build my church." He developed the idea of the *sedes apostolica*, the apostolic see, to which lesser churches appealed for judgment. From pagan custom, he inherited the old priestly title of pontifex, pontiff, although it would be some centuries before the popes acquired the full imperial title of pontifex maximus. He also reorganized the papal archives, an achievement that went far beyond any mere contribution to antiquarian scholarship. The archives were a rhetorical arsenal: any time a king or bishop made the slightest acknowledgment of papal prestige and power, the document went straight into the archives, ready to be retrieved when needed to prove a point a year or a century later. Some of these documents were authentic, others not. Among the influential forgeries were the Pseudo-Clementines, a collection of letters attributed to the first-century Christian Clement but actually created around 220. These documents had long appealed to the Roman church because they offered an explicit recognition of papal supremacy, with the bishops of Rome inheriting Peter's powers to bind and loose. By the end of the fourth century, they were translated into Latin, and Clementine ideas became part of the common currency of papal rhetoric.[12]

In the time of Damasus's successor Siricius (384–99), the title of *papa*, or pope, came to be applied especially to the Roman pontiff, rather than merely being a generic term for a bishop. Siricius promulgated Roman authority through decretals, statements modeled on imperial edicts. Although later generations would happily invent bogus early decretals, the first authentic example comes from Siricius's time in an edict that spells out detailed regulations for church life and policy in Spain. As Siricius boasts, "We bear the burdens of all who are oppressed, or rather the blessed apostle Peter, who in all things protects and preserves us, the heirs, as we trust, of his administration, bears them in us." Such words would seem quite normal for popes over the following 1,600 years, but they were a startling innovation in the 380s. The Roman bishop now claimed to sit in the *cathedra Petri*, Peter's throne.[13]

Later popes continued this march to supremacy. Pope Innocent I (401–17) as a matter of course issued decretals to churches across the Western Empire, and the papacy was now claiming that it could not be judged by other churches. Innocent also found a new basis for asserting a far-reaching primacy in the church. The idea depends on a passage in the sixth canon of Nicea, in which the council declared that the church of Alexandria should have the same jurisdiction over its home territories—Egypt and Libya—that Rome had in its area. But what exactly was the Roman jurisdiction implied here? The context makes it clear that the territory is definitely in Italy, in regions that would formerly have been subject to the city of Rome. Under Innocent, though, the papacy claimed that the passage recognized Roman supremacy through the whole Western church. A spurious Latin version of the canons pushed these assertions still further, with a declaration that the *ecclesia Romana* had always had the *primatum*, primacy, over the whole church. Later popes proudly cited this passage as the formal recognition of Rome's universal authority—and they continued to do so even after Eastern leaders scornfully pointed out that the words did not appear in the authoritative Greek originals.

Between 420 and 460—the era of the christological battles—successive popes built mightily upon these foundations. At First Ephesus in 431, Pope Celestine I's envoy explicitly used the Petrine inheritance to justify Roman authority. And when Leo became pope in 440, he consciously operated as vicar of Peter, Peter's earthly voice: as he said, "the blessed apostle Peter does not cease from presiding over his see." When Leo spoke—he believed—Peter spoke, and an insult to Leo was a direct blow at the fisherman. When Leo made a diplomatic approach to Dioscuros, Cyril's successor at Alexandria, it was no mere matter of Leo writing to Dioscuros, but rather, Peter was speaking to his old secretary, Mark. Of course, he claimed, the two churches were as one on points of doctrine. As Leo wrote, optimistically, "It is wicked to believe that [Peter's] holy disciple Mark, who was the first to govern the church of Alexandria, formed his decrees on a different line of tradition."[14]

Leo strove to transform spiritual headship into a true primacy of jurisdiction. If he was the heir of Peter, then under Roman law he inherited Peter's rights and powers, including the ability to bind and loose, to make and break laws. He spoke as *indignus haeres beati Petri*, the unworthy heir of blessed Peter, and the loaded word there was *heir*. Leo also asserted the papal right to act as a principate, a near-imperial role first asserted in the 420s.

Rome Recedes

The era of the papal revolution—roughly between 370 and 460—neatly coincides with the decline of Roman imperial power in Italy and the West, and of course the two trends are closely intertwined. The weaker imperial power became in Italy, the more space appeared for a substitute authority—in the form of the church—and the greater the need for a successor. The Roman Empire's link to the founding city shrank steadily. From the third century onward, emperors tended to make their homes elsewhere, usually close to military centers from which they could easily move to defend the frontiers. Milan, Trier (Germany), and Sirmium (in Serbia) all served as imperial capitals long before Constantine established his new city on the Bosporus, and later Western emperors favored Ravenna. The popes, then, usually did not live under the immediate shadow of the emperor or his court, and this benign neglect allowed the papal institution to develop without close interference or supervision.

From the end of the fourth century, Roman power in the West suffered from massive barbarian incursions, which repeatedly threatened the historic capital. In 378, at the battle of Adrianople, the Romans suffered an epochal defeat at the hands of Gothic-led forces, who moved progressively west. Further invasions followed the collapse of the Rhine frontier in 406. In 410, Visigothic forces sacked Rome, and Visigothic kingdoms were founded in Gaul and Spain, while a lethally powerful Vandal regime gradually took over North Africa. Britain fell away from the empire in 410. Imperial diplomacy gradually succeeded in bringing at least some of the barbarians to work within the Roman system, but the new order was deeply troubling for the church. Both Vandals and Visigoths were Arian Christians, whose church rejected the Trinitarian doctrines of the empire; and by the 420s these heretics were founding substantial new states on what had once been Roman territory. This political collapse did not cut the popes entirely off from the empire. In popular historical consciousness, the Roman Empire ended formally in 476, supposedly one of the great turning points in world affairs. In fact, this change was less epochal than it might appear, and the main alteration that occurred in 476 was that the now-sole emperor in Constantinople thought it best not to have a coemperor. Imperial power survived in Italy, although the church came to exercise many of its functions.[15]

Lacking a powerful or interventionist emperor resident in Rome itself, Pope Leo was left to act very much as a sovereign might have done in earlier eras, and his well-documented career amply demonstrates the Roman church's imperial outlook. His letters suggest a man who expected to be obeyed without question, whether he was commanding other bishops in many parts of Italy and Gaul or asserting his authority across Spain and North Africa. One later editor writes of the "dictatorial strain" of much of this correspondence, and other words like "imperious" and "arbitrary" also come freely to mind. He was desperately sensitive about any hints of inferior churches seizing new powers or breaking away to follow centers other than Rome. He battled to prevent the churches of Illyricum (modern day Croatia and Albania) drifting into Constantinople's sphere of influence. In one case, he had to deal with a dispute in Gaul, in which a synod under Bishop Hilary of Arles had deposed a bishop named Celidonius for violating canonical rules. Hilary, who had declared himself metropolitan of Gaul, was as much an empire builder as Leo himself. Celidonius appealed to Rome, forcing Hilary to make a personal appearance before the pope. This meant undertaking a trek that would not have been an easy matter in the best of circumstances but which was deadly dangerous on the barbarian-infested roads of the 440s. Even so, Leo was not satisfied. He reinstated Celidonius, limiting Hilary's powers, and continued to intervene in the management of the province. He was acting, in fact, like a strong Roman emperor dealing with restive provinces, or like an authoritarian medieval pope.[16]

But however strong the popes might have been in Italy and parts of Gaul, in the most ancient areas of Roman domination, it remained to be seen what influence they might enjoy in an empire that had moved decisively eastward in terms of demography and culture. Instead of serving as the impregnable heart of civilization, Rome itself was now an exposed outpost on the western fringes of empire. The city's population fell from perhaps 800,000 in the fourth century to 350,000 in 450, and to just 60,000 by the 530s.[17]

The political shocks had enormous cultural implications. In 330, the Roman Empire found its central axis roughly on a line from Rome to Carthage; but by 430, that axis would better be imagined as running much farther to the east, from Constantinople to Alexandria. The new geography would have been familiar to Herodotus nine hundred years earlier, or to Alexander the Great. And the Eastern world was thoroughly Greek. Greek was, of course, the oldest language of Christian thought and writing, and that dominance within the church continued after the conversion. As the empire shifted its focus, Greek steadily became the language of politics. It would not be long before "the Roman language" came to refer to Greek rather than Latin.

Corresponding to this change was the decline of Latin, which had once been a powerful force unifying the Roman world. A linguistic barrier now cut Rome off from the debates of the East Mediterranean. Already at the fifth-century councils, Roman participants had to use interpreters, and Pope Leo spoke not a word of Greek. Eighteen months after the Council of Chalcedon had concluded, he was pleading for a Latin translation of its decisions, as "we have no very clear information about the acts of the synod . . . on account of the difference in language." If they had known Greek, papal representatives would not have dared try to palm off the spurious Nicene canon about papal primacy. To put it mildly, Romans did not have the native familiarity with theological nuances that marked their counterparts in Antioch or Alexandria. When Eastern leaders insisted that popes be represented at councils, it was because of the prestige of Rome and Peter rather than for any intellectual contribution these Westerners could conceivably make.[18]

Nor did Latin scholarship have much currency in the East, where all the intellectual turmoil took place. For Westerners, the early fifth century seems like a time of towering intellectual achievement through the work of St. Augustine, but his writings made next to no impact in the contemporary Greek-speaking East for several centuries. Even the *City of God* never penetrated the Greek-speaking world. Nor did Easterners show any awareness of the lively Christian culture in contemporary Gaul—and they certainly knew nothing about a troubled missionary bishop working at just this time, whom Westerners remember as Patrick of Ireland. In contrast, quite minor Greek pamphlets and squibs circulated rapidly in the old Hellenistic world that stretched from Libya to Mesopotamia, and they were widely discussed shortly after their appearance.[19]

In other ways, too, the Roman church was now far out of the loop of church politics. All the councils that shaped the church from the fourth century onward occurred in the Eastern empire, and usually within easy striking distance of Constantinople itself. Of the first seven general councils recognized by the whole church, three were held at Constantinople itself (381, 553, 680), two at Nicea (325, 787), one at Chalcedon (451), and one at Ephesus (431). Ephesus was also the setting for the controversial council of 449. The only one of these locations that was not in the immediate vicinity of the capital was Ephesus, some 250 miles from Constantinople. The sites were chosen for the convenience of the court and the leading members of the church hierarchy. Being so far removed from the new center of ecclesiastical action forced Roman popes to react to decisions that had already been taken, rather than leading the way.

Rome was now just one player in a four- or five-power game, and by no means the strongest. Who knew how long the see of Peter might hold on to a primacy that was already looking anachronistic? In response, the Roman popes had to play the poor hand available to them. This meant exploiting differences between rival churches, while forming alliances with other centers with whom they shared common interests. But above all, it meant playing for all it was worth the memory of Peter, and the apostolic guarantee of strict orthodoxy.

Alexandria's Pharaohs

If Rome was fighting the threat of decline, the main question for the Alexandrian church was just how high its ambitions could rise. For over thirty years, Alexandria's patriarch Cyril played an aggressive and interventionist role in theological debates, and after he died in 444, his successors kept his tradition vigorously alive. So activist were they, so obstreperous, that it is often easy to forget that Alexandria was not in truth the capital of the Christian world or that the patriarchs were not its absolute rulers. In more recent times, the patriarchs had come to serve as the effective voices of a region as well as a faith, and they based their political power on tumultuous mobs and effective militias. If exasperated observers thought that the patriarchs acted like pharaohs or Hellenistic god-kings, these churchmen had excellent grounds for their pretensions.[20]

The Alexandrian church claimed a distinguished ancestry with a list of rulers that traced back to St. Mark the Evangelist, but we know very little about the succession of orthodox bishops before the famous theologian and philosopher Clement of Alexandria, around 190. This obscurity may reflect some embarrassed rewriting by later church historians. In fact, Alexandria had a very distinguished Christian history from apostolic times, but much of it was, by later standards, wildly heretical and overly willing to draw on the insights of pagan philosophy or Judaism. Egypt was the home of the greatest early Gnostics, Basilides and Valentinus, and probably several others, and before Clement, no non-Gnostic Christian enjoyed anything like the same degree of prestige in Alexandria. Only later, as orthodox non-Gnostics secured their position, did they feel the need to invent a respectable spiritual ancestry for themselves, in the form of an artificial list of suitably orthodox bishops.[21]

Alexandrian thinkers were thoroughly used to theologies that exalted Christ as a supernatural being. The fact that our oldest Christian manuscripts were all found in Egypt may just mean that ancient documents survived better in that dry climate, but many famous texts, canonical or heretical, probably did originate in that explosive cultural mix. Alexandria would have been a natural home for the gospel of John. John prominently uses the idea of Christ as the Logos, the creative Word of God, which draws on the ideas of Alexandria's greatest Jewish philosopher, Philo. Egyptian Gnostics loved John.[22]

Understanding those ancient roots also tells us a great deal about the likely attitudes of fifth-century church leaders. Cyril and his contemporaries were proud of Egypt's overwhelming Christian past and, beyond that, of its roots in an Egyptian culture that, as far as they knew, was the world's oldest and most influential. Even today, Egypt's Coptic Church preserves the ancient language spoken in the time of the pharaohs and the pyramid builders, and its calendar, too, dates back to pharaonic times. The very word *Coptic* comes from *Aigyptos*, Egyptian: the church was thoroughly rooted in Egyptian soil and speech. The Coptic Church still divides the year into the four seasons observed by ancient Egyptians, with appropriate liturgies and blessings for the transition points. But at the same time, the presence of so many pre- and non-Christian influences seemed potentially threatening in a melting-pot Alexandrian culture that so naturally mingled cultures and traditions and favored religious syncretism.[23]

Nervousness about cultural drift helps explain the ferocity of Egyptian church leaders against other religions, pagan or Jewish. In 367, Athanasius issued the strictest condemnation to date of noncanonical Christian gospels and scriptures, leading many to be concealed or destroyed. This may have been the point at which the famous Nag Hammadi gospels were hidden to forestall destruction. At the end of the fourth century, his successor, Theophilus, led Christian mobs in a comprehensive assault on the pagan temples. Not content with demolishing statues and buildings, the church organized public exhibitions to show how the pagan priests had contrived some of the miraculous tricks by which they overawed the simple. In 391, Theophilus led an assault on the Serapeum at Alexandria, one of the greatest pagan centers of the ancient world. Such shows were extraordinarily powerful in reinforcing Christian loyalties, in proving the superiority of the Christian Lord to the long-dreaded pagan powers. It is exactly such ritual destructions of pagan objects that have given so much momentum to Christian growth in modern-day Africa.[24] This aggressive attitude to other faiths also suggests why Cyril and his followers would fight desperately against any version of Christian theology that might offer the slightest concession to pagan ideas of multiple gods. Egyptian Christians must above all defend the oneness of God's nature.

Cyril's church had a powerful tradition of hands-on direct action, with several distinct constituencies available to break the heads of rivals. Alexandria itself was notoriously rowdy, and the church historian Socrates noted that, "The Alexandrian public is more delighted with tumult than any other people: and if at any time it should find a pretext, breaks forth into the most intolerable excesses; for it never ceases from its turbulence without bloodshed." That is actually a good summary of the city's church history. Once Christianity was legalized and churches became widespread, lower clergy used their sermons and homilies to disseminate the official patriarchal line throughout the city. They mobilized urban factions against the church's rivals—against pagans, Jews, or imperial officials. Through sermons, processions, and devotions, the church controlled the media through which urban opinion could be manipulated. If they chose, the church had the means to promote demagoguery, and it had a willing audience. Athanasius was certainly willing to use mob action when needed, to the point of beatings and kidnappings. In 361, a mob lynched a rival bishop who claimed his diocese. Even Cyril's election in 412 was only achieved following a "tumult" in which his followers overawed a rival faction that had the support of the Roman military commander on the ground.[25]

The patriarchs could also count on still more fearsome supporters from beyond the city limits. At least by the third century, Christianity had penetrated deep into the Egyptian countryside, where followers used native Coptic rather than urban Greek. These rural believers provided recruits for the booming monastic movement that originated in Egypt and then spread throughout the Christian world, especially in Syria and Mesopotamia. Neither for the first time nor the last, Egypt acted as a primary incubator of change within the churches.

Egypt's emerging native Christianity was a profoundly impressive phenomenon. Its most famous product was the pioneering monk St. Antony, who died at an advanced age in 356 and whose biography—written by Athanasius—served as wonderful publicity for Egyptian faith around the Christian world. Antony, incidentally, seems to have thought and worked entirely in Coptic. His spiritual successor was the awe-inspiring Aba Shenoute, who died in 466, allegedly at the age of 118. He led the White Monastery, a huge community several thousand strong, which included many nuns in addition to the male monks. Like other smaller settlements, his monastery became the center of life for neighboring lay communities. Ordinary Christians turned to the monks for spiritual sustenance, but also for social services, education, and disaster relief. Shenoute's vast body of writings and correspondence made him one of the very greatest figures of Coptic literature and faith. He made Coptic the basis of a proud new Christian tradition that defined itself aggressively against a Greek language that was tainted by paganism and, increasingly, heresy.[26] When all other resources failed them, the Alexandrian patriarchs could rely on the passionate faith of these native Christians.

Monks were, in theory, *monachoi*, solitaries, utterly detached from the world, but many became passionately engaged in worldly politics in the defense of orthodoxy. The most militant and active were those of the Nitrian Desert, the venerated Holy Desert that contained hundreds of houses and where Cyril himself had studied for several years. Egypt's monks served as a reliable clerical army. Most obviously political were the *parabolani*, a brotherhood sworn to perform charitable tasks such as the burial of the dead, and who enjoyed clerical privileges. By the fifth century, though, they served as a personal bodyguard for the bishops. In 416, an imperial law tried to fix their numbers at five hundred, but the patriarchs recruited these enforcers as they thought they needed them. Monks supported the powerful political machine that was the Egyptian church.[27]

The Egyptian church had an uneasy relationship with civil authority, if and when that authority ran contrary to enforcing what was seen as God's will. In constantly stressing the superiority of church power, the patriarchate was staking out a theocratic position. This tension became obvious in about 414–15 in a series of events that reveals much about the radical political aspirations of the church less than a century after the empire granted toleration to Christians. The affair also foreshadowed many of the wider church confrontations at the great councils.[28]

At this time, Cyril was the new patriarch of Alexandria. His main opponent was Orestes, the Roman prefect, a Christian, but one who still held traditional Roman notions about religious or ethnic diversity. According to this view, religious practices should generally be tolerated provided that their followers acknowledged imperial power, obeyed the law, and paid taxes. Toleration did not apply when groups became seditious or flouted the law, and in such cases Roman vengeance could be frightful. Until that point, though, it really was no business of Roman power to pick and choose between rival schools of thought. Cyril, in contrast, wished to destroy rival faiths and competing currents within Christianity, by force if necessary. Orestes was nervous about the growth of church power at the expense of imperial jurisdiction and had personal reasons for concern. He knew that Cyril had set spies to watch him, to note any slip from orthodoxy, or to find anything that could damage his reputation.[29]

The crisis began when Orestes issued regulations for the popular dances and theatrical shows held by Alexandria's large and old-established Jewish community. Jews protested the agitation of one Christian activist, "a very enthusiastic listener of bishop Cyril's sermons," and Roman authorities agreed that this troublemaker deserved silencing, and indeed torture. Orestes was sending a clear signal to Cyril about the bounds of this authority, but the attempt backfired. As relations between the patriarch and the Jews deteriorated, mob violence ensued. Cyril led "an immense crowd" to raid the synagogues, to rob and expel the Jews whose roots in the city dated back some seven hundred years. Although Orestes complained directly to the emperor, he could not reverse a patriarchal coup against civil authority.[30]

Several hundred Nitrian monks now stormed into the city. They denounced Orestes as a pagan idolater persecuting their beloved patriarch. As Orestes's military guard fled, the monks stoned and wounded the prefect in an outrageous act of rebellion that in other times and places would have persuaded a Roman emperor to sack an entire city. Orestes ordered the ringleader to be tortured to death, but once again, Cyril was not intimidated. Instead, he ordered the executed monk recognized as a martyr for the church, canonizing him on the spot—to the disapproval of mainstream Christians who otherwise supported their spiritual father.[31]

The conflict now claimed another victim. This was the woman philosopher Hypatia, a venerated thinker and teacher, who now suffered because of her alleged friendship with Orestes. (The recent film *Agora* makes Hypatia as glamorous as she is brilliant.) Taken in the streets by a Christian mob, she was dragged to a church where she was mutilated and dismembered and her remains burnt. While no direct evidence connects Cyril to her death, he had not tried to calm the mob fury that was its immediate cause. And criticisms of Cyril's conduct do not just arise from modern hindsight, which fails to take account of the different standards prevailing in the distant past. In the words of a near contemporary critic of the patriarch's conduct, "surely nothing can be farther from the spirit of Christianity than allowing massacres, fights, and transactions of that sort."[32]

By Cyril's time, then, Alexandria's patriarchs looked to a tradition that was royal in its aspirations, and near absolutist in its willingness to overwhelm opposition. Cyril presided over an impressive Egyptian hierarchy of a full hundred bishops, organized under ten metropolitans. The patriarchs even had an imperial role, as their ecclesiastical power extended deep into Africa, into the kingdoms of Ethiopia and Nubia, and Alexandria largely determined the beliefs and practices of these churches. This southward reach stretched much farther than that of any earlier pharaoh. This issue, incidentally, contributed still further to rivalries with Constantinople. While Alexandria naturally dreamed of an African empire, the imperial capital now claimed jurisdiction over all churches established beyond the frontiers.[33]

Looking at the church of Alexandria around this time, a modern observer is bound to ask whether the fervor inspired by Athanasius or Cyril was in some sense nationalistic, whether the monks and mobs were fighting for a concept of Egyptianness, and against Roman conformity. Certainly, Cyril and his followers were keenly aware of the dignity of their city and region, and Egypt's historic role in defending orthodoxy. At the same time, terms like nationalism would be anachronistic when applied to this early era, and there really is no evidence of secessionist feeling. Rather, the patriarchs saw themselves as effective rulers of Egypt within the context of a Christian empire, and their goal was not to leave the empire, an idea that was as unnecessary as it was bizarre. Instead, they wanted to use their homeland as a secure base from which they could spread the historic truth of Egypt throughout the Christian world. And the experience of Nicea above all had shown how useful church councils could be in this process. Athanasius had largely established Nicene orthodoxy throughout the empire, despite serious opposition from within the imperial family itself.

Constantinople and Antioch

Alexandrian ambitions faced two obstacles, which proved to be closely linked. One was the see of Antioch, with its rich apostolic traditions. It was here that the word *Christian* was first applied in apostolic times, probably as a dismissive term or insult within the Jewish community. The city also claimed St. Peter as its first bishop, before the fisherman had traveled to some strange city in the far west. In later centuries, Antioch earned more fame as the home of the martyr Ignatius, while its bishopric was one of the handful of leading patriarchal sees that held the highest places of honor within the church. Adding to its political pull within the Christian empire, Antioch dominated the rich land of Syria. Just as the Egyptian church looked south into Africa, so Antioch influenced the Syriac-speaking worlds of the Near East, reaching into Mesopotamia and beyond. Antioch was in its way quite as imperial as Alexandria.[34]

Culturally, Antioch was at least a match for Alexandria, however much the ideas the city produced disturbed or repelled the Egyptians. It was natural for emperors to look to Antioch's alumni for the monks and scholars who would fill the episcopal sees, and especially that of Constantinople. Antioch's weak point lay in its theology. If Alexandrians could portray Antioch as heretical, as less than totally devoted to the divinity and glory of Christ, that gave an opening for subversion. An Antioch-trained bishop in Constantinople would stand in real peril.

Constantinople itself suffered all the blessings and curses of direct imperial patronage. The see would not have existed if not for the imperial presence and certainly would not have held a rank second only to Rome. As the choice of a bishop was such a politically sensitive matter, emperors and leading courtiers played a key role in the selection, so that bishops should in theory have begun their tenure with the intimate support of the most powerful figures in the empire. These same laypeople also had a powerful vested interest in developing the city's Christian credentials, beautifying its churches, and stocking them with dazzling collections of relics. They worked to build up Constantinople as the special holy city of an empire under the protection of the Virgin Mary. And unlike the other great sees, this city was a purely Christian creation, with no need to purge the sins of a pagan past. The holier the city, the greater the prestige of its bishop.[35]

But having said that, leading the church in Constantinople did pose special dangers, as external forces found it easy to build and exploit factions within the imperial family and court. Through most of the fifth century, Alexandrian patriarchs ran a substantial and effective network for lobbying and intelligence-gathering in Constantinople. They backed up their efforts with gift-giving and bribery undertaken on an epic scale, a lavish generosity that suggests the vast wealth that Egypt could still produce. This Alexandrian manipulation shaped imperial religious politics.

By the fifth century, too, Constantinople was a sprawling, turbulent center with a strong history of riot and civil disorder. As many emperors found, controlling distant frontiers was not much use if they lost control of the streets within a mile of the palace. The centrality of religious issues in politics also meant that the bishops were likely targets of mob action. Constantinople had many prestigious monasteries, which the Alexandrians targeted for their diplomatic efforts. These monks easily became militant activists and potentially the dangerous leaders of a restive crowd. An unpopular bishop could rapidly find himself in a position that would make even a sympathetic emperor reluctant to defend him.[36]

The Fall of John Chrysostom

Long before the christological battles of Ephesus and Chalcedon, this interchurch rivalry brought down one patriarch in an affair that closely foreshadows later events. The main figure in this drama was John Chrysostom, one of the greatest saints of Christian antiquity and a legendary preacher: his name signifies "Golden Mouth." At every stage, his career exemplified the glories of Antioch. He was born in Antioch, and he studied under its last great pagan teachers, where his fellow pupils included Theodore of Mopsuestia. He was an early pupil of the new Christian school led by Diodore of Tarsus. Antioch was, naturally, where he was ordained a priest. In 398, against his better judgment, he agreed to become archbishop of Constantinople.[37]

Within five years, his career was in ruins, due to the machinations of Alexandria's patriarch Theophilus. Theophilus was engaged in a typical controversy with some dissident Egyptian monks, and he responded with the standard operating procedures of an Alexandrian patriarch, namely organizing a heavily armed force to destroy the monks' dwellings and maltreat their sympathizers. When the monks protested the persecution, the bishop was summoned to Constantinople to explain himself. But Theophilus turned the tables on his accusers, presenting both the exiled monks and John Chrysostom himself as fellow supporters of a notorious heresy based on the works of Origen. Theophilus also found a key ally in court, in the empress Aelia Eudoxia. Whatever she thought about the theological issues, she had come to loathe Chrysostom personally. She took personally his puritanical denunciations of excessive feminine luxury and vanity. Also at issue were the rituals that the Christian empire devised to celebrate the regime, which seemed to borrow from older pagan rituals. John expressed his horror when a statue of Eudoxia was dedicated with public festivities.[38]

With such powerful foes, Chrysostom's fall could not be long delayed. In 402, Theophilus arrived in Constantinople backed by an impressive phalanx of twenty-nine of his suffragan bishops—and reinforced by Alexandria's legendary capacity to dole out bribes. This show of force helped him assert his position against John, who was duly deposed at a provincial synod, the Synod of the Oak (403). In fact, John's abasement did not last long. The urban crowd admired him, while an earthquake convinced some of his enemies that they were struggling against a man beloved of God. Also foreshadowing later events, John Chrysostom found a powerful friend in the Roman pope, Innocent, who tried to call a council to restore the ousted patriarch. John himself maintained his resistance, comparing the empress to Herodias, the evil inciter of the death of John the Baptist. Chrysostom was briefly restored, but was once more deposed shortly afterward and died en route to exile in 407.[39]

Every aspect of this affair reappeared in some forms in the later councils, which were notionally so concerned with issues of Christology rather than church order. In later years, too, the patriarchs of Alexandria would play the role of ecclesiastical vigilantes, dabbling mercilessly in the affairs of other dioceses. Then, too, they would back up their authority by the massed presence of allied bishops, reinforced by extravagant bribes and gift giving. Theophilus's secretary on this occasion was Cyril, the later patriarch, who learned much about the art of politics in church and state.

By the 420s, then, Cyril's experiences had taught him some basic lessons about achieving policy goals. He had learned about the judicious use of violence, real or threatened; about the need to win favor at court; and about how councils and synods could be exploited to produce desired results. But if he learned one thing above all, it was that few problems or conflicts were so stubborn that they could not be resolved by enough bludgeoning and buffaloing.

But all the patriarchs always had to bear in mind one critical fact: however independent they might appear, however much they ruled as petty kings—often not-so-petty—they still, in fact, operated within a still-flourishing empire that had more than enough power to stop them in their tracks. If and when they forgot this fact, they could steer their patriarchates on the road to ruin. Throughout the fifth century, the outcome of church debates depended absolutely on gaining the favor of the imperial family—and especially the royal women.

4

Queens, Generals, and Emperors

That new heresies have not prevailed in our times, we shall find to be due especially to Pulcheria.

Sozomen

If patriarchs acted like kings, then emperors behaved like popes. Through all the christological debates, the empire acted as a force within the church, far more than merely an honest broker seeing fair play between contesting sides. Church leaders struggled to win the favor of courtiers or members of the imperial family, but many princes and empresses needed no encouragement to participate. The government was absolutely involved in church debates at all stages.[1]

Beyond the Emperors

Imperial politics meant much more than the office of the emperor himself and involved a complex world of court, bureaucracy, and royal family. Roman government was evolving into a military-ecclesiastical-courtier complex, a pattern it would retain through the Byzantine period.[2]

The empire became increasingly absolutist. From the third century, the emperor gave up the pretense of being just the first citizen, the *princeps*, and was openly proclaimed as lord, *dominus*, an absolute sovereign, untrammeled by republican institutions. The Greek word, which gives its meaning to another familiar English term, was *despotes*. The imperial court imitated the styles of absolutist Persia and the ancient god-kings of the Middle East, while the language of divinity permeated imperial life. The imperial finance minister bore the title of *Comes Sacrarum Largitionum*, the Count of Sacred Largeses; the empire's senior legal official—in modern terms, roughly, the attorney-general—was the Quaestor of the Sacred Palace.[3]

After Theodosius I, the Great, died in 395, his dynasty remained in power in both East and West. The fact that his immediate successors enjoyed such very long reigns might mislead us into thinking that these must have been eras of peace and stability. Just two incumbents held the Western throne for most of the period from 395 to 455, an impressive span of sixty years. One of Theodosius I's grandsons, Valentinian III, ruled the Western empire from 425 to 455, while another, Theodosius II, held the East from 408 through 450. But, in fact, this was anything but an enviable time of easygoing prosperity, and barbarian invasions repeatedly threatened to destroy both Eastern and Western empires. The long reigns rather suggested that at least some so-called despots—by no means all—were largely figureheads, so irrelevant to public affairs that they were scarcely worth replacing. Valentinian III was at best childish and petulant, and probably mentally unstable.[4]

Power within the empire had moved elsewhere, above all to the military, to quasi-independent warlords who served the Roman state but who naturally had their own agendas. This was a massive historical change from the older system, in which the army had been an integral part of the Roman state. By the fourth century, though, military forces were largely recruited and hired from external nations and tribes, who could handle the radically changed styles of mobile warfare that marked the great age of the barbarian migrations. Although each new wave of intruders posed its own problem, the most destabilizing force was the Huns, fast-moving horsemen using a deadly new type of bow. The empire was enduring a thoroughgoing revolution in military affairs.[5]

The Romans successfully employed some of these barbarians as allies and mercenaries, while others ran out of control and took over whole portions of the empire for themselves. Some peoples oscillated between the two courses, sometimes being predators, sometimes faithful defenders. Some warlords became kingmakers. From 430 through 470, the power behind the throne of the Eastern empire was Aspar, a member of the Alan nation that derived from eastern Europe, beyond the Roman frontier. As *Magister Militum*, commander in chief, the fate of the empire depended on him and whichever of his military protégés he chose to place in high office, including that of emperor. The Western empire, meanwhile, relied on the half-barbarian Aetius, the de facto military ruler of the Western empire from 433 through 450. Aetius owed his success to his close familiarity with the Hunnish tribes and his ability to deploy their own tactics against those terrifying invaders.[6]

Old and new ruling peoples intermarried freely. Although the Roman Empire had never aspired to racial purity, by the fifth century it was looking surprisingly multicultural and pan-European. In the West particularly, ruling elites represented the kind of Germanic/Latin blend that would dominate the region for the next thousand years. The Visigothic king Athaulf claimed that he had originally wanted to replace the Roman Empire, Romania, with a new Germanic Reich of Gothia, but he eventually despaired of making such a radical change and decided instead to use Gothic vigor as the foundation for a restored Nova Romania. What actually occurred was not too far from that design. Barbarian lords—Goths, Franks, and others—married their daughters and sisters into the imperial elite, so that a warlord like Aetius could plausibly hope to see a grandson in the imperial purple. Even the Vandal ruler Gaiseric, overlord of the North African kingdom that so alarmed

the empire, married his son to the daughter of the Western emperor
Valentinian. Barbarian influence in imperial politics was actually
stronger than we might think from merely looking at the personal
names of emperors or high officials. From 457, the new emperor
bore the impeccably Greek and philosophical name of Zeno, but
his real name—barely pronounceable to civilized Greeks—was
Tarasicodissa. He stemmed from the Isaurian highland tribes of
Asia Minor, possibly relatives of the modern Kurds.

The courts themselves contained other centers of power. Roman
sovereigns entrusted great power to eunuchs, who would not try to
seize power in the interests of their descendants, yet that limitation
did not prevent eunuch officials from struggling constantly for influence. In this world of backstairs politics, what mattered was not
one's birth or background or, often, ideology, but who had best
access to the emperor and his family. This access was commonly
sold to the highest bidder. Court politics were a matter of ins and
outs, with outsiders adopting whatever policies and alliances might
best serve to destabilize and discredit existing favorites. In some
cases, courtiers and court officials so controlled access to the emperor, so channeled the information available to him, that the leader
of the dominant court faction became a kind of shadow emperor.[7]

The power of the eunuchs reached new heights under the long-
lived emperor Theodosius II (408–50). One eunuch, Antiochus,
acted as his regent from 408 to 414, while the emperor was still a
small child. In later years, too, Theodosius II "was under the control
of his eunuchs in everything."[8] In the 440s, the eunuch official
Chrysaphius dominated the court and used this power to promote
Monophysite doctrine within the empire.

State as Church, Church as State

Another potent new force was the church, and the story of church-
state conflict in Alexandria suggests the difficulty of absorbing the
new religious reality within Roman state traditions. Modern observ-

ers find it hard to appreciate how slim were the distinctions that late Roman society drew between the church and the world, between religious life and the everyday doings of society. What we today would call religious issues served as vehicles for pursuing causes and grievances that were just as much political or economic in nature. That linkage of issues helps explain why ordinary people became so passionately involved in theological struggles.[9]

The rising popularity of the church coincided with the declining power and prestige of the state. Western historians have long debated the causes of the empire's decline and fall and have resisted simple, single-cause explanations, pointing instead to combinations of different types of weaknesses and stress. Some modern historians turn the question on its head, preferring to ask how the empire could possibly have kept going as long as it did, faced as it was by such a nightmare concatenation of military, social, and economic threats. But however we assess the role of the different threats, there is no doubt that they all were at their height in the era of Ephesus and Chalcedon, which was also the age of Attila the Hun.[10]

The imperial crisis had a direct impact on the lives of everyday people and ordinary Christian believers. Much of the impact was fiscal, as maintaining the empire became just too expensive a proposition. Throughout these years, external enemies repeatedly threatened the empire—Germanic barbarians, Persians, and Huns. These menaces forced the empire, as a matter of survival, to spend ever larger resources on its military apparatus, on supplying armies and fleets, maintaining fortresses and garrisons, buying the friendship of barbarian tribes, and paying tribute to buy off dangerous raiders. The imperial institution itself became ever more expensive, with the rich display and dress expected of emperors, all the court ritual, and the cost of a sizable bureaucracy.

Even in the best circumstances, those pressures would have stretched the capacity of the treasury and put enormous demands on the general tax burden. But in the fifth century, the regions available to pay taxes and tribute were shrinking steadily, with the secession or destruction of whole provinces. Even when the empire maintained its power over an area like the Balkans, Attila's repeated looting left the inhabitants with little ability to pay. Heavy tax demands fell on the remaining provinces and cities, which became progressively more disenchanted with civil authority, with its soldiers and tax collectors.

Nor did the empire offer much pretense of equal treatment, any sense of shared suffering. In Gaul, the prophetic Christian Salvian wrote that the empire was dying or drawing its last breath, "strangled by the cords of taxation as if by the hands of brigands"; but even at such a time, "still a great number of wealthy men are found, the burden of whose taxes is borne by the poor; that is, very many rich men are found whose taxes are murdering the poor." In an oft-quoted passage, a Greek merchant cited these economic burdens to explain just why he had opted out of the empire and defected to the Huns: "The exaction of the taxes is very severe, and unprincipled men inflict injuries on others, because the laws are practically not valid against all classes. A transgressor who belongs to the wealthy classes is not punished for his injustice, while a poor man . . . undergoes the legal penalty." More than ever, the state and its mechanisms became the face of the enemy. It was only natural, then, to turn instead to the comforting face of the church.[11]

By the start of the fifth century, churches had convincingly established themselves as clear forces of authority in individual cities, matching and in many cases overwhelming the symbols of secular power. The empire recognized the dignity and independence of the church by giving clerics a separate justice system, granting clergy the right to be tried in their own special courts. In the East, this right extended to bishops only, but Western rulers applied it to all clergy, of whatever rank. Bishops were now vital channels of government and were active in political and economic affairs as much as the strictly religious. As the Roman Empire crumbled in the West, local power in cities and regions passed to an alliance of counts and bishops, a pattern that would remain in place for a thousand years and more. In both East and West, institutional Christianity powerfully asserted its authority through the physical presence of church buildings and monasteries, which were now experiencing a massive building boom, supported by the empire and other secular magnates. At last, churches were beginning to challenge and even overtop the mighty temples, which were duly raided for building stone.[12]

The extensive social services provided by the church cemented popular loyalties. By the fifth century, wealthy laypeople were providing very large gifts and bequests to the churches as a means of promoting their eternal well-being. People gave money to help prisoners, for the ransom of captives (crucially important during wars and barbarian assaults), and for relieving victims of poverty and pestilence. Bishops distributed these moneys according to their discretion, and their charitable activities gave them immense prestige. If the state was always demanding money, the church cultivated a reputation for always giving it away. The empire might boast of its sacred largess, but the church actually practiced it.[13]

Just how substantial were the sums involved emerges from the frequent corruption charges that regularly surfaced in intrachurch fights, as each faction tried to make its enemies seem as greedy as possible. For present purposes, the truth of such charges matters less than the scale of wealth and patronage suggested. In 449, Edessa's bishop Ibas was accused of multiple offenses, mainly involving diverting charitable gifts to family members. And what gifts! They made up "an immense sum," "the bequests and the offerings, the contributions from every source, and the collection of dedicated crosses of gold and silver." His nephew, another bishop, reportedly gave all his money to a woman friend, who became rich lending the money out at heavy interest. The churches had vast capacity to help or harm, in the material world no less than the spiritual.[14]

We can easily understand the deep popular loyalty that clerical leaders attracted and the violent partisan contests that regularly arose over matters of succession and promotion. Clergy themselves were famously partisan, and not just in Alexandria. Constantinople's clergy were notorious for their "spirit of ambitious rivalry," and worse, they could expect mob support. When the city's archbishop died in 434, the emperor appointed a successor almost overnight, for excellent practical reasons. Desperately anxious "to prevent the disturbances in the church which usually attend the election of a bishop," he ordered the bishops who happened to be in the city to ordain a new incumbent, Proclus, even before his predecessor was actually buried. Tumult and rioting were natural ways for ordinary Christians to show their devotion to the institutional church.[15]

God's Warriors

The church's authority went far beyond its material resources. The people of the late Roman world believed firmly that they faced the assaults of evil spiritual powers, powers that could only be confronted by heroic spiritual champions. This meant above all the holy men and women who proliferated across the empire, the ascetics and hermits, monks and stylites, whose ostentatious rejection of the world allowed them to challenge the forces of evil. By the fifth century, the growing horrors of the secular world were encouraging mass defections into the spiritual life, as monasticism offered a whole alternative society.[16]

In the language of the time, monks and ascetics were holy warriors, engaged in constant religious combat, or else spiritual athletes. It was exactly in this period that celebrity saints took to living atop pillars, their food lifted to them daily by faithful disciples. Around 420, Simeon Stylites began occupying the pillartop where he would remain for some thirty incredible years. For the Christian public, rich and poor, such absolute devotion proved beyond doubt that a man like Simeon was close to God, and they anxiously sought his advice.[17]

The amazing popular devotion that such figures attracted shows the prevailing distrust of the material world, and especially of sexu-

ality: true holiness must involve an absolute rejection of these se-
ductive temptations. From this point of view, the ideal Christian
was not only celibate, but must also reject as far as possible any
form of material comfort, including any food beyond what was absolutely necessary to keep the person alive. They were to be "tombless corpses," dead men walking. Ascetics had a charismatic power
far greater than that of any secular figure, and the best that a lay
Christian could do was to try and copy them. Looking at such an
ideal must make us look very suspiciously at modern-day claims that
Christianity is inextricably linked to any kind of family values. In
this era, Christian values meant rejecting one's family as thoroughly
as possible.[18]

Just how far this estrangement from the worldly might go is suggested by the experience of the monk Severus, one of the most influential Christian figures of the sixth century and a founding father
of Syria's Monophysite church. When he became bishop of Antioch in 512, he was appalled by the luxurious living practiced by his
predecessors. His first step was to close the episcopal kitchens and
dismiss the cooks, so that henceforward, he would live on the
cheapest and nastiest bread he could buy in the marketplace. He
also destroyed the baths, an action that his admirers compared to
the ancient Old Testament kings' sacking temples of Baal. What
place did the vanity of bodily hygiene have in a proper Christian
regime? Cleanliness was very far from godliness. He was just as horrified to learn that earlier bishops had even slept in *beds*, and that
practice, too, had to change. Instead, "he practiced lying down on
the earth, refraining from washing, performing the offices with long
psalmody, eating vegetables."[19]

In a time of general political and social crisis, such otherworldly
figures acquired overwhelming authority and commanded respect
for their ability to lead their supporters and sympathizers to salvation. The fact that Simeon the Stylite supported the Council of
Chalcedon mattered enormously for that cause. Quite apart from
the spiritual superstars, their ascetic sacrifices meant that ordinary

monks also attracted popular awe and love, which made them a potent force in a city like Constantinople. Significantly for the political story, the upsurge of monasticism was much more rapid in the eastern portions of the empire, where the trend began, than in the west. At least before the sixth century, Roman popes and Western bishops did not face the task of disciplining legions of unruly monks, as was common in Syria and Egypt. Nor were they as tempted to deploy them in factional combat against secular officials or rival churchmen.[20]

In the East, though, holy men and women revolutionized the political world and served as a potent destabilizing force. Although they did not quite operate outside the law, in practice their charismatic authority gave them wide latitude to challenge official policies and to organize and channel popular resentment. When they spoke out on matters of theology or church politics, the world listened, and not merely the poor masses of city or countryside. Offending the empire could at its worst mean loss of life or property, but willfully disobeying the monks and ascetics would lead to everlasting suffering. In any conflict between spiritual and secular power, the church had immense advantages.

Holy Women

But if the church acted politically, the empire clearly conceived of itself in religious terms. The empire's rulers themselves thoroughly accepted the Christian worldview, and indeed personified charismatic notions of power. Although it was not until the 450s that patriarchs actually began crowning emperors, the notion of a holy empire absolutely rooted in Christian symbolism and ideology was much older. For better or worse, the concept of a Christian Empire went far beyond rhetorical verbiage.[21]

If emperors themselves might be figureheads, their relatives were very active indeed politically and religiously, and in the fifth-century context, this usually meant the imperial women, the empresses and princesses descended from the great Theodosius I. Some learned brilliantly how to play the political game, to manipulate the new Roman order of warlords, bishops, and courtiers. They became so influential that for long periods the empire looked like a matriarchate. In some cases, the Theodosian princesses who effectively dominated the empire for long periods were not only women, but startlingly young women or teenage girls, whose royal blood gave them the authority to overawe far more senior contemporaries. Adding to their potential influence, their royal lineage also made them attractive brides for ambitious generals or courtiers in search of a plausible claim to the imperial title. All the genius in the Theodosian line ended up in its womenfolk.[22]

In terms of religious politics, the imperial women were so personally invested in particular causes, so active in their respective movements, that the theological conflicts looked like battles between rival empresses as much as between patriarchs. This interventionist theme began early in the dynasty's history and endured well over a century. Theodosius I married a Spanish woman, Flaccilla, who fought staunchly for Nicene theology against Arianism and exactly set the pattern for the later Theodosian women.

Flaccilla was the mother of the emperors Arcadius, in the East, and Honorius, in the West. Arcadius in turn married Aelia Eudoxia, who was, despite her Greco-Roman name, the daughter of a Frankish barbarian warrior in Roman service. Like Flaccilla, she struggled hard for Nicene orthodoxy while building up the sacred character of Constantinople by importing and publicizing an impressive collection of sacred relics. She also imposed her will on senior appointments. In 403, she allied with the Alexandrian bishop Theophilus to destroy John Chrysostom at the notorious Synod of the Oak.

In tracing the history of the fifth-century councils, three queens, three Augustae, stand out above all as prime movers and manipulators—Galla Placidia and Pulcheria on the Catholic/Orthodox side, Aelia Eudocia for the Monophysites.

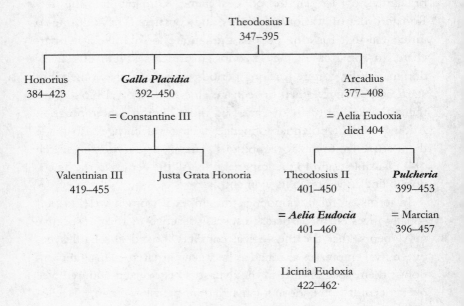

THE THEODOSIAN DYNASTY

Theodosius I
347–395

Honorius
384–423

Galla Placidia
392–450
= Constantine III

Arcadius
377–408
= Aelia Eudoxia
died 404

Valentinian III
419–455

Justa Grata Honoria

Theodosius II
401–450

Pulcheria
399–453

= Aelia Eudocia
401–460

= Marcian
396–457

Licinia Eudoxia
422–462·

(Valentinian III married his cousin Licinia Eudoxia)

The lives of some of these women seem almost incredible. One breathtaking example was Galla Placidia (392–450), daughter of Theodosius I by his second wife. Abducted by Goths when Rome fell in 410, she remained a prisoner until she formed a relationship with Athaulf, brother of the barbarian king. She married him and bore his son, raising the prospect of a new Gothic-Roman dynasty. However, her husband died early—an occupational hazard for a barbarian warlord—and she returned to Rome. There she married a prominent general, who used that link to establish himself as emperor of the West. When he also died young, in 425, the thirty-two-year-old Galla Placidia found herself the mother of the new reigning emperor, Valentinian, who was just six years old. In effect, this meant that she ruled the Western empire for another decade.

Working alongside the general Aetius, she remained a potent figure in the West until her own death in 450.[23]

In such a situation of shared power, the personal religious views of the empress and her circle mattered enormously, and Galla Placidia was passionately interested in matters religious and theological. The church and mosaics she commissioned in Ravenna are among the greatest treasures of early Christian art. She was also resolutely Orthodox/Catholic and anti-Monophysite. When Monophysites seemed to be gaining dangerous power within the Eastern empire, beleaguered orthodox believers begged Galla Placidia and her royal son to plead with their imperial kin in Constantinople, which they duly did. On the other side of the partisan gulf, the main court patron of the Monophysite cause before and after Chalcedon was Aelia Eudocia, wife of the Eastern emperor Theodosius II.[24]

Galla Placidia also left a daughter, Justa Grata Honoria, whose own career was as spectacularly improbable as her own. Together with her lover, Honoria plotted to assassinate her brother Valentinian and take over the empire. When the conspiracy was revealed, she was sent to a convent, but the prospect of that lifestyle appalled her. Seeking an escape route, she turned to a new prospective lover with a solid record of achievement in public affairs: Attila the Hun. Honoria wrote to Attila, offering to marry him if he would free her, and in exchange she would give him title to rule the Western empire. Attila used the correspondence as an excuse to launch his invasion of Gaul, which he presented as an attempt to take his promised bride and dowry.[25]

That particular plot would scarcely carry conviction in a bad romance novel, and its only excuse is that it actually happened. Pushing the bounds of credibility further, Honoria was not the only Theodosian woman to invite an invasion of her own empire out of personal reasons and family grievance. Just three years after Honoria's Hunnish flirtation, her example inspired her cousin Licinia Eudoxia to invite the Vandal king Gaiseric to attack Italy. He did so with gusto in the second sack of Rome (455). Although theological issues played no part in these particular soap operas, the stories tell us a great deal about the turbulent independence of the imperial women, their immersion in public affairs, and their absolute conviction that their views should be heard. All those features reappeared regularly in their religious politics.[26]

Like the patriarchs in their different way, these women were also prepared to imagine futures for the Roman world utterly different from familiar traditions. Once, it would have seemed inconceivable for the imperial capital to move out of Rome, yet Constantine had accomplished just that. So what else could happen? What might the empire look like in another couple of centuries? Might it be a Romano-Gothic or Romano-Hunnish hybrid? Might it be a Christian theocracy run from Alexandria or Antioch? Or even, to take an outrageous hypothetical, might the popes of remote Rome become the patrons of a new successor Western empire ruled by some rough Germanic tribe, even the Franks? The possibilities were limitless.

Pulcheria

By far the most important Theodosian woman in the religious story was Pulcheria (399–453), who was granddaughter to Theodosius I and Flaccilla. She was also the daughter of the Aelia Eudoxia, whom we have met as the enemy of Chrysostom, and sister to the current Eastern emperor Theodosius II. Pulcheria was also a niece to Galla Placidia and cousin to the dreadful Honoria. If genes exist for theology and conspiracy, Pulcheria had both.[27]

Pulcheria made superb use of the men who dominated the empire, especially the warlord Aspar, and in most cases, she never directly resorted to the appeal of sex or marriage. Instead, she made consistently shrewd use of a vow of virginity she had taken by the age of fifteen. More than just a personal dedication, she made a very public commitment:

She first devoted her virginity to God, and instructed her sisters in the same course of life. To avoid all cause of jealousy and intrigue, she permitted no man to enter her palace. In confirmation of her resolution, she took God, the priests, and all the subjects of the Roman Empire as witnesses to her self-dedication.

This act removed her from the field of plausible royal brides and allowed her to carry on political life as an independent agent. Even better, in contemporary minds, her virginity gave her an aura of holiness and charismatic power. When in 450 she eventually married Marcian, Aspar's henchman, she did so in order to give him a solid title to the imperial crown and to strengthen her own position in the theological struggles of the time. She married only after receiving a strict promise that he would respect her celibacy.[28]

Pulcheria's own spirituality represented a startling blend of beliefs. In official church history, she has been remembered as the holy amazon of orthodoxy, slayer of heresies. But she also said and did things that, if they had come from other women at different times and places, could well have got them burned at the stake. She had a powerful mystical devotion to the Virgin Mary, building churches and shrines to her. During the 430s, Constantinople acquired a dazzling series of new relics of the Virgin, including Mary's robe and belt and the icon of her painted from the life by St. Luke, and each was housed in a splendid new building. This Marian obsession was innovative at the time, but well within the familiar trends in church devotion—it was cutting-edge, rather than deviant. But Pulcheria also made astonishing claims about her own status within the church and identified herself with the figure of the Virgin Mary, the *Theotokos* or God-Bearer. The empress applied to herself exalted titles such as Bride of Christ and acted almost as matriarch of the church, as well as augusta. She became leader or pontifex of an extravagant cult devoted to Mary, and together with her following of

virgins and holy women, she played a visible role in the public liturgies of what were already some of the greatest churches of the
Christian world. However firm her loyalty to church teaching, her
own devotional life was not far removed from that of some of the
feminine-oriented Gnostic sects purged from the Christian mainstream two hundred years earlier.[29]

Although Pulcheria did not officially rule the Eastern empire, she
so influenced public policy that it certainly looked like she was in
sole charge from 414 through 440. She ruled, in fact, through her
position as imperial Big Sister. When her father, Arcadius, died in
408, she was nine, and her brother Theodosius II, the new ruler,
was just seven. She clearly matured earlier than he did, and by the
time she was fifteen, she was placing a personal stamp on religious
policy. She took effective power in 414, displacing the eunuch
regime. Her devoted admirer Sozomen records how:

> She caused all affairs to be transacted in the name of her
> brother, and devoted great attention to bringing him up as a
> prince in the best possible way, and with such information as
> was suitable to his years. She had him taught by the most
> skilled men, in horsemanship, and the practice of arms, and in
> letters. But he was systematically taught by his sister to be or-
> derly and princely in his manners; she showed him how to
> gather up his robes, and how to take a seat, and how to walk;
> she trained him to restrain laughter, to assume a mild or a for-
> midable aspect as the occasion might require, and to inquire
> with urbanity into the cases of those who came before him
> with petitions.[30]

Literally, she taught him to walk and talk. By some accounts, she
even chose and groomed a wife for him, in the form of Eudocia. If
the story is true, Pulcheria would have cause to regret her decision,
as Eudocia became a bitter foe.

Pulcheria also ensured that her brother followed the strictest standards of piety and devotion. "She taught him to frequent the church regularly, and to honor the houses of prayer with gifts and treasures; and she inspired him with reverence for priests and other good men."[31] Her efforts paid off richly. Theodosius II himself fasted often, especially on Wednesdays and Fridays.

> He rendered his palace little different from a monastery: for he, together with his sisters, rose early in the morning, and recited responsive hymns in praise of the Deity. By this training he learnt the holy Scriptures by heart; and he would often discourse with the bishops on scriptural subjects, as if he had been an ordained priest of long standing.

One later Monophysite story tells how Theodosius II wrote to Egypt's monastic leaders for advice about his failure to produce an heir. They responded that the lack of a son was God's plan, as the religious order of the world would change after his death, and God wanted to prevent him having a son who would participate in this wickedness. The emperor and his wife agreed to live together in celibacy thereafter.[32]

Beyond personal piety, Theodosius II and his sisters showed an attitude to the official enforcement of orthodoxy that would not have been out of place at the Spanish court of Queen Isabella in 1490. Coincidentally or not, the Theodosian family had Spanish roots: Theodosius I grew up in that land, and his wife Flaccilla was a Spaniard. To use a later term, Pulcheria had a crusading mentality. In many societies, young teenage girls develop a fascination with religious devotion, and some plan to become nuns or devote their lives to good works. Pulcheria had very much these impulses, but she also had a well-armed empire to play with. As early as 414, when she was still fifteen, she persuaded her brother to expel remaining pagans from the imperial civil service. In 421, she pushed the empire to declare war against Persia, the other superpower of the age, to avenge the persecution of Christians within the Persian realm.[33]

The Age of Intolerance

More than most of her contemporaries, Pulcheria had a potent vision of an empire that was not just Christian but militantly and uniformly so, a regime determined to use its full power to enforce orthodoxy. She has an excellent claim to rank as the pioneer of medieval notions of Christendom at their most aggressive. That resemblance grows all the stronger when we think of her Roman, Christian, empire fighting under the banner of the Virgin Mary.

Jews were particular victims of the new regime. Christian-Jewish conflict grew steadily during the late fourth century, and by the 380s John Chrysostom denounced Jews and Judaizing Christians in terms that would have a long and wrenching afterlife. John used the charge of deicide, holding the Jews guilty of the death of Christ, and thus of God himself, a theme later developed by Pope Leo. Of course, this concept was also intimately linked to the ongoing debate over the nature and person of Christ: to talk about killing God made a powerful statement about who or what had died at Calvary. One incident from these years suggests the worsening religious climate. In 388, the bishop of the city of Callinicum, in Mesopotamia, led a mob that destroyed a synagogue. The emperor, Theodosius I, ordered the rioters to rebuild it at their own cost, even if that meant using church funds. Church leaders were appalled, and the great saint-bishop Ambrose of Milan wrote a furious protest against this blasphemy, by which he meant not the original desecration, but the rebuilding. That same year, the emperor prohibited Christian-Jewish intermarriage, on pain of death.[34]

His descendants built on this tradition. From 415, Theodosius II withdrew the privileges traditionally granted to Jewish communities, and in 425 his government ordered the execution of the last Nasi or head of the Jewish Sanhedrin, from a line that had maintained its tradition for centuries. Theodosius II's policies—or, we should perhaps say, Pulcheria's—provoked the destruction of Constantinople's synagogues and the expulsion of its Jewish population.[35] In 439, Theodosius II issued a comprehensive law that excluded Jews and Samaritans from public office and dignity, and it was forbidden either to build new synagogues or to repair existing ones threatened with ruin. Converting a Christian to Judaism meant death for the Jew responsible and the confiscation of his property. Reflecting a poisonous new hostility, a version of the blood libel legend even made an early appearance in these very years. In Syria, a group of Jews allegedly staged the mock crucifixion of a Christian boy, who died of his maltreatment. The emperor, we are told, ordered the perpetrators severely punished. Just how bad things became is suggested by the incident in the 480s when Christian mobs in Antioch sacked a synagogue, digging up and burning the bodies in the cemetery. The emperor, Zeno, was appalled. If they were going to so much trouble, he asked, why had they not burned the bodies of living Jews together with the dead?[36]

Under Theodosius II, imperial repression was only tempered by the presence at court of another and more moderate voice in the shape of his queen, Eudocia. As the daughter of a sophist or teacher of rhetoric, she remained in dialogue with pagan intellectual circles and tried to provide limited protection to pagans as well as Jews. These differing religious attitudes split the court between Eudocia and Pulcheria, a domestic war that contributed to the growth of Monophysite influence in the 440s. Court rivalries shaped theological debate.[37]

True Christians and False Christians

Taken alongside the vigilantism of individual bishops in Alexandria and elsewhere, such official policies suggest a radical new intolerance toward religious minorities. This policy change would be so important for the christological debates in vastly upping the stakes at issue, in that the full force of government and law would be turned against the losing side. Theological debate became a zero-sum game, with far-reaching implications in the material world.

The fact that the new Christian empire was willing to persecute rival Christian sects demands explanation. Individual Christians might be so zealous as to tolerate no rival faiths, but imperial authorities did not necessarily have to accept such fanaticism, especially when it ran against the practical realities of governing a vast and complex empire. But matters changed toward the end of the fourth century. In the 360s, the utter failure of the pagan revival launched by the emperor Julian the Apostate showed just how strongly entrenched Christianity had become, and official pressures to conform mounted. The church became a dominant factor in imperial affairs, rather than just serving as a humbly grateful recipient of official favors.[38]

The turning point came under the first Theodosius, who was a pupil of Ambrose of Milan. Theodosius I also came to power as a result of the imperial collapse at the battle of Adrianople in 378, which at the time seemed to herald a near-terminal crisis for the Roman world. Although he succeeded in reconstructing Roman power, he always remained sensitive to the empire's need for divine protection and the dangers that might befall if God's patience were tested too far.[39]

Theodosius I made Christianity the empire's official state religion and began policies of strict religious conformity. Besides favoring Christianity in general, he showed a strong preference for the faith in its orthodox, Nicene form and hated the rival Arians, who denied the full equality of God the Father and God the Son. He systematically expelled Arian adherents, even in a city like Constantinople, where Arians clearly commanded a strong following. From 380, Arian-leaning bishops were removed from office or forced to conform, and ordinary Arian believers were forbidden to meet in churches. Nonorthodox groups, including Apollinarians, were forbidden from calling their leaders bishops or clergy or describing their meeting places as churches. By the end of the decade, the empire had a whole system of official investigation and persecution in place, a protoinquisition. Other groups were hit even harder. In 382, Theodosius ordered the death penalty for monks of the Manichaean faith.[40]

Theodosius I left a powerful inheritance for fifth-century church leaders, when they faced churchwide theological warfare. They recalled how mighty a threat Arianism had been before a great and determined emperor had joined the battle, and how successfully a few decades of persecution had reduced the Arians to insignificance—at least within the bounds of the empire. This offered an encouraging precedent for the extermination of the deviant creeds of their own day. And like Constantine before him, Theodosius had pursued his fight for orthodoxy by calling a great ecumenical council, at Constantinople in 381.[41]

Also during the 380s, the Christian church witnessed an ominous first, namely the official execution of a dissident heretical thinker. The protagonist was a bishop called Priscillian—another Spaniard—who formed a hyperascetic and puritanical sect that looked dubiously on marriage and the material world. He attracted the outrage of a warlord who had set himself as a rival emperor against Theodosius I and who wanted to prove himself a faithful son of Christian orthodoxy. Accordingly, the pretender had Priscillian beheaded. In this case, we can blame neither Theodosius I nor the church for the actual killing. The most visible and prestigious Western leaders of the time—including Pope Siricius, Ambrose of Milan, and St. Martin of Tours—all condemned both the trial and the execution. Nor, technically, was Priscillian punished for heretical belief, but rather for magic, a familiar criminal behavior in Roman law. But the precedent was set: the Christian state had killed a heretic. In terms of future religious debates, the ratchet had just turned several notches.[42]

In 390, clerical power grew alarmingly when Theodosius I made a remarkable submission to the church, of the kind that we associate more with the medieval heyday of papal power. The affair began when rebels in Thessalonica killed a Roman commander and, in the best imperial tradition, Theodosius replied by ordering his forces to sack the city. Appalled by the violence, Milan's bishop Ambrose refused to grant the emperor admission to the church and its communion, calling on Theodosius to submit to God's penance. The historian Theodoret then tells us that, "Educated as he had been in the sacred oracles, Theodosius knew clearly what belonged to priests and what to emperors. He therefore bowed to the rebuke of Ambrose, and retired sighing and weeping to the palace." For centuries, faithful Christians recalled the story as a telling example of the secular state recognizing its proper place in the divine order, and artists presented the story in great paintings. Modern observers though—including many Christians—are as likely to be alarmed by the aggressive ecclesiastical usurpation of state power. After doing public penance, Theodosius was restored to the church. Soon afterward, he issued new restrictions on pagan rituals and approved the destruction of pagan temples, initially in the cities. The order to destroy rural temples went out a few years later.[43]

This rigid Theodosian inheritance survived into the new century. Besides the tough new measures against pagans and Jews, the scope of state action expanded to competing Christian communities, to schismatics as well as heretics. Schismatics were believers whose faith was broadly orthodox, but who were separated from the official church hierarchy by disagreements of various kinds. Such differences could be personal or factional, or might involve some specific point of doctrine. Schism was a common fact in church life, and reasonable church leaders knew that such breaks came and went. At various points in the fourth century, no less than four rivals contested the see of Antioch. While schismatics might temporarily be out of communion with other believers, normal relations would likely be restored at some future point.[44]

Increasingly, though, as the fifth century progressed, the fact of being out of communion with the mainstream church meant that a schismatic was not just a principled opponent but an active enemy of the true faith, deserving the sternest sanctions. Such for instance were the Novatians, an otherwise orthodox group who maintained a separate hierarchy. By the 430s, though, in Rome, Alexandria, and elsewhere, the orthodox seized the Novatians' churches and forced them underground. Even being a Christian was no longer enough. One had to follow precisely the correct form of faith, as laid down by the church and the empire—assuming that any distinction could be drawn between those terms.[45]

Why Hate?

The religious world was becoming a much chillier place, but not entirely due to the hard-line ideas of the Theodosian family, or of individuals like Pulcheria. However important the imperial family might have been in driving religious politics, they could have had nothing like the impact they did unless their policies channeled powerful trends in popular belief and culture. In fact, some emperors found themselves trying not to encourage intolerance, but rather to moderate the persecuting whims of church leaders. Even without the Theodosian house in power, then, the empire's rulers probably could have done little to limit the pressures toward greater church activism in political life, and to an ever greater hostility toward rival faiths and creeds.[46]

Theology goes a long way toward explaining the strength of feeling, and supplying a cosmic dimension to intra-Christian battles. According to the beliefs of the time, some issues were so critical that any deviation from them meant not just falling into error, but actively leaving the Christian sphere. When dissidents lapsed into errors that seemed pagan or Jewish, they thus entered the service of the devil, and surely a Christian society should not tolerate Satan's wiles? The Old Testament contributed powerfully to deterring tolerance. Throughout those scriptures, prophets and priests repeatedly urge the duty to struggle constantly against false religion and to use the state to enforce true doctrine. A righteous king was a king who suppressed error. The same texts offered dire warnings about what befell the overtolerant.

Despite the empire's conversion, Christians had not lost their traditional sense of being engaged in warfare against the world. Even in the unprecedented atmosphere of political security, Christians were thoroughly used to expecting violent conflict and persecution, of seeing martyrs being faithful unto death. When the prefect Orestes opposed Alexandria's Cyril—on excellent grounds, most would think—the monks naturally accused him of being a pagan persecutor, on the lines they knew very well from the past three or four centuries of experience. Why else would anyone go against a holy Christian bishop? The popular cult of martyrology reinforced this suspicion of the civil power.[47]

Christians also still lived in a world where paganism was an everyday reality, and perceptions of external danger and internal subversion always supply a formidable boost to religious intolerance. Ramsay MacMullen has suggested that by 400, "the entire Levant from the Euphrates south to Egypt was not much more than half converted." Pagan survivals still abounded, in terms of evocative temples, and semiclandestine rituals. As late as 541, the emperor dispatched the famous cleric John of Ephesus to clean up paganism in western Asia Minor, an area that had first been exposed to Christianity in St. Paul's time. But despite all the Christian efforts in the previous five hundred years, John still found seventy thousand pagans to convert.[48]

In 430 or so, then, many Christians would still have been first- or second-generation converts, and they dreaded any relapse to the old faiths. In such an environment, church leaders were still trying to determine the acceptable limits and boundaries of faith on a daily basis. There were constant struggles over how much of these older beliefs and practices could safely be imported into the churches. (As so often, debates in that fifth-century world closely foreshadow conditions prevailing in modern-day Africa). It was devastating to claim that some theological stance was not Christian at all, but a version of pagan or Jewish teaching being smuggled into the churches. Fifth-century theological debates regularly featured charges of pagan revivalism.

The largest single mental marker separating the premodern or medieval world from our own was the belief that earthly error had cosmic implications. For a modern audience, the obvious question is why a church could not have tolerated a wide variety of beliefs and doctrines, allowing different schools of thought to contend, so that ultimately the truth would prevail. This liberal doctrine, after all, had scriptural warrant in the book of Acts. The Jewish sage Gamaliel reportedly warned against persecuting Christians, on the grounds that if their ideas were false, they would fail, but if they were true, they should not be opposed. But once in power, the church had a rather different answer to the question of "What harm could it do?" If, as they believed, errors arose from sinful pride or diabolical subversion, then tolerating them attracted God's anger, as expressed through different forms of worldly catastrophe: famine, drought, plague, floods, and earthquakes, or defeat in war. In the ancient world, it was not difficult to point to some event of this kind taking place somewhere, and in the fifth century, catastrophes erupted with a frequency guaranteed to give ammunition to the most moderate-minded preacher.

A regime that tolerated heresy, immorality, and error would suffer, and nobody could complain against this fulfillment of God's essential justice. But suppressing these horrors meant prosperity and victory for the regime, and the people. As an imperial representative declared at Second Ephesus in 449, "The demon who is the originator of evil can never relax in his war against the holy churches. The most pious emperor always opposed his unrighteous warfare, rightly realizing that he will have a defender for his empire if he himself takes up arms in the battles for religion." Nestorius himself urged the emperor, "Give me, my prince, the earth purged of heretics, and I will give you heaven as a recompense. Help me destroy the heretics and I'll help you conquer the Persians."[49] The other implication is obvious: tolerate the heretics, and God will give victory to the Persians, or the Huns. Being the great Christian empire was an enormous privilege, but it carried dire responsibilities.

Part 2

Councils of Chaos

My inclination is to avoid all assemblies of bishops, because I have never seen any council come to a good end, nor turn out to be a solution of evils. On the contrary, it usually increases them.
Gregory Nazianzus

5

Not the Mother of God?

Cyril presided: Cyril was accuser: Cyril was judge! Cyril was bishop of Rome! Cyril was everything.

Nestorius

The name of Nestorius has become attached to some of the most impressive chapters of Christian history. Through the Middle Ages, a great polyglot church carried out Christian missionary efforts across much of Asia, and historians recall this body as "Nestorian." Many eastern Christians venerated Nestorius as a brilliant teacher who had suffered grave injustice at the hands of the Roman Empire. Even today, the Assyrian Church of the East—the direct descendant of the great Nestorian church—still uses a liturgy credited to that founder, the so-called Hallowing or Consecration of Nestorius. But Nestorius himself was both greater and lesser than his legend claims. He was not, in fact, a heresiarch, one who would split both the personality of Christ, and his church, and he undoubtedly was a victim of double-dealing and intrigue. At the same time, his own acts of rigidity and intolerance make it hard to portray him as a passive Christlike victim: he gave as well as received.[1]

The career of Nestorius is a perfect example of being in the wrong place at the wrong time. Knowing as we do the religious alignments of the time, it is hard to see how his story could have ended except in disaster. When he became archbishop of Constantinople in 428, he was in the position of a thief entering a bank vault in which any movement is bound to activate some kind of alarm, and the only question is which sensor will go off first and loudest. Nestorius held the teachings of Antioch, at a time when those ideas were bound to draw fire from the church of Alexandria. He was dubious about the cult of the Virgin Mary, when any attack on that devotion was guaranteed to infuriate the empress Pulcheria, not to mention angering many monks and ordinary believers. And he was doing all this in Constantinople, where only a generation before an empress had allied with Egyptians to evict an obstreperous Syrian bishop. The precedents were awful. All in all, his destruction seems like just a matter of time.

Less predictable, though, was the outcome in the longer term. What should have been a faction feud in Constantinople itself generated an escalating series of theological wars that ultimately consumed many of Nestorius's enemies as well as his allies.[2]

Patriarch

Nestorius himself was a Syrian, born in the far south of what we would today call Turkey. He was an alumnus of the distinguished school of Theodore of Mopsuestia and became famous in his own right for his eloquent sermons. These roots in the Syrian church made him a friend of John, the new patriarch of Antioch. His move to Constantinople in 428 could only have been granted with the favor of the imperial family, and particularly of the first sister, Pulcheria.[3]

Nestorius was chosen as an outsider who could rise above the city's bitterly divided church factions, but he disappointed any such hopes. From his earliest days, he laid out an aggressive policy agenda that called for the elimination of non-Christians and heretics, ideas that would have delighted his royal patrons. Just five days after his ordination, he was busily destroying an Arian chapel, inciting a riot and an outbreak of arson in the process. Within months, he was striking out generally at deviant Christians, against Novatians, Quartodecimans, Macedonians, any and all remnants of long-defeated heresies and schisms, as he ordered the seizure of churches and the suppression of services. While he believed that these blasphemous rivals needed silencing, he also had other motives. He was an alien intruder in a great city, where many of the clergy did not want him in the first place, and he could only assert his position by demonstrating strength.[4]

Crisis

The irony of this story is that Nestorius himself would soon find himself labeled an archheretic. The crisis stemmed from a controversy over the correct term of address for the Virgin Mary. On the one side, powerful forces in Constantinople favored the term *Theotokos*, God-Bearer or Mother of God, which had been in circulation for perhaps two hundred years but which now became a standard form of praise. Favoring this usage were Pulcheria herself and important church leaders like Basil and Hypatius, who were archimandrites—superior abbots ruling over several monasteries. Other supporters included some bishops close to Pulcheria, such as Eusebius of Dorylaeum, and Proclus of Cyzicus. Adding to the likelihood of conflict, Proclus had been one of the candidates for the archbishopric when Nestorius was chosen, and his disappointment rankled.[5]

The Marian language troubled Nestorius's chaplain, a presbyter named Anastasius, and the other clergy that Nestorius had brought with him from Antioch. The logic behind *Theotokos* seemed perfect: if Jesus was indeed Christ, and Christ was God, then the Mother of Jesus was, in fact, the Mother of God. But that straight identification of the human Jesus with God seemed Apollinarian and ran flat contrary to Antiochene teachings.[6] The critique of the Marian language must be seen as a direct sequel to Nestorius's recent attacks on the leftover remnants of heresies. In this case, though, he was targeting a much more formidable enemy, namely the Apollinarian beliefs that were still so popular in Constantinople.

In a sermon preached in November 428, then, Anastasius cautioned, "Let no one call Mary *Theotokos*, for Mary was but a woman; and it is impossible that God should be born of a woman." The remark caused a sensation. If Mary had not given birth to God, who or what had she borne? Was Anastasius really saying that the child born to Mary was human, but not really divine? Or Jesus was perhaps a mere human being who later became God? Another supporter now threatened "Anathema, if any call the holy Mary, *Theotokos*." So horrible did this last warning seem that some listeners ran from the church, and many—especially monks and secular magnates—withdrew from communion.[7]

Nestorius now faced an impossible dilemma. Had he chosen, he could have publicly repudiated Anastasius and the others and avoided the theological firestorm, but that would immediately send an embarrassing message about his still-new regime and his choice of subordinates. Alternatively, he could justify Anastasius, with all the dangers that implied of himself being linked to heretical doctrine. And that is what he decided to do, in a series of lectures that condemned any failure to distinguish between humanity and divinity. For Nestorius, Christ's divine and human natures did not exist in total union (*henosis*), but rather formed a lesser union, a kind of conjunction (*sunapheia*). The two natures combined to form a common *prosopon*, a person, but in a much weaker sense than the hypostatic union that Cyril would advocate. Reporting to Pope Celestine in Rome, Nestorius complained that those who spoke of the *Theotokos* suffered from a grave theological sickness "akin to the putrid sore of Apollinarius and Arius. For they mingle the Lord's union in man to a confusion of some sort of mixture."[8]

Mother of God

In attacking the term *Theotokos*, Nestorius went to the heart of the Christian paradox. We today find the word less shocking than it properly is because memories of the Hail Mary prayer have made the words "Mother of God" so familiar in most Western languages. Pursued to its logical conclusion, though, *Theotokos* meant that the teenaged girl Mary, from a remote village on the fringes of the Mediterranean world, was the mother of the God who had created the world out of nothing, who made the sun and the stars, who had made his covenant with Abraham and Moses, who had appeared in fire and smoke on Sinai. The logical mind revolted.

So did the minds of many Christians who had grown up in a world dominated by images of the great and terrifying Mother Goddess who predated the gods, and who reigned with them, deities like Egypt's Isis and the Cybele of Asia Minor. Must not the Mother of God be a Goddess in her own right, even a greater figure than her son? As Nestorius preached, "Has God a mother?" Then how can we blame pagans for inventing all those mothers for their gods? No, he insisted: "The creature did not bear the Creator, but she bore a man, the instrument of deity."[9]

Nestorius did not want to see Christian doctrine contaminated by alien practices, especially through popular devotions, the expressions of faith that often drew on pagan precedents. In his era, devotion to the Virgin Mary was becoming an ever-larger part of popular Christian practice, as Mary became almost a divine figure parallel to Christ. Already from the second century, apocryphal gospels were putting forth an exalted image of Mary, who was perpetually virgin and whose own life paralleled that of her son. By the fourth century, we find the idea that she had not suffered an ordinary death, but was instead assumed into heaven. Images of the Virgin and Child—portraits and statues—were now a commonplace of religious art, and these imitated ancient pagan figures of the goddess and her divine son, of Isis and Horus. The fourth-century bishop

Epiphanius warned his readers to draw a careful distinction between the worship (*latreia*) due to God, and the veneration (*proskunesis*) rightly given to Mary. The fact he had to make the point suggests that at least some Christians were already crossing the line to Mary worship.[10]

Whatever its origins, Nestorius's sermons infuriated his listeners, who saw him as a bold heresiarch. Making matters worse, his preaching took place around Christmas, the feast of the birth of Christ. It appeared that Nestorius was underplaying the status of Christ and of Mary and thus—in the popular mind—insulting their honor. Devaluing Christ was a particularly sensitive theme for the monks, who saw themselves as heavenly warriors on the front lines of spiritual combat against the forces of evil. Such a struggle demanded constant nourishment in the form of the Eucharist, the Body of Christ; and suddenly the doctrine of the Two Natures threatened to make that sacrament less holy, less divine, and more of a symbolic recollection of Christ. Two Nature theory was a form of unilateral spiritual disarmament.[11]

The more Nestorius's enemies explored his ideas, the more alarming their implications. If, in fact, Christ had two natures, then both should be worshipped, both Jesus and Christ, so that the deity came to look more like the pagan assembly of gods on Mount Olympus. Or perhaps Nestorius was suggesting a cluster or consortium of divine personalities, recalling the Gnostic vision of the heavenly *pleroma*, the Fullness. The sixth-century historian Evagrius saw Nestorius as quite literally the agent of a diabolical conspiracy to subvert the church. The archbishop must also be a Judaizer, who presented Christ the man as a great prophet like Moses but one who fell short of true divine status. Nestorius was reviving the old heresy of the Ebionites, the Jewish-Christians.[12]

Nestorius was wandering into deep waters, and floundering. He won little support for giving Mary the compromise term of *Christotokos*, Christ-Bearer or Mother of Christ, because it suggested "Mother of a child who was born, and who would someday become Christ." (And when did that happen, exactly?) And once you admitted the idea of birth or bearing, a whole new set of theological problems arose. The gospel of John taught that the Logos existed from the beginning of time, but Nestorius's language suggested that Christ was somehow born again when he emerged from the womb. During one of Nestorius's sermons, Bishop Eusebius interrupted him to protest that if Nestorius were right, then "the eternal Word had undergone a second generation." Was Nestorius suggesting a dual creation?[13]

In fact, Nestorius's own view fell far short of such radicalism. Later historians have been much kinder to the patriarch and have argued that his views were quite mainstream in terms of Antiochene belief and were not too far removed from the interpretation that would win the day at Chalcedon. However badly he expressed himself, Nestorius was, in fact, fighting a worthy battle in his attempt to preserve a human image in Christ, to keep Christ's feet planted on the earth. In later centuries, too, Protestant writers found much to admire in Nestorius's resistance to what they saw as a superstitious worship of Mary, and they praised the Nestorians as precursors of rationalism and scientific inquiry. The praise is as ill-placed as the earlier criticisms, but the embattled patriarch was asking some excellent questions.

He did not understand the minefield he was entering. The historian Socrates offered a defense for Nestorius that is all the more convincing, given the otherwise hostile source. Socrates thought Nestorius was stupid and reckless, but he also argues that the archbishop was innocent of the worst charges of heresy raised against him. He certainly was proposing nothing as radical as Paul of Samosata had done in suggesting that Godhood had suddenly descended on Jesus when he entered the Jordan river. In Socrates's view, Nestorius was orthodox on key points of belief and his worst flaws arose from a lack of any real sense of the scriptural or patristic literature that he should have known. Far from denying the divinity of Christ, Nestorius's major problem was a misunderstanding of the buzzword *Theotokos*, which he feared "as though it were some terrible phantom."[14]

Enemies

Constantinople's clergy united to defend the Mother of God. Bishop Proclus justified the word *Theotokos* in an extravagant sermon that would endure through the centuries as a classic text of Marian devotion. No praise was high enough for the Mother. Mary was "the untarnished vessel of virginity, the spiritual paradise of the second Adam, the workshop of the union of the natures, the market place of the contract of salvation, the bride-chamber where the Word took the flesh in marriage . . . handmaid and mother, maiden and heaven, only bridge to mankind." Inextricably linked to such Marian doctrine was Proclus's high view of the Incarnation: "We do not preach a deified man," he protested. "We confess an incarnate God." Such sentiments appealed mightily to a community still muttering against Anastasius. Adding to the force of the reaction was Proclus's position as a former disciple of the beloved Chrysostom, still venerated in the city he had led as archbishop. He also had a close relationship with Pulcheria. A few years earlier, he had celebrated her devotion in panegyric verses that sound worryingly like hymns to the empress herself.[15]

Constantinople's monks and lower clergy united against their patriarch. They denounced Nestorius as a heretic unworthy to be bishop, challenging him directly, and loudly, during church services. When a monk tried to prevent him entering the church during the liturgy, Nestorius had him handed over to the secular authorities to be beaten and publicly paraded; he then had the monk sent into exile.[16]

Nestorius responded with the tactics he had already used against heretics and rivals. One prestigious victim, Archimandrite Basil, recorded his punishment in a petition to the emperor: "Immediately he had us seized, and thence, beaten by the crowd of the officers, we were led to the prison, and there they stripped us naked as prisoners and subject to punishment, bound us to pillars, threw us down and kicked us." This treatment seemed all the worse because clergy were used to immunity or mild treatment in the civil courts, but Nestorius knew no such restraints. "Oppressed, famished, we remained a long time under guard. . . . Loaded with irons we were led back to the prison, and afterwards were brought up in the Praetorium in the same way with chains. Since there was no accuser, we were again led back by the guard in the prison, and thus he again chastised us smiting us on the face."

Given the turbulent reputation of the city's monks and their popularity with the masses, this massive disaffection was a serious warning sign for the imperial court. Basil even told the emperor that Nestorius's misdeeds arose directly from the patriarch's powerful connections. Nestorius was "confident in his wrath, and in the might of some who have been corrupted, and (to speak fearlessly) in your Majesty." That was as close as a Roman subject could safely get to accusing the emperor of allowing a functionary to get away with gross oppression.[17]

But Nestorius faced still more powerful enemies, among the imperial women. He had already annoyed Pulcheria by preventing her from taking communion alongside the emperor within the sanctuary of the church. Although this right strictly belonged to the emperor alone, Pulcheria had previously insisted on it by right of her vow of virginity and, presumably, her special holy status. Nestorius also attacked the woman-oriented devotional life she had constructed. He removed Pulcheria's image from its place of honor above the altar in the great church and tried to limit women's participation in night services, seeing them as an excuse for immorality. He would also later charge that Pulcheria's much-vaunted virginity was a sham.[18]

The *Theotokos* debacle was the last straw for Pulcheria, who viewed such a denigration of the Virgin Mary as a personal attack on herself. In his autobiography, Nestorius laid many of his problems at her feet. He had no need to name the person he was denouncing,

> a contentious woman, a princess, a young maiden, a virgin,
> who fought against me because I was not willing to be per
> suaded by her demand that I should compare a woman cor
> rupted of men to the Bride of Christ. This I have done
> because I had pity on her soul and that I might not be the
> chief celebrant of the sacrifice among those whom she had
> unrighteously chosen. Of her I have spoken only to mention
> her, for she was my friend; and therefore I keep silence about
> and hide everything else about her own little self, seeing that
> she was but a young maiden; and for that reason she fought
> against me.[19]

Out of Egypt

Nestorius's sermons traveled far and fast. Cyril of Alexandria was
soon writing that "There is no one from any city or country, who
does not say that these things are in every one's mouth, and, What
new learning is being brought into the churches?" By the start of
429, they were being read and debated in the Egyptian monasteries.
Alarmed by the spread of deviant thinking on such a critical subject,
Cyril of Alexandria promptly wrote to the monastic communities,
reaffirming his view of orthodoxy. He was sincerely shocked by
Nestorius's ideas as they apparently created two gods in one person
and moved to a kind of polytheism. Or perhaps Nestorius was
saying that Jesus was a mere prophet, who should yet be worshipped, just as the pagans of old had worshipped god-men. This
was no less troubling an idea, and one equally far from anything
Nestorius had suggested.[20]

Cyril also had his own agendas for being outraged, as he was involved in a bitter fight within his own church. The immediate cir cumstance involved a group of Egyptian bishops whom he had disciplined, and who sought help from the emperor. Cyril protested that these were men of obvious bad character—one had wronged the blind, he claimed; another had drawn a sword against his mother. Still, Nestorius refused to support Cyril's plea to dismiss the case. The refusal aggravated Cyril and gave him a motive to create a new legal case that would divert attention from his own difficulties. That was exactly how the Egyptian assault on John Chrysostom had started thirty years before.[21]

Discrediting Nestorius worked for the long-term good of Alexandria over Constantinople. Legally, Cyril was in a weak situation, because emerging church law and custom limited the right of even the most senior bishops to operate outside their correct jurisdictions, and Alexandria had no power over Constantinople. Intervention could only be justified in situations of extreme emergency—if, say, a powerful bishop suddenly proclaimed some extreme heresy that threatened the survival of Christian orthodoxy. It was politically essential to make Nestorius's errors as outrageous as possible. Alexandria might be far from the imperial court, but at least, Cyril would show, it did a far better job of maintaining orthodoxy. As a bonus, destroying Nestorius would also blow back on his mother church at Antioch, so that two rivals could be taken out with one coup. Cyril's campaign against Nestorius was partly directed against better-known Antiochene thinkers, namely the disciples of Theodore of Mopsuestia.[22]

Whatever he thought at the time, Nestorius had plenty of leisure in later years to think over the crisis. Looking back, he complained that Cyril had created a strong party within Constantinople itself, and through a network of agents and legates—we would say lobbyists—he was undermining Nestorius within the church and the court. In fact, claimed Nestorius, Cyril's motives were based on a personal quest for power. He blamed Cyril for the resistance to his efforts at compromise:

Now the clergy of Alexandria, who were in favor of his deeds, persuaded those of Constantinople as persons deceived that they should not accept the word "Mother of Christ," and they were stirring up and making trouble, and going around in every place and making use of everything to help them; for his clergy were sending word to him.[23]

Nestorius believed that Cyril was only looking for an excuse to target him, because Constantinople had failed to supply the bribes that would have prevented the furor from arising. Cyril, in effect, was levying protection money to avoid the kind of crisis that had taken out John Chrysostom, and when the money was not forthcoming, the trouble began in earnest.

Cyril vs. Nestorius

The conflict escalated, as Nestorius read Cyril's letter to the monks, with its frank attack on his own views. Nestorius complained, and Cyril replied, ostensibly as a brother and fellow-minister seeking to correct a mistake, but in confrontational terms. Nestorius replied in kind. He began one response, "I pass over the insults against us contained in your extraordinary letter!" Seemingly unable to bear the mention of Cyril's name, Nestorius's reports to his friends thereafter usually speak only of what "the Egyptian" has done. From mid-429, the two began a correspondence that would have vast implications for later Christian thought.[24]

Cyril expressed his views most thoroughly in his second letter, which acquired an authoritative status almost equal to that of the great councils themselves. He stated his doctrine of the hypostatic union and powerfully reasserted the idea of incarnation in such a way that justified the word *Theotokos.*

This expression, "the Word was made flesh," can mean nothing else but that he partook of flesh and blood like us; he made our body his own, and came forth man from a woman, not casting off his existence as God, or his generation of God the Father, but even in taking to himself flesh, remaining what he was.

We should call Mary the Mother of God "not as if the nature of the Word or his divinity had its beginning from the holy Virgin, but because of her was born that holy body with a rational soul, to which the Word being personally [hypostatically] united is said to be born according to the flesh."[25]

Nestorius replied frankly, in letters that Cyril's partisans found "full of blasphemies" but which a modern audience is likely to read rather differently. His main goal was to deny that "the consubstantial godhead was capable of suffering, or that the whole being that was coeternal with the Father was recently born, or that it rose again." But in addition to philosophical argument, he raised vital questions about how human beings knew about God. Where his views will strike a modern audience more congenially than Cyril's is in his approach to authority, and specifically to interpreting Scripture.[26]

Nestorius based his doctrine firmly on biblical texts, and as a good Antiochene, he read his New Testament historically as a work rooted in time, not as an encyclopedia of mystical symbols. His basic point was that the New Testament "speaks of the birth and suffering not of the godhead but of the *humanity* of Christ, so that the holy virgin is more accurately termed mother of Christ than Mother of God."[27] Throughout the Gospels, passages clearly refer to Mary as the mother of Jesus, not of Christ. It would be anachronistic to find there such later theological terms as Mother of God, or of the Logos. As the Gospels wrote, "the mother of Jesus was there"; she was "Mary, the mother of Jesus."

He believed that Cyril's talk of hypostatic union served to undermine the humanity of Christ. Actually reading the Bible reminds us constantly of the human side of Christ and his sufferings, however much others may spiritualize them. It was a story of:

the human fear and the betrayal, . . . the crucifixion, the fixing of the nails, the gall which was offered unto him, the other distresses, the surrender of his spirit to the Father, the bowing down of his head, the descent of his body from the cross, the embalming thereof, his burial, the resurrection on the third day, his appearance in his body, his speaking and his teaching that they should not suppose him to be an illusion of the body, but truly body which had also flesh.[28]

Docetists and other heretics believed that Christ's body and human nature were illusions, and according to Nestorius, Cyril was reducing Christ's humanity in the same way. It was ludicrous for Nestorius's critics to accuse him of "making Christ out to be a mere man, I who at the very beginning of my consecration obtained a law against those who say that Christ is a mere man and against other heresies."[29]

Cyril responded with New Testament quotes but heavily weighted toward the more mystical and otherworldly passages. He shows a strong preference for two books, namely John's gospel, and the very Platonic and symbolic letter known as Hebrews. Naturally, he stressed two key Johannine verses: "He who has seen me has seen the Father," and "I and my Father are one." In other writings, though, Cyril's use of Scripture puzzles modern readers. Like all early Christians, Cyril had no hesitation in drawing doctrine from the Old Testament passages that supposedly prophesied the coming of Christ. But, as an Alexandrian, he pushed these supposed connections and parallels to the breaking point. He was particularly fond of what is called anagogical interpretation, by which a seemingly routine material object becomes a symbol or pointer through which the text reveals a spiritual reality. In his *Scholia on the Incarnation*, written about this time, Cyril proves his doctrines by drawing on a bewildering range of Old Testament authorities including the Pentateuch and the Psalms. In the Pentateuch, we hear how God gave specific instructions about building the ark in the wilderness, made of wood but covered with pure gold, and this text—he thinks—helped explain the Incarnation. "God the Word was united to the holy Flesh. . . . For the gold that was spread upon the wood, remained what it was, and the wood was rich in the glory of the gold; yet it ceased not from being wood." "Many proofs" showed that the ark was here a type (an image or prefiguring) of Christ.[30]

Cyril found rich evidence for Christ's divinity in the book of Isaiah, which Christians mined so enthusiastically that it almost enjoyed the status of a fifth gospel. In one passage, Isaiah records how an angel took a live coal from the altar and put it to the prophet's lips. Aha, says Cyril, "one may see in the coal, as in an image, the Word of God united to the human nature, yet not losing the being that He has, but rather transforming what He had taken, or united, unto His own glory and operation." Fire seizes hold of wood although not changing its nature of wood—and that's how you should think of Christ.[31] As mysticism or devotion, this might be inspiring; as a basis for a claim that Cyril could find biblical roots for his Christology, it is wildly unconvincing.

Nestorius warned, reasonably enough, that Cyril was going much too far in his reaction to the attempt to undercut Christ's divinity. Reading Cyril's letters today, we ask what remained of the human Jesus, or in what sense the God who died on the cross differed from the Father, creator of the universe? To quote one of the greatest modern scholars of this debate, W. H. C. Frend: "Cyril's Christ remained an abstraction, his humanity so much part of the divine world as to be unrecognizable in human terms. . . . There was no biblical ring in his thought, for all his commentaries on the books of the Bible."[32] So determined was Cyril to show that Christ was not just a man that he stressed and overstressed the theme of Jesus as God, reviving—said Nestorius—the doctrines of Apollinarius.

As Nestorius warned, Cyril was not only wrong in his main argument, but he might have been venturing into even graver heresies involving a dualistic division of the material and spiritual worlds. He urged Cyril to realize how he might have been deceived by clandestine heretics either in Alexandria or Constantinople, including some who had been expelled as Manichaeans. Cyril was in danger of seeing Christ as a purely divine visitor with no real human qualities, a nonresident alien. Nestorius's supporter Ibas of Edessa reported that Cyril "slipped up and was found falling into the teaching of Apollinarius." As Ibas recalled, the Gospels spoke of Christ's body as a temple, suggesting a distinction between a divine reality and a human frame. Cyril, however, failed to understand this. Like Apollinarius, Cyril "wrote that the very God the Word became man in such a way that there is no distinction between the Temple and the one who dwells in it."[33]

Nestorius also noted how cynically Cyril and his followers misquoted him for partisan effect. The Nestorius they hated was not the real person, but a straw man constructed from passages wrenched out of context. One of Nestorius's sermons had declared that "Mary, my friends, bore not the Godhead; she bore a man, the inseparable instrument of Godhead." Cyril misquoted that remark to read "Mary, my friends, bore not God." And as Nestorius objected, "Here to say God, and not to say the Godhead, makes very much difference." It did indeed.[34]

Cyril's Crusade

As is common in such pamphlet wars, each side presumably thought it had carried the day, but Cyril was not content with outarguing his opponent. Instead, Cyril now took positive steps to depose and destroy him, and entered crusading mode. The history of the Alexandrian patriarchate recalls how "Cyril availed himself of the weapons of his fathers, Alexander and Athanasius, and put on the breastplate of faith that his predecessors had handed down in the Church of Saint Mark the Evangelist; and he went out to war, as David did, with his heart strong in Christ who is God."

He called together the Egyptian bishops, who declared that the new situation was singularly dangerous—so dangerous, in fact, as to demand extraordinary intervention in the affairs of another province. They compared Nestorius with the most notorious heretical leaders of the previous two hundred years. "For Arius and his followers, and Paul [of Samosata] and Mani and the rest of the heretics were not patriarchs, and yet they led a multitude of men astray. How then can this man remain patriarch of Constantinople?"[35]

Cyril mobilized support from other bishops wherever he could find them, including—critically for later history—the Roman Pope Celestine. From the Egyptian point of view, the Roman see had many advantages, particularly the enormous weight attached to the primacy of Peter, but also because it was far removed from the traditional rivalries of the Eastern churches. In early 430, Cyril sent a dossier of recent texts and correspondence to various church leaders, including Celestine. In turn, Celestine had his own interests to pursue. He made no claim to be a skilled theologian (Nestorius thought he was too gullible and simple to stand up to Cyril), but Cyril's alarms genuinely convinced him. Moreover, he shared the familiar Roman fears about the growing status of the see of Constantinople, which could stand to be taught a lesson. Among other grievances, Nestorius had annoyed Celestine by writing to him as an ecclesiastical equal, brother to brother, boosting the claim that Old and New Rome stood on the same footing.[36]

Celestine ordered an inquiry into Cyril's charges, to be headed by his deacon Leo. After convening a synod, in August 430 the pope gave Nestorius an ultimatum, with a specific deadline. Nestorius had just ten days to "annul by an open confession in writing that faithless novelty which undertakes to sever what holy Scripture unites," and agree to teach the same doctrines about Christ that the churches of Rome and Alexandria held, and that Constantinople had before his time. Otherwise, he would be excommunicated.[37]

That November, with Rome firmly behind him, Cyril wrote a third letter to Nestorius, which presented his views in a more aggressive and extreme style than ever. Cyril was declaring war:

Who can help us in the Day of Judgment, or what kind of excuse shall we find for thus keeping silence so long, with regard to the blasphemies made by you against [Christ]? If you injured yourself alone, by teaching and holding such things, perhaps it would matter less; but you have greatly scandalized the whole Church, and have cast among the people the leaven of a strange and new heresy.[38]

In this much-quoted third letter, Cyril was demanding that all Christians accept his doctrine of the hypostatic union, rejecting any separation of the human and divine. Appended to the letter were twelve anathemas, each describing a theological error, and ending with the note that if anyone believes this, "let him be anathema." (See appendix to this chapter, The Twelve Anathemas.) These anathemas would serve as a charter for orthodoxy for decades afterward and helped shape what became the church's official Christology. But they were also open to other interpretations. So resolutely did Cyril oppose Nestorius that he now restated his doctrines in terms that could easily be cited in support of One Nature theory. Most egregious was the twelfth anathema, which condemned anyone who denied that "the Word of God suffered in the flesh and was crucified in the flesh and tasted death in the flesh." The anathemas were a frontal attack on Antiochene theology as much as on Nestorius himself.[39]

Together with other bishops, Cyril wrote to the emperor begging him to hold a council to enquire into Nestorius's beliefs and conduct. This was a delicate matter, given the possible implication that Theodosius II had chosen a thoroughly flawed archbishop. Nor could it be argued that Nestorius had been a fine choice when originally appointed but had somehow drifted into heresy while in office. He had held the job for only two years, and Theodosius should, in theory, have taken some responsibility for his beliefs. But Cyril played expertly on Theodosius's famous piety and his role as guardian of the church. Reinforcing Cyril's message was his envoy at the imperial court, Abbot Victor, whom Theodosius venerated for his holiness and asceticism. Also, Theodosius must have known just how disturbed the capital city was, so that some kind of urgent action had to be taken. In November 430 the emperor convened a council to be held in the ancient city of Ephesus, in western Asia Minor. The date would be June 7, 431, the feast of Pentecost that commemorated the original descent of the Spirit upon the apostles. Adding to the appropriateness of the date—and redounding to imperial glory—this would be just fifty years after the earlier Theodosius I had called his own great council, in Constantinople.[40]

But it was far from obvious that the new Theodosius had agreed to the kind of hostile tribunal that Cyril was demanding. If Nestorius had infuriated the court, then Cyril had also alienated the emperor by generating the present mess. A rough paraphrase of Theodosius's letter to Cyril would run as follows: You should have known that I take good care of these religious matters. Why on earth, then, did you choose to try and settle things yourself, spreading confusion and chaos everywhere in the church? Whatever happened to caution, prudence, restraint, good sense? Just know that, whatever happens, you are to blame for all this.[41] The emperor went on to complain about Cyril's attempts to win favor in the court and the royal family. When the council actually did meet, Cyril should turn up promptly and not expect to take any further liberties or to speak more freely than he was allowed. Reading such a letter today, it looks as if Theodosius expected the coming gathering to lead to an absolute defeat of Cyril, who should in theory have faced the new year in fear and trembling.

On the other side, Nestorius was surprisingly pleased by the turn of events—so much so, perhaps, as to give further evidence of just how out of touch he was. He had himself requested a meeting of scholars and theologians to discuss the controversy, but a general council was not necessarily bad news. In fact, he hoped that the outcome would be the condemnation of Cyril rather than himself, as Cyril had expressed views that (in his view) were clearly Apollinarian.

Pope Celestine marveled that Nestorius should rejoice at such an imminent battle. Partly, Nestorius knew that he had the sympathy of Theodosius, but he also had other powerful allies, especially Bishop John of Antioch. The empire now faced an alarming confrontation between Alexandria and Rome on the one hand, versus Constantinople and Antioch on the other. In fact, John was much more cautious in light of the overwhelming forces now arrayed against Nestorius, and he urged his friend to make an accommodation. The word *Theotokos* was not really that unacceptable, he said, when so many earlier Fathers has used it. But Nestorius pressed ahead.[42]

A Hot Summer in Ephesus

We can know the ins and outs of these events, all the gruesome details and sordid deals, with as much certainty as we can approach, for instance, backroom American politics of a century ago. In the fifth century, too, accounts of councils were preserved in exact detail because of the legalistic mind-set of the participants and the near certainty that the records would provide the basis of a later appeal.[43]

The council drew on a wide cross section of the Eastern church, with a token presence from Africa and the West. In some ways, Ephesus was an excellent meeting place, because it was an important communication hub by land and sea. But the city's associations worked against Nestorius's side. Ephesus boasted astonishing claims to connections with the apostolic age. One lively tradition claimed that St. John had brought the Virgin Mary there after the crucifixion, making it an appropriate site for discussions of the Virgin's status in heaven. Choosing Ephesus also raised delicate issues of church politics, as the bishop, Memnon, had long-standing grievances against Constantinople and had every reason to want to see Nestorius ruined.[44]

A phrase like "the Council of Ephesus" suggests a degree of structure and organization that was far removed from the reality.

For one thing, it conjures visions of a body of clergy meeting on a set day, gathering under one roof, debating and voting. In practice, the hardest thing was actually getting all the people together, a process that literally cost lives. Partly as a result of travel difficulties, different groups arrived piecemeal over a period of some weeks. Some set out around Easter, but many others were still arriving after Pentecost, seven weeks later. Cyril arrived with a formidable contingent of fifty bishops, against sixteen for Nestorius, and other bishops brought their own phalanxes—Juvenal of Jerusalem with the clergy of Palestine, Flavian of Philippi with his Macedonians.[45]

By the end of the proceedings, perhaps 250 bishops had attended at some point, each accompanied by two priests and a deacon. That suggests a total attendance of at least a thousand, although those figures would not include servants, slaves, bodyguards, and general hangers-on, nor the secular military forces intended to keep order. The city's population that summer probably found itself swollen by at least several thousand. In modern American terms, that would be equivalent to the impact of a very large convention on a major city, although Ephesus would have been far more stressed to provide accommodations.

But travel issues alone did not fully explain the patchy arrivals. Bishops were genuinely concerned about a range of threats they might face—risks of making a political misstep or of alienating powerful court factions. Some, too, had real fears for their lives and safety at a time of such heightened tensions. Cyril's Egyptian record showed just how willing he was to resort to mob rule, while his entourage included some ferocious Egyptian monks, like the doughty followers of Aba Shenoute. The threat of violence is stressed in the official history of the Alexandria patriarchate, which has nothing but good to say of Cyril. According to this account, Nestorius reputedly pleaded with the emperor, "The bishops are many, and I fear that they will kill me." (In 449, murder at a council was exactly the fate that would befall Flavian, Nestorius's successor at Constantinople).

Anti-Nestorian bishops pledged themselves to defend orthodoxy to the death if necessary.[46]

Finding Nestorius's fears plausible, Theodosius II sent with him Candidian, a patrician, together with the powerful official Count Irenaeus, supported by a military force, while the archbishop also brought "a great crowd of his adherents." Candidian's role would be controversial. Although he was acting under imperial orders to observe strict neutrality, some accounts portray Candidian as a friend and partisan of Nestorius, always looking out for his interests. His soldiers, meanwhile, showed little respect for the bishops following Cyril and Memnon. In fact, most of Candidian's controversial decisions genuinely seem to have been undertaken in the cause of neutrality, as he tried to avoid seeing the proceedings turning into a rout stage managed by the Egyptians. Alexandrians, in turn, viewed him as the familiar kind of secular official who had blocked the church's ambitions back home and who eventually succumbed to enough bluster. They remembered the prefect Orestes, whom Cyril had thoroughly bested some years earlier. They were duly shocked when Candidian failed to cave in, and demonized him accordingly. Charges of Candidian's bias would be important in later councils, as the Egyptians would bring their own armed strength, notionally to provide self-defense.[47]

By far the most important of the reluctant participants was John of Antioch himself, whose long-anticipated arrival dominated the early proceedings. On June 6 he sent messengers promising that he would be there within five days, or at worst six, but he was still conspicuously absent on June 21, and so were most of his bishops. His absence gave Nestorius an excellent excuse for refusing to go ahead with the hearings: how could any council claim to speak for the church if it lacked the chief representative of Syria and the East? Candidian agreed that no valid council could be held without the key Eastern dioceses, so they must delay.[48]

Yet hanging on indefinitely in Ephesus was intolerable for so many bishops, so far from their dioceses, and having to cope with unfamiliar and unhygienic food and water. This was what we would today call southwestern Turkey in June, in the middle of a heat wave, and bishops were literally starting to die off. In imagining the scene, we also recall that this was just the era when the well-bathed and scented Roman world was giving way to an ascetic Christianity in which the holiest and most committed believers, as a matter of pious principle, refused to wash. Especially when gathered in large groups, monks must have stunk to a degree that a modern Westerner would find inconceivable. As pro- and anti-Nestorius factions glared at each other, it was an open question which side would crack first. Participants were beginning to place John's arrival in an indefinite future, rather like that of the second coming of Christ himself.

By June 22 the anti-Nestorius forces achieved their goal, by actually beginning the hearings without John. Participating were 155 bishops, while sixty-eight others signed a petition pleading with Cyril not to start without Antioch. But the majority claimed higher authority. They met in the presence of the Gospels, which were placed on the main throne to symbolize Christ's presence. In worldly terms, the real head was Cyril, serving as president in his own name and that of the Roman pope, who had authorized proceedings against Nestorius. And as before, Cyril had secured his position with generous gifts to all concerned.[49]

But the proceedings raised multiple legal problems, quite apart from the continued absence of most Syrian bishops. While the pope's order gave some authority, the imperial summons had superseded it, and even the most ambitious claims for church power agreed that emperors still trumped popes. Nor was there any pretence of any balance between pro- and anti-Nestorian parties. This was in no sense a contest between two competing forces, each with a valid position that needed to be presented and duly judged. Technically, Nestorius himself was already excommunicated, as he had not fulfilled the conditions laid out in the pope's letter the previous year. His opinions did not count, and (at least according to the strictest interpretation) he should certainly not be seated at the council. Memnon of Ephesus had already closed the city's churches to the Nestorians, who were not to be treated as Christians in good standing.[50]

Ideally, though, Nestorius and his allies should at least be present to make the proceedings look properly judicial; but they refused to play along. Nestorius and his friends withdrew from most of the council, refusing to acknowledge its validity without the presence of the Antioch clergy and of some more representatives from the West. They tried to ensure that it would be regarded as a purely partisan, local event. Candidian also lodged a protest and registered a complaint with the emperor.

The game continued awhile, with Nestorius and allies ensconced in his house, being approached repeatedly by delegations from the council. His critics suggest that he was hiding behind fortified walls and Candidian's armed soldiery, as if he were in arms against the council and the world, but it all depended on where you stood. As Nestorius himself said, the soldiers were not to threaten the council, but to defend himself. "I needed to post soldiers around my house to guard myself, that they might not come against me with violence and destroy me!"[51]

With Nestorius out of the picture, the council proceeded under Cyril's choreography—as Nestorius observed, "Is it not evident even to the unintelligent that he was in everything?" Apart from Memnon, Cyril's deputy on this occasion was Juvenal of Jerusalem, who served as vice president of the council. This choice was daring, as Juvenal was notionally a patriarch, but legally he was subject to the metropolitan of Caesarea and the patriarch of Antioch. Yet on this occasion, he was acting as the equal of any of the "real" patriarchs. This power grab was also ironic, as in earlier years Cyril himself had opposed Juvenal's daring claims for the status of his see of Jerusalem. On this occasion, though, Juvenal was a valuable ally.[52]

With the Cyrillians so clearly in control, little doubt remained about the result of the proceedings. Cyril's scribe read to the council a series of incriminating documents, including the patriarch's earlier correspondence with Nestorius. The council had to determine which of the two was in accord with church doctrine, as expressed in Scripture and the earlier church councils. Naturally enough under the circumstances, they sided wholly with Cyril, concluding with cries of "Anathema to Nestorius!" Two alleged friends of Nestorius provided damaging reports of their recent conversations with him. One, Bishop Acacius, shocked the assembly when he reported Nestorius's seemingly blasphemous remark that a child of two or three months could not properly be called God. The council then heard relevant passages from key scriptural texts and church authorities, all reflecting the Alexandrian standpoint.[53]

The council then approved the papal letter of excommunication. Besides everything else, they wrote, Nestorius has not accepted their summons, "nor to receive the most holy and god-fearing bishops whom we sent to him." By default, then, they continued, we have been forced to examine his impieties in his absence. And based on these, "with many tears," we have no option but to agree with the sentence of excommunication. Nestorius is therefore deposed as a bishop. Including proxies, an impressive two hundred bishops signed the document. Nestorius was notified by a letter amicably addressed to "the new Judas."[54]

In Search of an Exit

Matters ran still further out of hand when John of Antioch finally arrived on June 26, with his Easterners. Candidian brought him up to date on the council, telling how he had tried to prevent it from rushing to judgment. Horrified by the state of division, John blamed Cyril wholly for the disaster. He responded by convening a council from forty-three of the bishops present, and this body now deposed Cyril and Memnon. This was not so much from any loyalty to Nestorius or his ideas, but out of John's fury at the kangaroo-court aspect of the earlier proceedings. The Syrians also charged, rightly, that Cyril's gold had tainted the proceedings. But Cyril's theology was at issue, as well as his conduct, and the Syrian churchmen demanded that the council repudiate his twelve anathemas, which so stressed Christ's unity with God. How, they asked, could Cyril possibly declare that the "Word of God" had really been crucified in the flesh? Theodoret of Cyrrhus denounced the anathemas as heretical in their own right, a revival of the opinions of Apollinarius and Arius. Ibas of Edessa, too, thought The Twelve Anathemas were "packed with every form of impiety. . . and contrary to the true faith." The rival council was deeply unpopular among the people of Ephesus itself, who remained faithful to Memnon: a crowd stoned the Syrian bishops as they tried to make their way to the church. Matters now reached the point where, as Ibas complained, "no one dared to travel from city to city or from region to region, but everyone persecuted his neighbor as if he were an enemy."[55]

Both sides now appealed to the emperor, who learned that what should have been a straightforward hearing was fast turning into a divisive potential schism. "In bitter regret," Nestorius declared: "Let Mary be called *Theotokos*, if you will, and let all disputing cease!" But his statement came a year too late.

Under imperial orders to make peace, the council reconvened on July 11. The weather was now getting hotter, and the assembled bishops were growing angrier and desperate to leave Ephesus. The council reported to the pope that "many, both bishops and clergy, were both pressed by sickness and oppressed by expense, and some had even deceased." Bishops complained, "We are being killed with the heat through the heaviness of the air, and someone is buried almost daily; so that all the servants are sent home, and all the other bishops are in the same state."[56]

Only the arrival of fresh papal legates offered any hope of a chance to reconcile the impasse. So ecstatic, in fact, was the reception that when their credentials from Pope Celestine were read, the bishops responded with cries that, to a modern audience, sound disturbingly Stalinist: "This is a just judgment!" cried the bishops. "To Celestine the new Paul! To the new Paul, Cyril! To Celestine, the guardian of the Faith! To Celestine agreeing to the Synod! The Synod gives thanks to Cyril. One Celestine, one Cyril!" It was the sense of relief at finding a way out that led the council to make such florid acclamations of Roman prestige, which later papal supporters would quote when arguing for papal supremacy. St. Peter had now cast his weight entirely behind Cyril, and the envoys confirmed the sentence against Nestorius.[57]

Even so, the council remained deeply divided with the Syrian statement against Cyril. In turn, Cyril and Memnon persuaded a majority of the council to depose John and thirty-three of his followers. Open war loomed among the churches of the East.

On to Constantinople

Although the majority party had written their damning judgment of Nestorius, it had to be delivered and accepted, much like a modern court subpoena, and it had to be published, in the sense of being made known at the imperial court. Nestorius fought on both fronts, refusing to accept the letter. Candidian, meanwhile, suppressed popular demonstrations in favor of the council and ordered copies of the letter torn down from public walls. Alexandrian accounts report that he arrested Cyril, although the chronology of events is not clear. Candidian's soldiers seized Cyril by night, an act that for the Alexandrians undoubtedly recalled the arrest of Christ and made even more explicit the patriarch's messianic role.[58]

Although Candidian was forced to free Cyril, he kept his stranglehold on the city and on the flow of information. His control of the roads leading out of Ephesus prevented the letter reaching Constantinople until one of the bishops found his way out of the city in disguise, carrying the letter hidden inside a cane. He brought it to two anti-Nestorian monks, one of whom—Eutyches—would himself play a key role in later theological battles. Meanwhile, Nestorius and Candidian sent their own letters presenting the other side of the case and denouncing Cyril and Memnon.[59]

Even with the hostile letter in Constantinople, the anti-Nestorian party still had to convince a reluctant Theodosius. Critical to the change in opinion was the archimandrite Dalmatius, who pleaded Cyril's cause. Dalmatius was a veteran soldier who had retired to a monastic cell that he never left and where he acquired a reputation for ferocious holiness and asceticism. His intervention in 431 was all the more amazing because Dalmatius had not even left his cell when the emperor had requested him to say a litany to prevent earthquakes. Now, though, "a voice came down from heaven bidding him go forth. For [God] did not will that His flock should perish utterly." Earthquakes, the city might withstand; but not Nestorius.[60]

Nestorius himself—obviously, not an impartial witness—describes the tumult in Constantinople in a torrid July. "Assemblies of priests and troops of monks" condemned him. Most could not normally agree to get along with one another, but all lesser rivalries gave way to the greater purpose of bringing down their archbishop. They mobilized a threatening mass demonstration, clothed in all the available symbols of heroic piety and charismatic religious power:

And they took for themselves as organizer and chief, in order to overwhelm the Emperor with amazement, Dalmatius the archimandrite, who for many years had not left his monastery. A multitude of monks surrounded him in the midst of the city, chanting the offices, in order that all the city might be assembled with them and proceed before the Emperor to be able to hinder his purpose. For they had prepared all these things in advance in order that there might not be any hindrance, and they went in with the chanting of the office even to the Emperor.[61]

If any emperor was strong enough to stand up convincingly against this sight, it was not the priest-ridden Theodosius.

Nestorius reported the dialogue between the emperor and Dalmatius in terms that are explicitly designed to remind the reader of the trial of Christ, with himself representing Jesus. Here, more than anywhere in Nestorius's account, we can be sure that he is spinning a tale. Dalmatius is given the part of the Jewish priests constantly demanding punishment, while the good Theodosius washes his hands of the matter. And just as the Jews at the trial of Jesus reportedly cried, "his blood be on us and our children," so Dalmatius allegedly offers to take eternal blame for the evil and impious actions being taken against Nestorius. But once Theodosius had received this vindication, he accepted and confirmed the sentence.[62]

The mob then launched a citywide demonstration, an outburst of popular passion that in other circumstances could very easily have turned into a riot to threaten the empire itself.

They carried Dalmatius around, reclining on a couch which was spread with coverlets, and mules bore him in the midst of the streets of the city, so that everyone knew that a victory had been gained over the purpose of the Emperor, amidst great assemblies of the people and of the monks, who were dancing and clapping their hands, and crying out the things that can be said against one who has been deprived for iniquity.

Reportedly—and this time, plausibly—the happy throng was swelled by many of Nestorius's old enemies, including the heretics and schismatics he had himself treated so roughly when he held the upper hand. All joined in the demonstration, clapping their hands and shouting over and over the memorable slogan of the day, the proclamation of the unity of persons in Christ: "God the Word died! God the Word died!"[63]

At the end of July, the council reaffirmed the decrees against Nestorius, and that ended the gathering. All that now remained was for the emperor to sort out the mess within the Eastern churches.

Initially, he tried to accept the acts of both rival councils, favoring the depositions of John, Cyril, and Memnon, as well as Nestorius. Such a clean sweep of high offices must have seemed very tempting in the circumstances. Eventually, though, the emperor reinstated all the protagonists except Nestorius. After a brief incumbency in the see, Constantinople's bishopric passed to Proclus, a strong Cyrillian and Pulcheria's favored cleric. The crisis left Pulcheria even more firmly in control than hitherto and ready to pursue her scheme of making Constantinople the capital of a great empire dedicated to the *Theotokos*.

Alexandria and Antioch now had to patch up a truce. Long negotiations followed until, by 433, under heavy pressure from the emperor, Cyril and John recognized each other's claim to his patriarchate. They also reached a historic pact on doctrinal issues, the Formula of Reunion, which was near-miraculous to the extent that it reflected a common ground between the two irreconcilable cities. This agreement—probably put together by Theodoret— marked a major step toward the formula that would eventually win at Chalcedon, "the unconfused union of two natures." Jesus Christ was acknowledged as

> perfect God and perfect man, composed of a rational soul and a body, begotten before the ages from the Father in respect of His divinity, but likewise in these last days for us and our salvation from the Virgin Mary in respect of His manhood, consubstantial with the Father in respect of His divinity and at the same time consubstantial with us in respect of His manhood. For the union [*henosis*] of two natures has been accomplished.

As Ibas was delighted to report, the document acknowledged two natures, both "the temple and the one who dwells in it."[64]

Speaking of the two natures marked a real concession to Antioch, but Alexandria also won victories. Antioch distanced itself from Nestorius and explicitly accepted the word *Theotokos*:

In virtue of this conception of a union without confusion, we confess the holy Virgin as *Theotokos* because the divine Word became flesh and was made man, and from the very conception united to Himself the temple taken from her.

The two churches acknowledged a difference of opinion among theologians in how they interpreted the biblical and patristic statements about these issues. They "employ some indifferently in view of the unity of person [*prosopon*] but distinguish others in view of the duality of natures."[65]

Both politically and theologically, this was a huge achievement. Cyril announced the pact with words of high celebration: "Let the heavens rejoice, and let the earth be glad!"

Aftermath

Once removed from the archbishopric of Constantinople, Nestorius retired into a comfortable exile in a monastery near his old home of Antioch, where he "received all sorts of honors and respectful presents." However, that was too close to the world of intellectual debate to be comfortable for his critics. They sought a more lasting removal, which would leave him unable to spread his heresies. In 435, the emperor banished him for life, sending him to Arabia—roughly to what we might call Jordan or eastern Syria. The sentence was then changed to a life sentence in Upper Egypt. Egyptian residence was a particular insult since that land was the heart of the anti-Nestorian true believers. Also in 435, the emperor denied Nestorians the right to call themselves Christians.[66]

If Nestorius was the villain in a pious legend, then the rest of his life should have been spent in agony and disgrace, culminating in a suitably gruesome finale—his bowels split asunder, perhaps, or death in a snake pit. Some accounts do offer such a saga of misery, but the reality was more complex. One story comes from the historian Evagrius, who loathed "Nestorius, that God-assaulting tongue, that second conclave of Caiaphas, that workshop of blasphemy."[67] Evagrius tells how barbarian nomad raiders overwhelmed Nestorius's refuge, and in the process they unwittingly inflicted upon him the ultimate atrocity, of setting him free and moving him to another city. Although this act may not sound too savage, the consequences were potentially devastating. Apart from the privations and hardships of the journey, they had caused Nestorius to break imperial law by leaving his place of banishment, and he wrote at length to excuse his misdeed:

> I was conducted by barbarous soldiers from Panopolis to Elephantine, a place on the verge of the province of the Thebaid, being dragged thither by the aforesaid military force; and when, sorely shattered, I had accomplished the greater part of the journey, I am encountered by an unwritten order to return to Panopolis. Thus, miserably worn with the casualties of the road, with a body afflicted by disease and age, and a mangled hand and side, I arrived at Panopolis in extreme exhaustion, and further tormented with cruel pains: whence a second written injunction from you, speedily overtaking me, transported me to its adjacent territory. While I was supposing that this treatment would now cease, and was awaiting the determination of our glorious sovereigns respecting me, another merciless order was suddenly issued for a fourth deportation.

All this for a man past fifty, who according to the standards of the time was entering extreme old age. Evagrius gloatingly concludes that "when his tongue had been eaten through with worms, he departed to the greater and everlasting judgment which awaited him."[68]

Evagrius was wrong. Nestorius lived on well into his seventies, probably until around 452, which allowed him to hear news of the Council of Chalcedon and the ruin of all his old enemies. If he was not actually vindicated, his long life must have given him some grounds for satisfaction, not to mention teaching important lessons about the transience of human affairs. Not only did Nestorius live on for twenty years after his ruinous defeat in 431, but he survived to write a scurrilous commentary, an account that almost literally tells us where the bodies were buried. He wrote this lengthy memoir, *The Bazaar of Heracleides*, in order to justify himself and damn his foes, and although edited and interpolated over the centuries, it clearly reflects his own positions. The work survived in Syriac translation in a monastery in what later became Kurdistan, where European scholars rediscovered it in the late nineteenth century. It finally appeared in English translation as late as 1925.

Whatever we may think of his theological views, it is not easy to find much good to say about Nestorius. He was arrogant, he was intolerant of other believers, Christian and otherwise, and his political skills were abysmal. Yet we should admire his bullheaded determination never to surrender, even in the face of overwhelming odds. Such a position might have been plausible when he was backed by soldiers, but he kept it up even in exile, when he had no hopes of regaining favor.

One story tells how a royal chamberlain conducted him into exile in Egypt. At one point, Nestorius pleaded for rest, but the official said, "The Lord also was weary when he walked until the sixth hour, and he is God. What do you say about that?" Nestorius answered: "Two hundred bishops got together to make me confess that Jesus is God Incarnate, but I wouldn't do it. Am I then going to admit to *you* that God was tired?" Perhaps he left the chamberlain struggling for an answer, as the man grappled with the wrenching question: did God really get tired? Was it in his nature?[69]

Appendix to Chapter Five:
The Twelve Anathemas,
Proposed by Cyril and Accepted by the
Council of Ephesus (431)

1. If anyone does not confess that Emmanuel is God in truth, and therefore that the holy virgin is the mother of God (for she bore in a fleshly way the Word of God become flesh), let him be anathema.

2. If anyone does not confess that the Word from God the Father has been united by hypostasis with the flesh and is one Christ with his own flesh, and is therefore God and man together, let him be anathema.

3. If anyone divides in the one Christ the hypostases after the union, joining them only by a conjunction of dignity or authority or power, and not rather by a coming together in a union by nature, let him be anathema.

4. If anyone distributes between the two persons or hypostases the expressions used either in the Gospels or in the apostolic writings, whether they are used by the holy writers of Christ or by him about himself, and ascribes some to him as to a man, thought of separately from the Word from God, and others, as befitting God, to him as to the Word from God the Father, let him be anathema.

5. If anyone dares to say that Christ was a God-bearing man and not rather God in truth, being by nature one Son, even as "the Word became flesh," and is made partaker of blood and flesh precisely like us, let him be anathema.

6. If anyone says that the Word from God the Father was the God or master of Christ, and does not rather confess the same both God and man, the Word having become flesh, according to the scriptures, let him be anathema.

7. If anyone says that as man Jesus was activated by the Word of God and was clothed with the glory of the Only-begotten, as a being separate from him, let him be anathema.

8. If anyone dares to say that the man who was assumed ought to be worshipped and glorified together with the divine Word and be called God along with him, while being separate from him, (for the addition of "with" must always compel us to think in this way), and will not rather worship Emmanuel with one veneration and send up to him one doxology, even as "the Word became flesh," let him be anathema.

9. If anyone says that the one Lord Jesus Christ was glorified by the Spirit, as making use of an alien power that worked through him and as having received from him the power to master unclean spirits and to work divine wonders among people, and does not rather say that it was his own proper Spirit through whom he worked the divine wonders, let him be anathema.

10. The divine scripture says Christ became "the high priest and apostle of our confession"; he offered himself to God the Father in an odor of sweetness for our sake. If anyone, therefore, says that it was not the very Word from God who became our high priest and apostle, when he became flesh and a man like us, but as it were another who was separate

from him, in particular a man from a woman, or if anyone says that he offered the sacrifice also for himself and not rather for us alone (for he who knew no sin needed no offering), let him be anathema.

11. If anyone does not confess that the flesh of the Lord is life-giving and belongs to the Word from God the Father, but maintains that it belongs to another besides him, united with him in dignity or as enjoying a mere divine indwelling, and is not rather life-giving, as we said, since it became the flesh belonging to the Word who has power to bring all things to life, let him be anathema.

12. If anyone does not confess that the Word of God suffered in the flesh and was crucified in the flesh and tasted death in the flesh and became the first born of the dead, although as God he is life and life-giving, let him be anathema.

SOURCE: E. B. Pusey, preface to E. B. Pusey and P. E. Pusey, eds., *St. Cyril of Alexandria: Five Tomes Against Nestorius* (Oxford: James Parker, 1881), xi–xiii.

6

The Death of God

There is many a Nestorius!

Dioscuros of Alexandria

In August 449 the ghosts of the earlier council gathered once more at Ephesus. Once again, a patriarch of Alexandria brought his followers to confront heresy by any means necessary. And once again, there were winners and losers. A patriarch of Constantinople was deposed, and a new definitive statement of church doctrine proclaimed. But in terms of its impact on the future of the church, the participants of this council might well have been ghosts. In most accounts of church history, which give such prominence to earlier gatherings like Nicea, we look in vain for a Second Council of Ephesus. For all the numbers and prestige of those attending, all the weighty issues discussed, Second Ephesus—the Gangster Synod—became The Council That Never Was.[1]

At the time, though, the council seemed like a revolutionary event, building aggressively on the victories of 431. It marked the high-water mark of Alexandrian influence in the church. For a few years, it also seemed likely to uproot any form of Two Nature teaching within the empire as thoroughly as the Arians had been defeated in earlier decades. And condemned as heretical would have been the whole structure of what would ultimately become Christian orthodoxy.

The Last Romans?

By the 440s, the generation that had dealt with the Nestorian crisis was fading away. New leaders were in power in Rome, where Pope Leo succeeded in 440, and in Alexandria, where Dioscuros followed Cyril in 444. In each case, though, the rising men had served long apprenticeships under their predecessors and had full access to older memories. And just as Cyril had accompanied Theophilus to overthrow John Chrysostom in 403, so Dioscuros had been present at the fall of Nestorius in 431. A rising young cleric could have no better form of on-the-job training than witnessing his mentor overthrow a patriarch.

Other new men had risen to power elsewhere. The new bishop of Antioch was Domnus, who in 440 succeeded his uncle John. This was an unfortunate inheritance, as Domnus was a peaceable character who wanted nothing more than a quiet life and was ill-suited to deal with the kind of enemies he would soon face. The emerging dangers were nowhere clearer than in Constantinople, where (also in 440) Eutyches succeeded the abbot Dalmatius, who had played such a key role in shaping the emperor's religious policies. Both had been violent opponents of Nestorius, and both were willing to resort to aggressive political activism.

The most significant shift in power was at the imperial court, where the augusta Pulcheria was driven from favor and withdrew from public life. Partly, this followed a long-running feud with her sister-in-law, Eudocia, who was herself forced into holy exile in Jerusalem. In theory, this should have meant that the emperor Theodosius might have exercised some independence, but he now turned his favor to the eunuch Chrysaphius. Unlike the other transfers of power, that change marked a real change in policy and ideology.[2]

Just as significant for religious debates were changes in secular politics, as the empire moved into new and deeply dangerous territory. At the time of First Ephesus, in 431, the Roman world was enjoying a breathing spell of relative stability. The empire was recovering slowly from the shocks of barbarian invasions that had overrun whole provinces and learning to live with a drastically changed political landscape. Through the 440s, though, the situation had become massively more dangerous, to the point that one or more centers of power, Rome or Constantinople, would probably fall wholly under foreign rule, and it was an open question which part might be lost first.[3]

Living in an era of perpetual military danger had practical effects for debates within the churches, in making travel and communication much more difficult, and making it harder for particular bishops to participate in wider gatherings. But the crisis also raised the stakes of debate. Every month, it seemed, brought new evidence of the failure of Roman power, of defeats and massacres, of the defeat of orthodox Nicene Christianity. All were evidence of God's anger with his people, for their lack of faith and drift into heresy, and the church could only find peace by driving out error.

Much of the old empire was slipping into chaos. Romanized society in Britain was wiped out following a barbarian revolt in the 440s, and old-style civilization—*Romanitas*—was eroding along other frontiers, in the provinces along the Danube and Rhine. Gaul was torn asunder by class warfare, as the wealthy so manipulated the taxation system that ordinary people were driven to ruin. In retaliation, bands of peasant rebels, *Bagaudae*, devastated the countryside. But the greatest danger was not so much the collapse of authority as the replacement of Roman rule by a new barbarian empire, a new kind of regime, at least as brutal as the old order at its worst. Modern stereotypes of ancient barbarians imagine mobile raiders, perhaps causing much damage, but moving on swiftly. By the 440s, the Roman Empire's worst barbarian nightmares found their focus in two individuals who had evidently come to stay. Both were kings or emperors in their own right and might well succeed in carving out vast and permanent new realms out of Roman territory.[4]

One was Gaiseric, the Vandal king, who ruled his people for what was by the standards of a violent age an incredibly long time, from 428 to 477. For decades, Vandal pirates and raiders marauded over the Mediterranean, ruining trade routes and disrupting communications. But Gaiseric had higher aspirations and built up an impressive Vandal kingdom in North Africa. When St. Augustine died in 430, his city of Hippo was under Vandal siege, and shortly after its capture, it became Gaiseric's capital. The seat of the new kingdom moved only in 439, when Gaiseric's forces captured Carthage. The city had been a heartland of the Western empire, not to mention the breadbasket of Rome itself, but now it was under the heel of Arian Christians, anti-Trinitarians who persecuted Catholic Romans. As Gaiseric was known to have ambitions on the city of Rome, a wider Vandal empire spanning the western Mediterranean—Arian in religious loyalties—might easily lie on the horizon. Egyptians thought that it was only a matter of time before Vandal ambitions turned to Alexandria itself.[5]

The empire's other persistent bad dream was Attila the Hun. Through the 440s, both the Eastern and Western empires struggled to deal with the Hunnish threat, which was all the more serious because the Huns were not even heretical Christians, but aggressively pagan. Worse, the Huns represented a racial threat. Although many of their forces were Germanic subject peoples, the Huns themselves were of Central Asian origin, and Roman writers offer stereotypes of sadistic Orientals, slant-eyed and misshaped, and scarcely human. Huns sacked the Balkan provinces in 441, inflicting destruction that was astonishing even for an age not known for restraint in warfare. The great city of Aquileia, for instance, was one of the glories of late Roman Italy. After Attila's forces left it in 452, it literally ceased to exist, leaving only some confused survivors who sought a new protected site, in what would someday become the city of Venice.[6]

Attila was so dangerous that he forced the Romans to take steps that would once have been inconceivable. The Eastern empire recognized the independent Hunnish kingdom in 442 and in 443 began paying Attila huge regular sums of gold as the price of peace and survival. In 447, the Eastern empire experienced a disaster that became one of the great might-have-beens of history, when an earthquake breached Constantinople's legendary defensive walls. If Attila's forces had been closer to hand, the story of Christian Byzantium might have ended right then, a thousand years earlier than it actually did. Only desperate efforts by the city's population—soldiers, clergy, circus factions, and street gangs—rebuilt the wall to withstand any possible threat. This crisis passed, but both Eastern and Western empires knew that Attila's forces were biding their time before striking again.[7]

By the late 440s, the Roman Empire was facing enemies almost too many to count. As the historian Priscus remarks, apart from Attila,

They also feared the Parthians who were, it chanced, making preparations for war; the Vandals who were troubling the sea coasts; the Isaurians who had set out on banditry; the Saracens who were overrunning the eastern part of their empire; and the united Ethiopian races.[8]

The cumulative impact of these wars and natural disasters was overwhelming. As Nestorius described,

They had been worn out with pestilences and famines, and failure of rains, and hail, and heat, and marvelous earthquakes, and captivity, and fear and flight, and all kind of ills, but they did not perceive the cause . . . and there was no place of refuge. A twofold upheaval on the part of the barbarians and the Scythians [Huns], who were destroying and taking every one captive, had shaken them and there was not even a single hope of rescue; and hitherto they understood not that all this was not simply human.[9]

The great earthquake happened right in the middle of the theological wars that split the city in 447–48:

> And some things appeared openly in one part of the city in one way, and others in another part otherwise, and things had not been shaken by a common earthquake but to convince men that He who was doing these things was immortal and had authority over them.[10]

Any rational person should see that God was angry with his church, and it was up to his true followers to seek out and purge the errors that threatened Roman survival.

Eutyches

These international events provided the setting for a new religious conflict that, as in 431, began in Constantinople itself. In reaction to the Nestorian crisis, One Nature thought was moving in radical directions, more extreme in fact than the theories prevailing in Alexandria itself. The main advocate for these ideas was the archimandrite Eutyches, who believed that Cyril had made too many concessions to reach peace with Antioch in 433. Eutyches rejected any attempt to separate the divine Son of God from the human son of Mary. After the Incarnation, he thought, Christ had only one nature, one *physis*, in one person. For Eutyches, "God is born; God suffered; God was crucified." If so, what became of the human Christ? Eutyches said that after the union of human and divine, Christ contained no *ousia* [being] except the divine. Nor did he concede "that our Lord, who is our Lord and our God, is consubstantial with us; but he is consubstantial with the Father in the divinity." Whatever the Gospels might say, Christ could have felt no human pains or temptations, no hunger or thirst. God was emphatically *not* one of us.[11]

If Eutyches were an isolated cleric, his ideas would not have drawn much attention, but he was much more than that. He held a powerful church rank, and he gained new political clout as his godson and disciple, Chrysaphius, rose at court. Chrysaphius himself had strong One Nature views, and so, by this stage, did the emperor. In fact, we may ask whether the writers at the time were correct to put so much weight on the sinister role of Chrysaphius. Conceivably Theodosius II himself was more significant in the One Nature reaction than commentators dared say at the time, especially as this would have placed him on what would become the losing side.[12]

Within Constantinople's church, formal power rested in the hands of Flavian, who became archbishop in 446; but Eutyches was the power behind the throne, as Flavian himself became a docile cipher. Flavian suffered from multiple disadvantages. As he was not an effective speaker, he used the archimandrite as his public face. In the secular world, too, he blundered repeatedly. Even when first taking office, he made a disastrous mistake when he ignored Chrysaphius's request for a substantial gift or bribe. Flavian was too honest, or else too piously naive, to realize the importance of placating the royal favorite. And in the circumstances, he could not try and get around Chrysaphius by turning to Pulcheria, who was herself discredited. Flavian was in a dangerously exposed position, and, worse, he did not realize the fact.[13]

Eutyches, like Dalmatius before him, had a powerful influence in the city's monasteries, which might have served as a solid political power base. As the hot summer of 431 had shown, bringing monks onto the streets could potentially bring an emperor to heel. Quite possibly, Eutyches had looked enviously at how Cyril had used his monks to overawe Alexandria's civil authorities and establish a church hegemony over a great city. Certainly, Constantinople and Alexandria enjoyed close and frequent contacts.

Pushing Forward

Eutyches owed his prominence in the church partly to his speaking ability, but that fluency could be a mixed blessing. He also suffered from a take-no-prisoners style of debate, a sharp temper, and a tendency to see all critics as malicious or even demonic. He had a familiar academic tendency to pursue arguments to their logical conclusions, however risky or unsettling the consequences. The more Eutyches spoke and wrote, the more other church leaders were concerned at his proclamation of what appeared to be a dangerous new doctrine.

Eutyches found his deadliest enemy in a man who had been a firm ally in the earlier campaign against Nestorius, when bishop Eusebius had denounced the error of the Two Natures. Eusebius, though, was an ally of Pulcheria, and had no sympathy for extremism on the other side of the spectrum. As he talked with Eutyches, Eusebius became alarmed at the implications of his teaching. Was Eutyches really daring to deny the human nature of Christ? If so, that would mean that Christ was not consubstantial, of the same being, with us: "the very *ousia* [substance] of the flesh has thereby been suppressed." What should have been a rational discussion between the two degenerated into an embarrassing fit of name-calling, with Eutyches denouncing Eusebius for his lying and impious views, for hypocrisy, and adding for good measure that "all hypocrites ought to be extirpated!" Eusebius, though, was not to be bullied. A powerful and well-connected figure, his complaints carried weight, and he now called for a special council to investigate Eutyches.[14]

Flavian himself was frightened. He knew "that the churches were disturbed anew over these things, and the monasteries were divided and the people were rising up in parties, and that already the fire was kindling in all the world owing to those who were going and coming and were preaching various things that were full of impiety."[15] But even Flavian's timid protests became too much for Eutyches. No doubt thinking back to the fall of Nestorius, Eutyches thought it intolerable that a heretic should occupy a great see, but above all that of the holy city of Constantine's Christian empire. Flavian had to go; and if he did, then Eutyches himself was the natural successor.

Eutyches and his monks struck back against any and all critics, in ways that often recalled Cyril's campaigns in Alexandria. By 447–48, they had created a police-state atmosphere in Constantinople. They

> were carrying off men, some from the ships and others from the streets and others from the houses, and others while praying from the churches, and were pursuing others that they fled; and with all zeal, they were searching out and digging after those who were hiding in caves and in holes in the earth. And it was a matter of great fear and of danger for a man to speak with the adherents of Flavian, on account of those who were dwelling in the neighborhood and keeping watch, and were as spies to see who entered in unto Flavian.[16]

This sounds just like Cyril's intelligence system in Alexandria.

The War of the World

But Eutyches had plenty of other enemies, especially in Syria and the East, and events here turned the local dispute into a matter for the worldwide church. These regions had not forgiven the old campaign against Nestorius, and many Easterners insisted that the former patriarch's ideas were, for the most past, orthodox. But now, Eutyches was preaching a far worse and more extreme heresy, and because of his court connections, he seemed to have imperial support. Hence, "all the East was disturbed at these things, and there was no place that had not been stirred up."[17]

But while Easterners had their grievances, the fact that they were so tolerant of Nestorius's ideas further angered One Nature believers, in Constantinople and elsewhere. In theory, the Formula of 433 should have brought peace between Antioch and Alexandria, but new conflicts continued to arise. With Nestorius out of the way, Cyrillian followers turned their wrath against his teachers, to the now-dead theologians who had created and formed his thinking. They targeted the legendary Antiochene teachers, Diodore of Tarsus and Theodore of Mopsuestia, and tried to anathematize them. But such attacks threatened chaos. In order to challenge the legitimacy of the Eastern churches, they were seeking to condemn men who could not defend themselves. The attack on Nestorianism turned into a crusade against Antiochism.[18]

The war against Theodore's memory began very shortly after the Formula of Reunion. One early skirmish came in Edessa, where Bishop Rabboula tried to condemn Theodore, and in so doing, he created a deep division in his diocese. The move was reversed by his successor, Ibas, who thought that Cyril himself was a much more pernicious heretic than Theodore had ever been and probably should have been condemned alongside Nestorius. In 437, Proclus of Constantinople convicted a number of statements associated with Theodore, but he phrased his declaration in such a way that it targeted no specific individual.[19]

By the 440s, Alexandrians were campaigning for an explicit condemnation of Theodore. As at First Ephesus, Egyptians found their main villains in the Orient, that is, the empire's eastern regions, and in the churches that looked to Antioch. John of Antioch had refused to comply with these demands, and so (more timidly) did his successor Domnus. Domnus also supported or defended several bishops who infuriated the Alexandrians. Ibas of Edessa was the most provocative example but not the only one. Irenaeus, for instance, was the secular official who had helped see fair play at First Ephesus, and the Alexandrians saw him as too friendly to Nestorius. But despite those worrying Nestorian associations, he was consecrated as bishop of Tyre in 447. If the East was not actually rehabilitating Nestorius, Syrians at least were not condemning him as zealously as they should.[20]

The most influential thinker in the Antiochene church was Theodoret of Cyrrhus, who served as the main theological adviser to the successive patriarchs. Theodoret was not easily bullied, an essential quality when dealing with Dioscuros and the Alexandrians. Indeed, we can usually tell when Theodoret was advising Domnus, because those were the moments at which Antioch's patriarch showed unusual backbone. One letter plausibly attributed to Theodoret shows his reaction to the death of Cyril, at an advanced age. Cyril's case, wrote Theodoret to Domnus, just proved the saying that the good die young. "At last, and with difficulty, the villain is gone!" The main danger, thought Theodoret, was that the inhabitants of the underworld would be so appalled to have Cyril in residence that they would send him back to the living. It would do no harm to lay a particularly heavy stone on his grave to keep him down.[21]

Theodoret never doubted the divine nature of Christ. But he argued, against Eutyches, that Christ still had two natures after the Incarnation, united in one divine person (*prosopon*). In 447, Theodoret presented these ideas in his tract *Eranistes*—loosely, the Beggar's Banquet. The name is meant to suggest intellectual beggars or ragpickers, those who clothed themselves by patching together whatever fragments they could find of forgotten heresies that denied the humanity of Christ. In the context of the time, that had to be a not so veiled reference to Eutyches. If so, then Theodoret was denouncing the powerful archimandrite as a gross heretic, the heir of every Gnostic error through the centuries. To argue that

God the Word took nothing of the Virgin's nature, is stolen from [the Gnostics] Valentinus and Bardesanes, and the adherents of their fables. To call the godhead and the manhood of the Lord Christ one Nature is the error filched from the follies of Apollinarius. Again, the attribution of capacity of suffering to the divinity of the Christ is a theft from the blasphemy of Arius and Eunomius.

Invoking Valentinus was doubly effective, as he was not only a notorious heretic but also an Egyptian, so that bringing him into the picture served to discredit Alexandrian thinkers.[22]

Early in 448, the different controversies began to merge into a general churchwide war. Irenaeus was deposed as bishop of Tyre. Meanwhile, Dioscuros complained about Theodoret's seemingly Nestorian doctrines. He began with a protest directed personally to Theodoret himself and then followed up with an indictment addressed to Domnus, as Theodoret's superior. For the historically inclined—and most church leaders in that age had a weighty sense of precedent—Dioscuros's correspondence with Domnus was bringing back uncomfortable memories of Cyril's interchanges with Nestorius twenty years earlier. And everyone knew how that story had played out.[23]

Eutyches Fights Back

The main question now was which of the two sides would first find itself facing charges at a council. Although Eutyches was facing his own problems, he tried to invoke Roman assistance against his enemies. He wrote to Pope Leo, warning of the revival of Nestorian influence. Leo's reply was polite but cautious. Beloved son, he wrote, how wonderful to know that you are so vigilant against a revival of the awful heresy of Nestorianism and this pernicious belief in the Two Natures! "And *when we have been able to ascertain more fully by whose wickedness this happens*, we must make provision—with the help of God—for the complete uprooting of this poisonous growth which has long ago been condemned." A wise reader would have noted the critical clause—I will indeed do something, once I have carried out my own investigation. I'm not just going to take your word for it.[24]

In November 448, Constantinople's archbishop Flavian convened the so-called Home Synod, with the goal of settling several pending disputes in the Eastern churches. Comprising over thirty bishops and eighteen archimandrites, this was a heavyweight body. Among its other tasks, the group heard Eusebius's indictment of Eutyches. Eutyches followed the earlier example of Nestorius in refusing to appear personally for most of the sessions, and when he did appear, it was with the backing of a mob of monks and soldiers. He also brought a patrician ally, one Florentius, who was to be seated as the representative of the emperor or, more accurately, of Chrysaphius.[25]

But even with so much support, Eutyches could not save himself from himself. Under examination, he admitted his belief that Christ, after the Incarnation, had just one nature, and he even failed to make clear that at some point this divine being had become incarnate. "The Lord Jesus Christ," he declared, "is from two Natures, but after the union I affirm one Nature."[26] Like Nestorius before him, then, he was condemned. Flavian called him an Apollinarian and a Valentinian Gnostic.

But rather than ending the matter, Eutyches now sought church-wide help as he appealed to the bishops of Rome, Alexandria, and Jerusalem. He presented himself as the victim of the case, old and frail, and suffering for his defense of ancient Christian orthodoxy. He appealed to Leo, "defender of religion and abhorrer of factions." Surely, he pleaded, the popes who had condemned the awful heretics of the past would see his point of view? Like them, he anathematized "Apollinarius, Valentinus, Mani, and Nestorius, and those who say that the flesh of our Lord Jesus Christ, the Savior, descended from heaven and not from the Holy Ghost and from the holy Virgin, along with all heresies down to Simon Magus. Yet nevertheless I stand in jeopardy of my life as a heretic!" And whatever his theology, Eutyches did have technical grounds for protest, because the record keeping at the synod had violated established standards, and in those narrow terms, he received a vindication of sorts in April 449.[27]

But matters were also developing their own momentum. Chrysaphius persuaded the emperor to send his own supportive letter to Leo, while Dioscuros asked Theodosius to call a general council. In March, Theodosius agreed. The new council was to meet in August, and as before, Ephesus was the chosen venue.

Back to Ephesus

What did the different parties expect from this new meeting, and what lessons had they learned from the previous event? Theodosius himself should have greeted the forthcoming event with dread, remembering the largely unnecessary division and violence incited before. Yet by 448 he was clearly sympathetic to Eutyches and became a strong partisan of his against Flavian and Eusebius. According to Nestorius, Theodosius enthusiastically allowed Eutyches to deploy the full imperial power against his personal enemies. He encouraged clergy to secede from Flavian and reinforced this policy through financial pressure. The emperor reinstituted taxes and charges on the churches, burdens that he had relaxed in easier-going times, and demanded that these be paid, with arrears.

> Prelates were openly seized and rebuked before the crowds, and every bishop who was not of the party of Eutyches was seized; and he commanded every tax upon the possessions of their churches which had been remitted to them by him and by the emperors before him, even the tax of all these years, to be exacted of them at one time. . . . He commanded vengeance to be exacted of Eusebius, the accuser of Eutyches, without mercy.

Using "the assaults of hunger and of usury and of captivity. . . he made the Roman nobility fall at his knees and groan." Even when Flavian prostrated himself before the emperor at an Easter service, pleading for reconciliation, the emperor scorned and insulted him.

Theodosius had become a violent partisan, who called the council to depose Flavian and to restore Eutyches. As Nestorius wrote from personal experience, "Ephesus . . . is appointed and destined for the deposition of the bishops of Constantinople."[28]

Dioscuros hoped for a more comprehensive victory, certainly the defeat of Flavian and (for the third time in half a century) the humbling of Constantinople. But he also wanted a reaffirmation of Alexandria's leading role as the center shaping Christian thought and belief. He wanted a world in which Alexandria decided what Christians everywhere would think and where Rome used Peter's authority to rubber-stamp what Egyptians decided. Dioscuros had also learned other lessons from Ephesus, especially concerning the role of the secular power. The Alexandrians bitterly recalled the role of Candidian and his military forces. Expecting the worst, they came prepared, with Dioscuros's thuggish *parabolani*, who intervened at will, bullying and beating.

We might be making a mistake in judging what Dioscuros wanted in terms of his memories or of rational self-interest. Like any good machine politician, he wanted to help his friends and harm his enemies, but such politicians usually have a sense of the limits of what they can reasonably get away with. They also know that any enemies who are not absolutely destroyed have powerful friends who might help them stage a comeback. It rarely pays, then, to unleash total war against all enemies at once, which is roughly what Dioscuros did at Second Ephesus. It almost seems as if he deliberately went out of his way to infuriate or alienate virtually every other church leader, who was then forced either to accept defeat at his hands or fall into some subordinate position.[29]

Why did he act like this? Almost certainly, he was misled by the absolute support he seemed to be getting from the emperor, who was in a position to overawe any opposition. Or perhaps he was just Alexandrian, in that he came from a church that had over a century's history of trampling all opposition, using a mixture of intimidation, manipulated piety, and the invocation of martyrdom. On the international scene, too, the Alexandrian patriarchate had long succeeded in getting virtually everything it wanted, running rings around its opponents and exercising power at the heart of empire. As Nestorius remarks, "Dioscorus had received from Cyril the primacy, and a hatred for the bishop of Constantinople."[30] If Dioscuros had witnessed what Cyril achieved, he might have felt that only a little more effort would be needed to make the whole empire as docile and compliant as the more distant regions of Egypt. What he failed to register was the sophisticated court politics and coalition building with which Cyril had operated, or Theophilus or Athanasius before them.

But one final possibility, not to be dismissed, is that he really was suffering from some kind of personality disorder, which drove him to extremes of paranoia and uncontrollable rage. Historians are justifiably shy about undertaking psychiatric diagnoses on the long dead, if only because the track record of such postmortem analyses is so dismal, but we should at least consider the possibility. There is such a thing as bullying, and then there is what Dioscuros did on a regular basis.

Leo the Roman

Based on his experience at First Ephesus, Dioscuros probably had little regard for Roman popes, but the new incumbent, Leo, was a very different creature from his predecessors. Like most popes, Leo wanted Constantinople kept in its proper place, but he insisted that matters proceed according to custom and legality, without the vigilantism of 431. Leo, the ultimate Roman, cared deeply about procedure and proper channels, and he was nervous about Eutyches's action in going behind the back of his properly constituted superior, Flavian. At the same time, he was also very conscious of the dignity of his own office, which was always in peril of falling out of the loop of communication that united the Eastern churches.

Problems of communication meant that the first news he had of proceedings in Constantinople came from the emperor himself and from Eutyches, rather than from Flavian, who should have kept him informed. Accordingly, Leo's first responses made him sound quite sympathetic to Eutyches and angry with Flavian. When he received a full transcript of the Constantinople synod, though, his sympathies turned decisively against Eutyches. In June 449 he reaffirmed the judgment in a substantial letter that has become known as the *Tome* of Leo. The Tome not only showed his disgust with Eutyches ("very unwary and exceedingly ignorant") but utterly rejected his ideas. His statements at the synod "reached the height of stupidity and blasphemy."[31]

The Tome has become a classic definition of the orthodox view of the person of Christ, and it marks a critical moment in the developing history of the papacy. Although Leo long received immense credit as the author of the Tome, it is only fair to note that it was largely drafted by one of his secretaries, drawing heavily on—some would say plagiarizing—the work of other theologians, including Augustine.[32] But the exact authorship is less important than Leo's willingness to stand behind it, to wager his safety and the fortunes of his office. The stakes were very high indeed.

For Leo, the forthcoming council would be so vital because it would mark the destruction of a pernicious theory that challenged the full reality of Christ and of Christian doctrine. Eutyches, he said, showed his basic ignorance of Christian doctrine as exemplified in the Bible and the creeds. He should have listened to "the whole body of the faithful confess that they believe in God the Father Almighty, and in Jesus Christ, His only Son, our Lord, who was born of the Holy Spirit and the Virgin Mary. By which three statements the devices of almost all heretics are overthrown." The pope showed at length how all these texts could be used to prove the belief in the Two Natures.[33]

Although the Tome can be discussed at book length—and often has been, through the centuries—a couple of examples will suggest its content. He used the battery of texts that clearly showed the human descent and nature of Christ. Did not two of the Gospels begin with a genealogy, stressing his human descent? And the New Testament only made sense as the fulfillment of the Old, especially of the prophecies of Isaiah. Leo denounces arguments that seem to show that Christ had but one nature. Look for instance at the words of the angel to Mary: "The Holy Ghost shall come upon thee and the power of the Most High shall overshadow thee: and therefore that Holy Thing also that shall be born of thee shall be called the Son of God." Didn't that suggest she was going to bear the Son of God and that divine nature would overwhelm or eliminate the human? Absolutely not, says Leo:

> Though the Holy Spirit imparted fertility to the Virgin, yet a real body was received from her body; and, "Wisdom building her a house," "the Word became flesh and dwelt in us," that is, in that flesh which he took from man, and which he quickened with the breath of a higher life.[34]

Throughout, Leo stresses the idea of balance and harmony, suggesting that any overemphasis on either aspect of Christ, either the divine or human, would produce a result that was illogical or even absurd. Humanity and divinity met in Christ: "For each form does what is proper to it with the co-operation of the other; that is the Word performing what appertains to the Word, and the flesh carrying out what appertains to the flesh. One of them sparkles with miracles, the other succumbs to injuries. And as the Word does not cease to be on an equality with His Father's glory, so the flesh does not forego the nature of our race."[35]

Many features made Leo's Tome such an impressive text, above all its comprehensive gathering of biblical texts and a sound, clear logic running throughout. Like an accomplished Roman rhetorician, he not only makes his own case but marshals any and all possible counterarguments and shows why they would not convince. With the Tome in hand, any opponent of One Nature theory had a readily available collection of knock-down texts and arguments ready for instant deployment. Even better, of course, was the source, the chair of Peter.

Not long after, Pope Leo would make his condemnation even more brusque. Eutyches's followers were in practice allied with Manicheans in denying the Incarnation: like them, they "maintain that all His bodily actions were the actions of a false apparition." Leo would make this allegation again in other forms. Eutyches, he wrote, "crosses over into the mad view of Mani and Marcion, and believes that the man Jesus Christ, the mediator between God and men, did all things in an unreal way, and had not a human body, but that a phantom-like apparition presented itself to the beholders' eyes." Eutyches was reviving heresies that should have died out a century or more before.[36]

Leo's Tome found one interesting reviewer at the time of its publication. Nestorius, the exiled heretic, wrote that "when I found and read this account, I gave thanks to God that the Church of Rome was confessing correctly and without fault, although they were otherwise disposed towards me myself." Although Nestorianism was still listed as an awful heresy, most of what Nestorius actually believed now stood an excellent chance of being publicly reaffirmed.[37]

Gangsters

The Second Council of Ephesus met in August 449, again in sultry weather that did nothing to reduce tensions. Today, temperatures in that region would certainly be in the nineties at that time of year, and air conditioning was fifteen hundred years away. Present were 127 bishops, a much lower number than at Nicea (notionally 318) or First Ephesus (some 250 in all). And again, they met in the Church of the Theotokos, so that the notion of Mother of God would never be too far removed from their minds.

Dioscuros presided, just as Cyril had in the first council, although on this occasion the papal legates could not offer any moderating force. The bishop scheduled to lead the Roman delegation had died, while the others spoke little Greek and were accordingly ignored. Although Rome had sent a personal legate, the council refused to seat him. Dioscuros, in contrast, was very much present together with his Egyptian phalanx, including ten powerful metropolitans. And this time, Alexandrians did not have to face the rival threat of a powerful secular armed force. Bishops old enough to remember Candidian's interventionist role at First Ephesus probably thought longingly of the fairly peaceful debate he had managed to supervise. But this time, the emperor had no wish to intervene.[38]

When the council began on August 8, Dioscuros exercised his full powers as president to rig the event in his favor and that of Eutyches. The council in theory had one simple question before it, namely, whether the previous November gathering had justly deposed Eutyches for his refusal to admit Two Natures. But in practice that meant that bishops who had participated in the verdict were excluded, and that promptly removed Flavian and six other bishops from any anti-Alexandrian voting bloc. As Syrian bishops later recalled, "Flavian went in as if already condemned."[39] Moreover, the emperor had specifically forbidden Theodoret from attending, which kept Syria's best theological mind out of the fray.

While Rome had no effective representative, Dioscuros was careful to include the archimandrite Barsaumas, a monk whose hostility to anything that sounded vaguely Nestorian was fanatical even by the standards of the time. But several things made Barsaumas a very unlikely participant, not least the question as to how good his Greek was: he did best in his native Syriac. The decision to admit him at Ephesus also broke precedent in admitting to such a council a monk who was not a bishop. But he was not invited because of either his eloquence or the charm of his personality. He was there primarily because of the armed strength he provided, and he had no compunction about using his militias. The bishops he targeted complained that he had "destroyed all Syria. He incited thousands of monks against us." And although Dioscuros was responsible for his presence, it remained open to question whether the patriarch—or anyone—could actually control Barsaumas's actions.[40]

With the outcome clearly determined, the council proceeded quickly to its decision. It read the documents relevant to the case, but Dioscuros carefully selected what was admitted to the proceedings. The Romans, naturally, wanted to read Leo's Tome, the definitive Western statement on the issue, but this was refused. Dioscuros excluded the symbolic presence of Rome and of papal authority.

At least according to the council's proceedings, the hearing then moved easily and logically—but a great deal of selective rewriting and bullying went into creating that record. Eutyches spoke, declaring his orthodoxy and his loyalty to the principles of Nicea and First Ephesus. He quickly won the support of an overwhelming majority, 114 bishops, and some of those who had originally condemned him now changed their minds. Vindicating Eutyches segued into a defense of his doctrines and a furious attack on anything that suggested the Two Natures, or the ideas of Nestorius (chants of "Burn Nestorius!" erupted from time to time). Once the council had officially proclaimed correct doctrine, then it followed that opponents of this belief must themselves be wrong and unfit to hold high office in the church.[41]

At that point, the campaign turned against Eutyches's critics, Eusebius and Flavian. Dioscuros here arranged a skillful parliamentary maneuver. He first asked the council to confirm the canons of First Ephesus, which condemned anyone who brought in new teachings contrary to the Council of Nicea. Once this was established, Dioscuros asserted that Flavian and Eusebius had violated that rule and must be deposed. Dioscuros silenced the restive crowd, while "crying aloud in his unruliness: 'Be silent awhile; let us hear also the other blasphemies. Why do we blame only Nestorius? There is many a Nestorius.'"[42]

Neither Flavian nor Eusebius was permitted to speak in his defense, and pro-Eutychians rigidly controlled the final record. When the bishops looked back at these events two years later, they repeatedly expressed surprise at what had been noted down. "During the reading, the most devout Oriental bishops and those with them exclaimed 'We didn't say this. Who said this?. . . Let [Dioscuros] bring in his notaries, for he expelled everyone else's notaries and got his own to do the writing.'" Dioscuros and Juvenal denied the charge, until Stephen of Ephesus explained how his own followers had taken notes, "but the notaries of the most devout Bishop Dioscuros came and erased their tablets, and almost broke their fingers in the attempt to snatch their pens."[43] And that was the treatment received by the bishop of one of the church's oldest and greatest sees. Overwhelming censorship of that sort explains just why the actual surviving record is such a neat affair, a story of simple adulation for the Dear Leader Dioscuros. If we go by the doctored record, the council swelled into messianic mood, with cries of "To Archbishop Dioscuros, the great guardian of the faith." When the great man spoke, he was greeted with "These are the sayings of the Holy Spirit! . . . The fathers live through you. To the guardian of the faith!"[44]

Those exclamations give no idea of the gathering's real fears and concerns. The move against Flavian was an arrogant and near-revolutionary act. Particularly after the insult to the Roman pope, Alexandrian high-handedness alarmed even those bishops who were prepared to go along with virtually anything Dioscuros wanted. The meeting degenerated into a riot, marked by mass intimidation. Seemingly, 101 bishops agreed to vote for Flavian's deposition, but violence and threats persuaded another thirty or so to sign the final document. Probably, they signed a blank sheet of paper, the actual details to be filled in later. Looking back at the event, "the bishops of the Orient, Pontus, Asia and Thrace exclaimed 'We signed blank sheets. We suffered blows and we signed . . . we were threatened with deposition. We were threatened with exile. Soldiers with clubs and swords stood by.'"[45] Other bishops describe being held in the church the whole of a long torrid day, not being allowed out for any reasons—reading between the lines, including for toilet visits.[46] But even after they had signed, the bishops remained unconvinced. Some went on their knees to beg for mercy toward Flavian.

Now, it should be said that when the bishops in question described the atrocities to which they had been subjected, they were struggling to explain votes that seemed hard to justify in the light of subsequent political changes. They had good motives for exaggerating the degree of intimidation at Second Ephesus, and similar behavior manifested itself at other, more reputable councils. But the accumulated evidence of bullying in 449 was unusual and pervasive. We hear of one bishop, Atticus, who had signed the condemnation of Eutyches at Constantinople. Now he faced a ferocious cross-examination, in which Dioscuros treated him like a naughty child. The conversation proceeded in a tone of "Have you stopped beating your wife?" or rather "Have you now abandoned that frightful heresy you used to hold?" Ultimately, a browbeaten Atticus was led to go along with what Dioscuros suggested, denying his earlier signature and allowing the assault on Flavian to continue. What Nestorius terms "the wickedness and the wiles of the Egyptians" triumphed.[47]

At this point, someone also launched a direct physical attack on Flavian himself. Different sources suggest that Dioscuros and Barsaumas themselves were responsible, and either version is quite possible, but in the melee it could equally well have been someone from the Alexandrian retinue or Barsaumas's monks. Later witnesses reported hearing Barsaumas utter the words "Slaughter him!"[48] Worse maltreatment followed. Once Flavian was deposed,

> he was carried off as if by bears and by lions by the counts. . . . And he was isolated and perturbed by all of them, and his spirit was vexed. And they delivered him up to the soldiers and commanded them to lead him away and remove him from the holy places. They led him away and incarcerated him, a man who was fainting, in prison. And before he came to himself and was revived, and was breathing fresh and pure air, and

taking nourishment that strength might be a little restored in him, they delivered him up to the officer and threatened to send the man away, bruised. And he was unable to endure the hardship of the journey.[49]

Flavian died three days later. Orthodox churches list him as a martyr as well as saint.

As that day's session wound up in chaos, the pope's legate Hilarius managed to yell the single word *Contradicitur*, objecting to the sentence against Flavian in the name of Rome.[50] At the time, though, the gesture seemed desperate, not least because he said the dread word in Latin, a language that virtually no other participant understood. It was almost as if he had spoken at the meeting of a modern-day U.S. denomination. A few erudite participants would know what he meant, but otherwise he would meet only baffled stares. Yet the move had important legal consequences. Although precedent held that the pope had to have some representation in order for any council to be truly universal (ecumenical), Dioscuros now decided to dispense with even that show of legality. Immediately after his brave intervention, Hilarius fled in disguise.

The Eastern Front

Although the council would seem to have accomplished more than enough damage, they went on to enact more decisions in their second session, on August 22. The council deposed several other key Eastern bishops in what was intended as a clean sweep of anyone who had failed to be sufficiently outspoken against Nestorius. These included Domnus of Antioch himself, as well as Theodoret of Cyrrhus, Ibas of Edessa, and Irenaeus of Tyre. And then the council went on to start deposing the friends and relatives of Irenaeus and other enemies on charges that included magic, heresy, bigamy, and everything a fevered mind could produce on a sultry Mediterranean afternoon. The council reaffirmed Cyril's Twelve Anathemas, condemning in the most demanding terms any backsliding toward the idea of Two Natures. New men were appointed to enforce the new Alexandrian order. At Constantinople itself, Flavian's successor, Anatolius, would not have held office had he not been acceptable to Dioscuros and Eutyches. He was himself an Alexandrian by birth, and he had served Dioscuros as *apocrisarius* or envoy to the court. Anatolius then (illegally) ordained one of the Constantinople clergy as bishop of Antioch.[51]

As well as attacking Constantinople, the council struck at the see of Dorylaeum, so that Eusebius was deposed and imprisoned. He managed to escape and found his way to Rome, where he joined the swelling anticouncil faction surrounding Leo. Besides Dorylaeum, the council had now acted against Antioch and Edessa, Tyre and Harran, Byblus and Tella—this was beginning to sound like a gazetteer of historic churches and cities of the Roman East. The diocese of Cyrrhus alone included eight hundred parishes. Then, Dioscuros—or rather, the council through which he acted—circulated a statement of the council's decisions to the Eastern churches, demanding that they sign on pain of becoming the next targets. The main exception to the Eastern purge was Juvenal of Jerusalem, who supported Dioscuros and would venture more or less anything to see his beloved city raised to patriarchal rank. Second Ephesus granted him this, as well as allowing him to carve territory out of Antioch's jurisdiction for himself.[52]

The attempted sweep of Eastern bishops was not as rash as it might appear. Most of the Eastern sees had strong One Nature factions, which would over the next half century or so come to dominate those regions, even in Antioch itself. Dioscuros had plenty of allies who could provide a foundation for later growth. The problem was the means by which he and his allies were proceeding, which trampled rules of procedure and fairness.

Although modern Americans sometimes apply the word McCarthyism to relatively minor acts of political maltreatment, it is difficult to think of an alternative here. At Second Ephesus, bishops' names were cited on the grounds that they were friendly with bishop X, who had just been deposed and must therefore be deposed, in their turn, without even knowing that they were being accused. As Theodoret complained to Leo,

> Me, too, [Dioscuros] murdered with his pen in my absence, without calling me to judgment, without passing judgment on me in person, without questioning me on what I hold about the Incarnation of our God and Savior. But even with murderers, tomb-breakers, and ravishers of other men's beds, those who sit in judgment do not condemn until they either themselves corroborate the accusations by their confessions, or are clearly convicted by others. But us, when thirty-five days' journey distant, he, though brought up on Divine laws, has condemned at his will.[53]

The case against Ibas illustrates the amazing fury of this event and how far its mood had degenerated into what a modern audience thinks of as the spirit of the Inquisition or the witch hunts. In several theological controversies over the previous year, Ibas had been accused of various misdeeds, mainly financial in character, although his alleged Nestorianism also featured. Domnus acquitted him. His enemies then demanded that the emperor grant a new trial, which again went in his favor.[54] The new council at Ephesus therefore became a kind of triple jeopardy. As the report was read, the episcopal mob responded with well-drilled rage. At one point, responding to the reading of a letter by Ibas, bishops protested variously, "These things pollute our ears. . . Cyril is immortal. . . Let Ibas be burnt in the midst of the city of Antioch. . . Exile is of no use. Nestorius and Ibas should be burnt together!" Somewhere in the previous decade or so, the idea of burning heretics had entered the commonplaces of ordinary discourse.[55]

After such a stormy month, Dioscuros really had only one bridge left to burn, which he did as he and his Egyptian clergy made their royal progress to Constantinople in 451. Stopping at Nicea, a place rich with symbolic associations, he joined his Egyptian metropolitans in judging and excommunicating Pope Leo.

Leo himself was appalled by the events, all the more since they were so unexpected. In the lead-up to the council, his main recommendation to Flavian had been to exercise mercy when—not if—Eutyches saw the error of his ways and repented. Now, the new arch-heretic had overcome his enemies, backed by the full weight of the empire. And the means by which this was all accomplished stunned a Roman with any sense of decent order. Leo now heard the full testimony of his envoy who "[escaped] the violence of the bishop of Alexandria who claims everything for himself." At Eutyches's demand, many had been forced to sign an unrighteous document, "knowing they would suffer harm unless they obeyed his commands, . . . that in attacking one man, he might wreak his fury on the whole Church." The papal delegates would never have agreed to what was proposed, "since the whole mystery of the Christian Faith is absolutely destroyed . . . unless this abominable wickedness, which exceeds all former blasphemies, be abolished."[56]

Leo duly denounced the *Latrocinium*, the synod of robbers or thugs. His response would have been even more forceful had he known that Flavian was actually dead, a horror that did not reach the West for some months afterward. He would summarize these evils in a letter to Pulcheria. This was a meeting

> not of judges but of robbers, at Ephesus; where the chief men of the synod spared neither those brethren who opposed them nor those who assented to them, seeing that for the breaking down of the Catholic faith and the strengthening of execrable heresy, they stripped some of their rightful rank and tainted others with complicity in guilt.[57]

In Leo's eyes, Dioscuros's followers were actually more cruel to those they forced over to their side than to those they beat and persecuted. At least when they attacked Flavian and Eusebius, these victims gained the glory of having suffered for the faith. Much sadder was the situation of those who compromised the faith through intimidation or bribery, who had been "divorced from innocence."[58]

Leo urged Theodosius to hold a new council safely far removed from all the plotting and conniving. Let it take place in Italy, where such violence can be avoided. All the Eastern bishops could come there, so that they could be duly reconciled to the church if possible and cast out if not. He followed up with a separate appeal to the imperial women, Pulcheria and Galla Placidia.[59]

By the end of 449, One Nature believers had carried off an astonishing putsch that potentially transformed the whole Christian world. Not only had the council proclaimed their ideas as the absolute foundation of correct belief, but the movement had removed from office anyone who threatened its supremacy. One Nature adherents now sat as bishops in Antioch and Constantinople. Eutyches was vindicated, Dioscuros ruled supreme, and Pope Leo was left to organize a desperate rearguard action, holding on against a potential Monophysite challenge in Rome itself. It was not far-fetched to imagine Rome as the last refuge of an embattled minority, in a Monophysite-dominated Christian world, in which the seat of power within the church had shifted definitively to Alexandria. However much such a radical reorientation might appall the churches of Italy or Syria, little could be done to stop it as long as the emperor reigned and as long as the Monophysite faction dominated his court.

If alternate worlds exist, in at least one the histories of early Christianity end in the year 449, at the great Second Council of Ephesus. Possibly, too, famous paintings depict the triumph of Saints Dioscuros and Eutyches and the defeat of the Dyophysite heresy. Demonic figures represent the villains of the story, Flavian and Leo, each depicted with a forked tongue to symbolize the evil doctrine of the Two Natures. Conceivably the greatest exemplar of this work would hang in the patriarchal palace of the leader of the Christian world, in Alexandria itself. Imagining such a painting, of course, assumes that this other world does not have grave doubts about depicting the human figure in art.

7

Chalcedon

Controversy about the orthodox religion of Christians has been put away. . . . Let profane wrangling cease!
Emperor Marcian

And then the emperor died. In July 450, the horse that Theodosius II was riding stumbled, and the emperor fell badly. On the 28th, he died, leaving no heir. Pulcheria would have made a fine successor, as her record of government was as lengthy and at least as distinguished as her brother's, but no woman could take the imperial throne. For the good of the dynasty, and for the security of the Christian world, the fifty-one-year-old Pulcheria abandoned her decades-long vow and agreed to marry the tough soldier Marcian, on the condition that he respected her celibacy. Marcian succeeded, giving the empire the best and most active emperor it had known since the first Theodosius.[1]

One Nature believers were stunned. Coptic historian John of Nikiu described the events as a sordid coup, the replacement of the excellent and pious Theodosius II by his Two Nature–inclined sister. Pulcheria, after all, acted without consulting the Western emperor, Valentinian, or most of the senators or leading state officials. But whatever the circumstances, a new political order now took shape. Major church leaders kept up the pressure for change. As

befitted the heir of St. Peter, Leo, of course, was—well, a rock.
And on this occasion, he found support from Anatolius of Constantinople, who owed his career to Alexandria's Dioscuros. But
Anatolius knew that Pulcheria was an even more powerful ally
close at hand and potentially a deadlier foe. He also realized that a
religious revolution could cement the position of his own patriarchate as second only to Rome.

The immediate outcome was the Council of Chalcedon, one of
the largest and most impressive arrays of church leaders in the history of Christianity. Yet contrary to what its enemies feared, this
event was not a simple clear-cut victory for any side or faction. Its
immediate importance was political, in reversing the Alexandrian
stranglehold on the church, but its theological implications were less
clear.

Many generations of students have learned Chalcedon as a critical benchmark in the making of Christian doctrine. They learn
something like this: "Ephesus, 431, rejected the separation of the
human and divine in Christ; Chalcedon, 451, insisted on the two
natures in one and drove out the Monophysites. This wise compromise ended the christological debates." At the time, though, Chalcedon was much more a balancing act between the two sides, in which
One Nature believers had a strong say. The importance of the
council, and its bitterly divisive effects, emerged mainly in its long
aftermath.[2]

Counterrevolution

The new emperor faced a situation as nightmarish as any of his predecessors had imagined, with the prospect of general collapse close
at hand. Marcian's first act was to end the empire's tribute payments
to Attila, making it certain that the Huns would invade a major portion of the empire, East or West. Attila actually crossed the Rhine in
force in early 451. At the least, he intended to sack Gaul, and probably to annex it. Equally likely was an imminent assault by Gaiseric

on Rome. So dreadful was the situation that it seems remarkable that the regime would devote so much of its time to settling the religious controversy, but in fact that was their first priority.

Partly, this urgency was a practical matter, in that restive and riotous cities were much more difficult to defend and impossible to mobilize for men or taxes. Some kind of religious settlement had to be reached, quickly. No less vital was the sense that the empire could survive only with God's help, by being the orthodox Christian realm, and that recent defeats and disasters proved beyond doubt that the divine relationship was under grave stress. Only the full and immediate restoration of orthodoxy could save the Christian world. Monophysites and Nestorians exactly shared this perspective about the workings of divine providence, although with a different view of the factions and individuals involved; but in terms of imperial policy making, their views were suddenly irrelevant. The court now turned sharply to the views of Pope Leo and the late Flavian. In terms of the party colors of the day, Monophysite Green suddenly turned Catholic Blue.[3]

The One Nature faction was painfully aware of the new environment and suggested that God in his heaven was quite as troubled as they were themselves. Knowing the aftermath of the political change—and the outcome of Chalcedon—John of Nikiu claims that

on the day of Marcian's accession there was darkness over all the earth from the first hour of the day till the evening. And that darkness was like that which had been in the land of Egypt in the days of Moses the chief of the prophets. There was great fear and alarm among all the inhabitants of Constantinople. They wept and lamented and raised dirges and cried aloud exceedingly, and imagined that the end of the world was at hand. And the senate, the officers, and the soldiers, even all the army, small and great, that was in the city was filled with agitation and cried aloud, saying: "We have never heard nor seen in all the previous reigns of the Roman Empire such an event as this." And they murmured very much, but they did not express themselves openly.[4]

An early casualty of the counterrevolution was the eunuch Chrysaphius, who perished in 451. Accounts of his death vary. He probably attempted to stir Green sedition. Either Marcian executed him, or else Pulcheria subcontracted the task by handing the hated eunuch over to one of his many personal enemies. Alternatively, he was murdered by a mob protesting high taxes. With the favorite also fell the members of his patronage network, in court and church. Eutyches followed Nestorius into exile, although he did not live long enough to claim vindication. Orders also went out to restore the exiled clergy. And now returned home was the deceased Flavian, whose remains were brought back to Constantinople in great honor and given the burial befitting a martyr.[5]

The Council

Although there was no mistaking the empire's new religious coloring, logic demanded an official proclamation of belief in the form of yet another council. Calling such a gathering was not as simple as it appeared, because of the overwhelming threat of fast-moving Hunnish raiders. Nor did Marcian himself want to commit his time to such an event when he might need to move to a highly fluid military front at very short notice. Pope Leo himself did not think a council was really necessary, as all the recent problems could be traced back to just a couple of malevolent individuals—Dioscuros and Juvenal—so that selective actions against them should set things right. But realistically, it simply was not possible to leave Second Ephesus on the record as the final statement of Christian belief, and that left little alternative to a council. Pulcheria above all wanted a public vindication of orthodoxy, and throughout she was the guiding force in shaping the new gathering.[6]

Marcian and Pulcheria ordered a new council to meet in September 451, on the hallowed ground of Nicea, and preparations began. Invasion threats meant, however, that Marcian did not even consider such a close venue as safe, so he commanded a move to Chalcedon, in the suburbs of the capital. The location helps explain the very large attendance, with perhaps five hundred bishops present at least legally, although at least some were there only through the action of proxies. Probably around three hundred were physically present, not counting attendants and secretaries. And significantly for the coming proceedings, a large minority of them—at least a hundred—had signed off on the decisions of Second Ephesus and had a lot of backtracking and self-justification to perform.

The new council met on October 8, incidentally in cooler weather than previous councils. And other lessons had been learned. This time imperial forces secured the meeting to prevent the influence of troublesome hangers-on. This was strictly a bishops' event with no roaming herds of monks or laymen.

The choice of site was important. Yes, it was conveniently close to the city, but the place also boasted its location as a suburb of heaven. The meetings would take place in the church of the martyr Euphemia, and thus, according to the thinking of the time, in her immediate presence. Since her martyrdom in the early fourth century, Euphemia had become the focus of a popular miraculous cult favored by the imperial family as well as surrounding churches and cities. The tomb was reputedly surrounded by a heavy and easily noticed odor of sanctity, but it also had other supernatural virtues. The saint would on occasion appear in dreams to bishops or other favored followers and invite them to harvest a vintage of her holy blood. Led by the archbishop of Constantinople, eminent visitors could touch the relics, using a sponge attached to an iron rod. When they removed the sponge, they found it "covered with stains and clots of blood," and that blood was then freely distributed to the faithful.[7] The bishops were meeting in the presence of the holy: surely, God was in this place. But the blood was not, so to speak, constantly on tap. It appeared only as a sign that the martyr was pleased and wished to pass on her blessing, so that it was a way of testing divine approval. And a cynic might say that if the organizers needed to reaffirm a doctrine by means of a miracle or apparition, one could easily be arranged.

The Council of Chalcedon had two major goals: to repeal Second Ephesus and reverse its political effects; and also to reject false teaching, Nestorian as well as Eutychian. The first day accomplished most of the task of repeal, with a direct attack on Dioscuros as the first order of business. Leo's representatives made it clear that they would not take their seats if Dioscuros was allowed his.[8]

The events began with a recitation of the horrors of the earlier council and of Dioscuros's misdeeds. Eusebius of Dorylaeum declared, "I have been wronged by Dioscorus. The faith has been wronged. The bishop Flavian was murdered, and, together with myself, unjustly deposed by him."[9] Appealing to the emperor, Eusebius recalled the events of the previous synod. "Would that it had never met, nor the world been thereby filled with mischiefs and tumult!" At that gathering, he reported, Dioscuros

> having gathered a disorderly rabble, and procured an overbearing influence by bribes, made havoc, as far as lay in his power, of the pious religion of the orthodox, and established the erroneous doctrine of Eutyches the monk, which had from the first been repudiated by the holy fathers . . . his aggressions against the Christian faith and us are of no trifling magnitude.[10]

The minutes of Second Ephesus were read, with many participants explaining the intimidation and distortions that had gone into the making of that record. Flavian was rehabilitated. Apart from Dioscuros's obvious crimes, the offense heading the indictment was that he had insulted St. Peter's dignity by barring the reading of

Leo's Tome. As the council later agreed, such sins could only have resulted from Dioscuros's succumbing to Satan's temptations: "The adversary would have been like a wild beast outside the fold, roaring to himself and unable to seize any one, had not the late bishop of Alexandria thrown himself for a prey to him."[11]

Although not directly concerned with Dioscuros's doctrine or beliefs, the council gave an opportunity for the patriarch's many enemies to parade their stories of oppression and injustice suffered at the patriarch's hands. The catalogue of atrocities suggests the megalomania of a Hellenistic god-king rather than a Christian pastor. Dioscuros had allegedly crushed his enemies by seizing their lands and properties, fining them, and wantonly cutting down their trees. When the emperors sent grain to feed starving Libyans, he had intercepted it and sold it for his own profit. The stories recounted also suggest the power that could potentially be exploited from the control of charitable donations and social services. Dioscuros, we hear, had diverted charitable bequests to support his dissolute living, his gambling and whoring: "Openly disreputable women wallow all the time in the episcopal residence and its baths." "Even murders have been committed at the instigation of this marvelous preacher!"[12]

Writing to Marcian, the council concluded that "We in session sought the cause of the storm that had rocked the whole world and discovered that its originator was Dioscuros, formerly bishop of Alexandria."[13] Dioscuros was deposed, together with his followers and allies. Other former followers managed to conform in time to the new order, including Anatolius of Constantinople and Maximus at Antioch. Particularly impressive in his coat-turning skills was Juvenal, who had spent twenty years plotting together with the Alexandrians, but who now decided that he no longer held the theology he had once affirmed. He kept his patriarchate.

Hymning victory, at the end of the first session the bishops spontaneously broke into the *Trisagion*, the proclamation of God, the Thrice Holy:[14]

Holy God, Holy and Mighty, Holy Immortal, have mercy
on us
   Hagios o Theos, hagios ischyros, hagios athanatos, eleison himas.

Particularly given its association with Chalcedon, the hymn later
became one of the most popular and powerful in the Byzantine and
Eastern Orthodox tradition, and it is commonly sung in the ancient
liturgical traditions of the Christian East. Even today, hearing it can
still overwhelm listeners of any Christian tradition, or indeed those
of no conscious religious belief. But its choice at Chalcedon was
important. Although the hymn itself was ancient, it had become
popular during the recent Constantinople earthquake: reportedly, a
child taught the words to the people before he himself died. The
Thrice Holy proclaims an absolute reliance on God, envisioned in
full heavenly splendor, but it also commemorates divine intervention in this life, a miraculous rescue from catastrophe, as, for instance, when a Christian empire is rescued from satanic plotting.

Defining Belief

Over the following week, the main agenda was the definition of
belief, which involved much more than a simple repudiation of One
Nature teaching. Certainly, Eutyches had to be rejected, but most of
the participants also spurned anything that might be seen as Nestorian, or too favorable to Two Nature ideas. When the council broke
into expressions of outrage against Nestorius, as it regularly did,
this was not just a shallow attempt to provide balance. Nor was it a
ruse to divert attention from a pervasive anti-Monophysite agenda.
If we can speak of a mainstream feeling at Chalcedon, it utterly rejected Dioscuros, while venerating his predecessor, Cyril. Significantly, many bishops were nervous about any attempt to issue a new
statement of belief over and above Nicea and First Ephesus, precisely because those documents both lent themselves so happily to
One Nature interpretation.[15]

Just how hostile to Nestorian thinking the bishops actually were became obvious when the Antiochene theologian Theodoret entered the assembly. When he appeared, "the most devout bishops of Egypt, Illyricum and Palestine exclaimed 'Have mercy, the faith is being destroyed. The canons exclude him! Drive him out! Drive out the teacher of Nestorius!'" The Egyptians went further (as always): "'Do not call him a bishop!'" they cried. "'He is not a bishop. Drive out the enemy of God! Drive out the Jew!'" "Jew," in this context, was not merely a term of abuse, but referred to Theodoret's focus on Christ's human nature, which made him an Ebionite, a Judaizer. They continued, "'We exclude Cyril if we admit Theodoret.'" In reply, the Eastern bishops called out their own imprecations against Dioscuros the murderer—but significantly, against his worldly misdeeds, rather than his doctrines.[16]

We still have minutes of this conference from more than 1,500 years ago, minutes that record quibbles and disagreements in immense detail. And this time the scribes were recording accurately, and nobody was breaking anyone's fingers in an attempt to grab their pens. Just to give an example of the tone of debate, we can look at one exchange from the fourth session, on October 17, when the council was determined to force the Egyptian clergy to separate themselves from Dioscuros.[17] The main body of Egyptian bishops signed a statement that seemed orthodox enough but did not go far enough to satisfy the assembled Fathers, who complained that they had not explicitly rejected Eutyches or accepted Leo's Tome. The conflict was lethally sensitive. The Egyptians were desperate not to go on the record with anything that could be used against them when they returned to Egypt. On the other hand, at Chalcedon they were in the hands of imperial authorities who demanded a thorough repudiation of anything linked to Dioscuros or Second Ephesus.

For the Egyptians, the only solution was to decide not to decide. When pressed to issue a clearer doctrinal statement, the leading Egyptian demurred, citing procedural issues. No, he objected, the Council of Nicea declared that Egyptian clergy have to follow the lead of the patriarch of Alexandria, but Dioscuros's removal had left the position vacant. If you don't mind, then, we'll wait for a new incumbent and get his opinion before stating ours. Matters grew poisonous, all the more so as the other participants had scarcely forgiven the Egyptian bullying at Second Ephesus:

Eusebius of Dorylaeum:	They are lying!
Florentius of Sardis:	Let them prove what they say.
All the bishops:	If their beliefs are not orthodox, how can they elect a bishop?
The Egyptians:	The dispute is over the faith.
Cecropius:	They don't know what they believe. Are they willing to learn?
Acacius of Ariaratheia:	Just as at Ephesus they confused everything and scandalized the world, so their aim now is to disrupt this holy and great council![18]

The Egyptians literally threw themselves on the ground to plead not to be forced to sign Leo's Tome. As they said—knowing Egyptian conditions much better than did their hearers—"We shall no longer be able to live in the province. . . . We shall be killed. Have pity on us." They weren't exaggerating.

This atmosphere made it difficult for any attempt to reach a formula for belief, as all the different factions could scarcely be accommodated. They had to reach a text that echoed Cyril, though without some of the extreme positions that he had reached in the last stages of his assault on Nestorius. Any compromise would have to lavish praise on Cyril and his blessed memory, lauding his writings but leaving individual readers to decide which parts of that varied correspondence might actually be under discussion. Ultimately, the council moved toward a common position that drew from one of

Cyril's more moderate letters to Nestorius, from Cyril's pact with Antioch in 433, and from Leo's Tome. In its October 17 session, the council accepted "The Rule of Faith as contained in the Creed of Nicea, confirmed by the Council of Constantinople, expounded at Ephesus under Cyril, and set forth in the Letter of Pope Leo when he condemned the heresy of Nestorius and Eutyches."[19]

On October 22, the council met in its fifth session, the most critical point of the whole gathering, and the debates that followed were genuine confrontations over significant matters of belief. Proceedings began with the reading of a draft statement of doctrine, which has deliberately been excluded from the minutes. The council's fathers knew they would have to work hard enough to convince critics about the statement that eventually did achieve consensus, without having to argue over every stage of debate along the way. But the draft had problems. Strikingly, it failed to include the word *Theotokos*, God-Bearer, which was such a symbol of Cyril's thought and a barrier to any concessions to Nestorians. Given the number of supporters, the word was added by overwhelming consensus.[20]

By far the touchiest part of the debate depended on the question of whether Christ was *out of* Two Natures [*ek duo physeon*] or *in* [*en*] Two Natures. Almost certainly, the draft used "out of," which could be interpreted in different ways, and that was at once its virtue and its peril. A true Monophysite could happily assert that Christ came from two natures, which were later joined in one: Eutyches believed just that. To speak of *in* Two Natures offered no such loophole and clearly stated that both natures existed after the union. This was the stance of Leo and the Westerners, and of the Antiochene school, and it was the Romans and Antiochenes insisted that the draft proclaim "in" rather than "out of."

Their protests sparked a furious response from the majority of bishops, who shouted against the Nestorians, the "fighters against God." When Romans threatened to hold a new council in Italy if they had to, some bishops responded with cries that roughly translate

to "So go back to Italy! We don't need Nestorians here." Other recorded yells—"acclamations" is the technical term—are important for
what they suggest about the continuing hatred of anything that
sounded vaguely Nestorian. "The augusta expelled Nestorius," some
shouted—that is, remember that Pulcheria took the leading role in that
struggle, and we should not do anything that brings Nestorius back.
"Drive out the heretics! The Virgin Mary is Theotokos. . . . Drive out
the Nestorians! Christ is God!"[21]

The issue of *ek* and *en* almost wrecked a conference that otherwise seemed so obviously destined for success. Unity was saved only
by the intervention of the imperial officials, who did not want to
deal with a catastrophic church split at a time when the borders
might be on the verge of collapse. They were also determined to see
some kind of official statement to come out of the council, to rein-
force Marcian's boast to be the new Constantine. If Constantine
had given the world the Nicene Creed, Marcian deserved some
comparable memorial, at least a Chalcedonian definition, if not a
full-scale creed. Pushing hard for compromise, the officials formed
a committee to reconcile the draft definitions, and they ensured that
this body had strong representation from Rome and Syria. Throughout the proceedings, imperial agents reminded the bishops that they
had already agreed to documents based on the "in Two Natures"
view. Also, surely a reference to the *Theotokos* in the revised text
proved that nothing Nestorian was intended?[22]

Grudgingly in many cases, the bishops reached agreement; 452
bishops signed on, a much larger body than met at Nicea or First
and Second Ephesus, and with a geographical span that fully justified the council's claims to ecumenical status.[23] This broad support
gives special weight to the Definition that was now issued.

Proclaiming Faith

The council first recapped the beliefs asserted at the first three
councils. As they said, these statements should have been clear

enough, but the devil was always trying to subvert the church.[24] Various babblings had arisen since, including those of the Nestorians, but the larger and more pressing problem was One Nature believers like Eutyches. Their wickedness lay in "bringing in a confusion and mixture, and idly conceiving that the nature of the flesh and of the Godhead is all one, maintaining that the divine Nature of the Only Begotten is, by mixture, capable of suffering."[25] Instead, the council admitted the writings of Cyril and Leo as authoritative. The Tome was highly praised:

> For it opposes those who would rend the mystery of the dispensation into a Duad of Sons; it repels from the sacred assembly those who dare to say that the Godhead of the Only Begotten is capable of suffering; it resists those who imagine a mixture or confusion of the two Natures of Christ; it drives away those who fancy his form of a servant is of an heavenly or some substance other than that which was taken of us; and it anathematizes those who foolishly talk of two Natures of our Lord before the union, conceiving that after the union there was only one.[26]

The council declared its belief in:

> one and the same Son, our Lord Jesus Christ, at once complete in Godhead and complete in manhood, truly God and truly man, consisting also of a reasonable soul and body; of one substance with the Father as regards his Godhead, and at the same time of one substance with us as regards his manhood; like us in all respects, apart from sin; as regards his Godhead, begotten of the Father before the ages, but yet as regards his manhood begotten, for us men and for our salvation, of Mary the Virgin, the God-Bearer [*Theotokos*].

On the subject of the Natures, the definition asserted faith in:

> one and the same Christ, Son, Lord, Only-begotten, recognized in two Natures, without confusion, without change, without division, without separation; the distinction of Natures being in no way annulled by the union, but rather the characteristics of each Nature being preserved and coming together to form one person and subsistence, not as parted or separated into two Persons, but one and the same Son and Only-begotten, God the Word, Lord Jesus Christ.[27]

The assembled bishops cried out, "This is the faith of the fathers: . . . this is the faith of the Apostles: by this we all stand: thus we all believe." The letter was then laid on Euphemia's altar and presumably taken thence to heaven. As the council reported to Leo,

> For it was God who worked, and the triumphant Euphemia who crowned the meeting as for a bridal, and who, taking our definition of the Faith as her own confession, presented it to her Bridegroom by our most religious Emperor and Christ-loving Empress, appeasing all the tumult of opponents and establishing our confession of the Truth as acceptable to Him.[28]

Definitions

But what exactly had Euphemia approved? Something made this statement so valuable that it has stood, in effect, up to the present day. If it was not the end of a story, it provided a solid foundation for all future development. However convoluted the Chalcedonian text looks, it repays closer reading. Examined more closely, we appreciate just how powerful are the ideas expressed, and how economical. The American Declaration of Independence offers a good parallel, in concentrating such a wealth of ideas into a very narrow space. And like the Declaration, the Definition cannot be appreciated except as a compressed commentary on a long previous history that is only alluded to in a brief document. In the Greek, the Definition runs only to a couple of hundred words.

The Chalcedonian Definition takes on several rival theological stances of the previous two centuries and rejects them, often with brief incidental comments that meet possible objections to orthodoxy. Take for instance the phrase, "of a reasonable [rational] soul," *psyches logikes*. What does that mean? Had anyone ever suggested that Jesus had not had a rational soul? Yes, indeed they had. Apollinarius had, in fact, and said that the Incarnation involved nothing more than an irrational, animal soul (*psyche alogos*) taking on a human body that was filled by God's Logos.

The text also targeted Nestorius, or at least Nestorian ideas as they had been caricatured at Ephesus. "Our Lord Jesus Christ" was absolutely both God and man,

> complete in Godhead and complete in manhood,
> truly God and truly man....
> Consisting, of one substance (*homoousion*) with the Father as regards his Godhead,
> and at the same time of one substance (*homoousion*) with us as regards his manhoood;
> like us in all respects, apart from sin;
> as regards his Godhead, begotten of the Father before the ages.

But what about the title of *Theotokos*, the Mother of God? What about all the absurdities of God as toddler? Christ, "in these last days for us men and for our salvation, was born of the Virgin Mary, the Mother of God *according to his manhood (kata ten anthropoteta)*." This final clause is critical. To quote Philip Schaff again: "Mary was the mother not merely of the human *nature* of Jesus of Nazareth, but of the theanthropic [divine/human] *person* of Jesus Christ; yet not of his eternal Godhead . . . but of his incarnate person, or the Logos united to humanity."[29]

The Definition proceeds to explain how the two natures must be regarded, in words that unequivocally condemn Eutyches. In reality, said the Chalcedonian fathers, the two natures are

> [united] without confusion, without change, without division, without separation
>   *(asyngchytos, atreptos, adiairetos, achoristos)*
>   the distinction of Natures (*physeon*) being in no way annulled by the union,
>   but rather the characteristics of each Nature being preserved,
>   and concurring in one Person (*prosopon)* and one Subsistence (*hypostasin*)
>   not as parted or separated into two Persons (*prosopa*)
>   but one and the same Son, and only begotten,
>   God the Word, Lord Jesus Christ.[30]

The four terms "without confusion, without change, without division, without separation" may sound like a ritual chant or hymn, but they carried real weight in terms of the alternatives they excluded. Asserting to this phrase allowed no chance of recognizing Christ as a mingled God-man whose flesh was not real flesh. Nor could the two natures be divided into "two Christs."[31]

New and Old Rome

Other issues also remained to be dealt with, including the restoration of Theodoret and Ibas, which made a very bitter pill indeed for most of the participants. Theodoret himself had to make very substantial compromises to be restored to favor. Although he understood that political realities forced him to anathematize Nestorius, Theodoret had to be pushed and driven to say the actual words. But ultimately he spoke them and was reconciled. The restoration of Domnus, deposed at Second Ephesus, came close to creating another potential crisis. Domnus's successor at Antioch was Maximus, but Maximus had gone on to be legitimately ordained, and the thought of two equally qualified claimants was nightmarish. Would both men claim the see, creating yet another schism? Fortunately, Domnus was, as always, happy to accept a deal that avoided confrontation or unpleasantness, so that he accepted a pension and honorable retirement.[32]

Still more contentious in the long run were the decisions concerning the rank and status of other great sees, including Jerusalem, now a patriarchate. On October 26, Juvenal and Maximus of Antioch announced a pact they had reached, in which Jerusalem would have the three provinces of Palestine. Antioch kept the regions that we would call the nations of Lebanon and Jordan.[33]

The council's canons enhanced the status and privileges of Constantinople, which received special privileges because it was the imperial city, suggesting parity with Rome. The new council recalled that the earlier assembly at Constantinople in 381 "rightly granted privileges to the throne of old Rome, because it was the royal city." But those same bishops "gave equal privileges [*isa presbeia*] to the most holy throne of New Rome, justly judging that the city which is honored with the sovereignty and the Senate, and enjoys equal privileges with the old imperial Rome, should in ecclesiastical matters also be magnified as she is, and rank next after her." Chalcedon proclaimed Constantinople as the second patriarchate and made it a court of appeal from provincial synods. The patriarch also received the right to ordain the metropolitans of neighboring regions—Pontus, Asia, and Thrace—and, potentially even more significant, bishops from these dioceses who were "among the barbarians." At a time of thriving missionary effort throughout eastern Europe and western Asia, this clause offered Constantinople the basis of a vast ecclesiastical empire.[34]

Leo was troubled by all this and tried unsuccessfully to void the new canon on Constantinople's status. Rome was always nervous of any attempt to raise other sees to anywhere near its level. Who knew that in a few decades another council might place the imperial capital as equal to Rome, or even superior? Also, raising Constantinople meant lowering the status of other ancient sees like Antioch and Alexandria. Leo reasserted the apostolic claims of each see, no matter what the misdeeds of individual bishops. Yes, Dioscuros had behaved abominably, but even so, "the See of Alexandria may not lose any of that dignity which it merited through St. Mark, the evangelist and disciple of the blessed Peter, nor may the splendor of so great a church be obscured by another's clouds . . . the See is on a different footing to the holders of it." Nor should the church of Antioch be demoted. It was here that "first at the preaching of the blessed Apostle Peter, the Christian name arose," and Leo was not about to tolerate any disrespect to Peter. Antioch should never be lowered below third place. "Never" of course is a long time, and taken literally, Leo was suggesting that such honors should still apply even when Antioch, say—or Rome itself—was a depopulated archaeological site.[35]

Leo also protested that a Christian bishop should not pursue status and glory as avidly as Constantinople's Anatolius was doing, especially when his own personal record left so much to be desired. After all, Anatolius had only come over to the orthodox position after thoroughly compromising himself under the previous regime. He only held office by reason of the murder of the sainted Flavian. Leo urged, "Let him realize what a man he has succeeded, and expelling all the spirit of pride, let him imitate Flavian's faith, Flavian's modesty, Flavian's humility, which has raised him right to a confessor's glory." For many reasons, Constantinople should exercise much greater humility.[36]

After Chalcedon

The council of Chalcedon ended with a grand session on November 1 in the presence of Marcian and Pulcheria, and the mood was ecstatic. Marcian himself was welcomed as a "second Constantine." But whatever Chalcedon's reputation in history, at the time, the council seemed less of a finality than a stage in a process. Soon, the different participants would have many other concerns.[37]

For the imperial court, Chalcedon offered only a temporary respite. The imperial family was deeply divided, as Pulcheria's sister-in-law Eudocia strongly favored the Monophysite cause and despised those timeservers who accepted the new order. Later sympathizers regarded her as a near saint, and Egypt's John of Nikiu later supplied this obituary:

> The empress Eudocia went to her rest in the holy Jerusalem, full of good works and a pure faith. And she refused to communicate with Juvenal, bishop of Jerusalem, and the men who had assembled in Chalcedon; for she knew that they had changed the true faith of our holy Fathers and of the orthodox emperors.

John, on the other hand, gave only the most slighting obituary to Marcian and rejoiced indecently at his gangrene ("his feet mortified and he died"). Pulcheria herself died in 453.[38]

By the time Marcian died, Rome had been sacked once more, this time by Vandals (455), and the Western empire was left immeasurably weaker. With the Theodosian dynasty close to extinct, the selection of emperors was left wholly to the military commander Aspar, who at least chose competent men. Marcian's Eastern successor was Leo, an able soldier, who succeeded in keeping most of the Eastern empire's territories out of barbarian hands.

We might think that the Roman emperors in this time would be entirely focused on mere survival, but for thirty years after Chalcedon, many of the issues faced by the Eastern rulers involved theological debates. Furious protests against the council raged across the Middle East. The degree of reaction may seem strange when we think how heavily Chalcedon had drawn on Cyril's thought, but this was a thought world in which even the slightest concession to error in such essential matters was a betrayal of the whole substance of

Christian truth. Moreover, One Nature believers were deeply disappointed. As recently as 450, they had every reason to believe that
they absolutely dominated both church and empire, but they suddenly found themselves forced to compromise, to accept the provocative phrase "in Two Natures." From the Monophysite point of
view, Chalcedonian orthodoxy was Christian only in name and out-
ward guise and the words Chalcedonian and Nestorian were virtually identical. An empire that accepted Chalcedon was not Christian,
a fact it proved repeatedly by the persecutions it inflicted upon the
true believers who accepted the Single Nature.[39]

Many in Egypt and the Near East viewed Chalcedon with quite
as much disgust as the Catholic/Orthodox saw the Gangster Synod
of Ephesus. The resentment detonated a civil war within many
churches, as lower clergy, and particularly monasteries, rebelled
against compliant bishops. The *Life of St. Peter the Iberian* summarizes
these reactions:

> It was then that the apostasy of all those schismatic bishops,
> sanctioned by the godless Tome of Pope Leo, and attended by
> the adoption of the scandalous doctrine of Nestorius, resulted
> in Dioscorus, chief of the bishops of Egypt and a zealous
> fighter for truth, being driven into banishment; while Juvenal,
> who bore the tide of bishop of Jerusalem, signed the act of
> apostasy, and thereby assumed the role of the traitor Judas.[40]

Some of the monks who had been at Chalcedon returned to Palestine and Egypt determined to stir up trouble. Juvenal might have
made his peace with the regime, but when he traveled to Constantinople, opponents staged a coup in his Jerusalem diocese, appointing
one Theodosius as rival bishop. Hard-line anti-Chalcedonians like
Peter the Iberian served other Palestinian sees. Alarmed at the
emerging schism, Marcian urgently sent Juvenal back to restore
order.[41] Or as Peter's biographer interpreted matters, the problem

could be traced back to Satan, "that prince of renegades and arch-counselor of apostates," who could not bear to see the church making such progress.

Accordingly he entered into the monarch who now held the reins of government, the Emperor Marcian, who readily listened to the devil's commands, and he incited him to issue a decree deposing the righteous bishops who had been appointed throughout the towns of Palestine by the apostolic patriarch Theodosius. In case of resistance, they were to be forcibly expelled from their sees and killed, while the patriarch Theodosius was condemned to death.[42]

Marcian—or Satan, as we choose to read it—succeeded in keeping control, but at a huge cost to public order.

Alexandria Burns

Chalcedon had its worst effects in Egypt, where Dioscuros's fall disrupted the near-pharaonic regime painstakingly constructed over the previous 150 years. Not just in titular precedence, Constantinople now established itself as the second patriarchate, taking the lead over Alexandria, and that dominance grew ever more apparent over the coming decades.

Alexandria itself plunged into political and religious turmoil. Even a simple list of the patriarchs suggests the acute contrast to the long stability of the previous era, when incumbents held their posts securely for decades, able to avoid any and all challenges. From then until the end of the century, the story of Alexandria's patriarchate was a lengthy series of depositions and insurgencies, exiles and reinstatements. The only constant was the fundamental battle between the Chalcedonian views of the empire and its agents, and the One Nature faith of the mass of Egyptians.

The growing crisis is recounted in *The History of the Patriarchs of the Coptic Church of Alexandria*, compiled by the Coptic Church. According to this official record, the "holy patriarch" Cyril was followed by Dioscorus who

> endured severe persecution for the orthodox faith at the hands of the prince Marcian and his wife; and they banished him from his see, through the partial action of the council of Chalcedon, and their subservience to the will of the prince and his wife. It is for this reason that the members of that council and all the followers of their corrupt creed are called Melkites, because they follow the opinion of the prince and his wife, in proclaiming and renewing the doctrine of Nestorius.[43]

Dioscuros died in exile in Paphlagonia (Asia Minor) in 454, but his sympathizers—the Coptic or Egyptian party—never lost hope. Several Egyptian bishops had gone over to the imperial side at Chalcedon, and they now tried to elect a Chalcedonian patriarch, one Proterius. But the imperial loyalists represented only a minority, and the election was seen as an attempt to impose an unpopular outsider. The consequence was "a very great and intolerable tumult" that exhibited Alexandria at its worst.[44] One protest erupted from a demonstration at the theater, as factions started shouting slogans: "'Up with Dioscorus and the orthodox! Burn Proterius' bones! Throw out the Judas!' They demanded the return of the pious Dioscorus from his unjust exile, and the expulsion of the ravening wolf and anti-Christ Proterius, the new Caiaphas. Soldiers intervened, killing many in the crush."[45]

A visitor described the scene on another occasion, as Egyptians tried to defend the central tenets of Christian truth: "He saw the populace advancing in a mass against the magistrates: when the troops attempted to repress the tumult, they proceeded to assail them with stones, and put them to flight, and on their taking refuge in the old temple of Serapis, carried the place by assault, and committed them alive to the flames."[46] The emperor responded by sending two thousand soldiers, a major commitment at a time when they could have been put to much better use on the frontiers. But even this intervention only stirred new troubles, as the soldiers behaved as if they were in a conquered city, with unrestricted rights of rape against local women. The military ran a tightly repressive regime, restricting food supplies and denying access to the baths and public shows that were the basis of all social life. The state of siege eased after a while, but grievances remained.[47]

From 454, the Copts maintained a separate patriarchate and a parallel hierarchy, choosing as their head the monk Timothy. He was a small-framed man known as Aelurus, which may mean "cat" but in this case probably suggests "weasel." His roots were also firmly in the Alexandrian tradition, as he had been ordained by Cyril and had accompanied Dioscuros to Second Ephesus. But the Weasel was an extraordinarily powerful figure in his own right who exercised influence far beyond Egypt itself and who set the stage for the creation of the later independent Monophysite church. In different circumstances, he would certainly have been as famous as either of his predecessors in the wider Christian world.[48]

When Marcian died in 457, Alexandrians rose against Proterius, as "the God-fearing populace breathed again, and gave thanks to our Redeemer Christ." They found bishops to proclaim Timothy the Weasel as patriarch, and try as they might, the military could not keep order. Imperial forces stormed the church that was the headquarters of the opposition, where they "murdered many laymen, monks and nuns. Since the multitude could not endure this, they were inflamed with the zeal of martyrdom and daily resisted the soldiery with all the bloodshed of civil war."[49] This time the army could not save Proterius from receiving the divine gift of martyrdom:

Some of the Alexandrians, at the instigation of Timothy . . . dispatched Proterius when he appeared, by thrusting a sword through his bowels, after he had fled for refuge to the holy baptistery. Suspending the body by a cord, they displayed it to the public in the quarter called Tetrapylum, jeering and shouting that the victim was Proterius; and, after dragging it through the whole city, committed it to the flames; not even refraining themselves from tasting his intestines, like beasts of prey.

By another account, "they left him lying in the road like a pig or a dog, which he resembled in his manners and ferocity."[50]

Chalcedonians were shocked both by the time of the murder (Easter) and the place. Even barbarians and savages, they wrote, respected the baptistery. Although pagans might not understand the theology of baptism, they certainly recognized its spiritual power. The roots of the crime were not hard to find. "Of all these transactions Timothy was the guilty cause, and the skilful builder of the scheme of mischief." Pope Leo never forgave Timothy for the murder. He compared him to Cain and called him a *parricida*, a father-murderer, who was *sacrilegus* or *impius*—in Roman thought, both terms of ultimate condemnation and eminently deserving the death penalty.[51] Copts, of course, had a quite different memory of the matter and glorified the Weasel as a virtuous sufferer for the faith. According to one tale, a governor who maltreated him "was eaten of worms and died," a phrase that recalls the death of King Herod. That was what happened to worldly lords who persecuted God's apostles.[52]

Just how far the Weasel was prepared to go remains open to debate, but in 458—the year after Proterius's murder—Anatolius of Constantinople died violently, probably assassinated by diehard supporters of Dioscuros and Timothy. Alexandrians loathed Anatolius as a native son who had betrayed his home church. Worse, Timothy himself had once described him as a "brother," which need not be taken literally but suggests how close the relationship had been prior to a violent split. Anatolius had betrayed their common father, Dioscuros. Whether or not Timothy was actually responsible for the killing, he would not have condemned it. Alexandrian blood feuds recognized no geographical limits and knew no expiration dates.[53]

The new emperor Leo deposed the Weasel, replacing him with another, orthodox Timothy, who held on to his office with interruptions until his death in 481. Yet the new Chalcedonian patriarch was always conscious of his tenuous position. His name *Salofakiolos* means something like Wobbly Cap, with the suggestion that just as a hat does not fit on somebody's head, so he did not belong in that job. His weaselly Coptic rival, Timothy, was always waiting in the wings as "secret patriarch."[54]

Rome

If the councils ruined the see of Mark, they hugely strengthened the successors of Peter. Few figures of late antiquity enjoyed a more active life than Leo, or one that touched great events at so many points. In October 451, he had secured an overwhelming political victory, but perhaps his greatest triumph was still to come. However terrifying Dioscuros or Eutyches might have been, neither was on a par with Attila, who threatened to pay his own visit to Rome. Shortly before Chalcedon, and unknown to the participants, Roman and allied forces had defeated Attila at the battle of the Catalaunian Fields, probably at modern Châlons in France. This battle was all the more historic because, for the first time in history, an overwhelmingly Christian force struggled against a pagan invader. Legend turned the battle into a precursor of the medieval Crusades, with the great general Aetius lauded as a warrior for Christian civilization. But Attila was not destroyed, and the following year he launched an invasion of Italy, still using the excuse of his marriage invitation from the princess Honoria.[55]

At Marcian's request, Leo joined a delegation to Attila to plead for the city. For whatever reason, Attila turned away, a withdrawal that has gone down in legend and art as the result of a miraculous intervention by heavenly powers, summoned by Leo: during the Renaissance, Raphael painted the scene to commemorate one of the greatest moments in papal history. Attila, reportedly, "was so impressed by the presence of the high priest that he ordered his army to give up warfare and, after he had promised peace, he departed beyond the Danube." We need not believe in the saintly apparitions to be impressed by Leo's courage, and his determination to defend his city and church, against overwhelming odds. Although he was not the only man in the delegation, history remembers Leo as the savior of the city.[56]

Rome's salvation lasted for exactly three years. Leo, unfortunately, never held the position of Western emperor, a job at which he would have excelled. The incumbent at that time was the worthless Valentinian III, whose regime survived only through the loyal service of generals like Aetius. However, Aetius had rivals at court, and the favorite Maximus persuaded the emperor that his faithful general was becoming dangerously popular. Accordingly, Valentinian personally stabbed Aetius to death. One courtier dared to rebuke him, with the words, "My lord, I don't know what exactly made you do this, but I do know you have acted like a man who has used his left hand to cut off his right."[57]

That murder set off a sequence of events that deserves reporting if only because it gives an idea of the utter political chaos in Italy at this time, amongst which Leo stood out as such a beacon of sanity. Maximus himself killed Valentinian, taking his predecessor's wife Eudoxia as his own (she was the daughter of the recent Eastern emperor Theodosius II). Maximus reigned as emperor for a couple of months, struggling to fight off other claimants before he was himself murdered. Meanwhile, Eudoxia took her own revenge by inviting Gaiseric to invade Italy, which he was happy to do. (The connection made some sense: Licinia Eudoxia's daughter was betrothed to Gaiseric's son). As before, disaffected empresses proved very useful to ambitious barbarians. Once again, Romans begged

Leo to save their city, and he did his best to plead with Gaiseric. On this occasion, though, in 455 the best he could achieve was a kinder and gentler sack, in which churches and places of refuge were respected, while the barbarians concentrated on their primary task of carrying off everything of value that remained in the eternally vulnerable city. When, some years later, the Eastern emperor tried to punish Gaiseric by a massive naval/amphibious assault against Carthage, the Romans suffered one of the worst military disasters recorded in the ancient world.[58]

Nestorius was quietly triumphant. Although he approved of most of Leo's theological views, he could not forgive the failure to rehabilitate him together with Flavian and the other victims of Egyptian malice. Leo, he wrote, "has indeed held well to the faith but has agreed to the things which these have unjustly committed against me without examination and without judgment." Nestorius, or a later editor, portrayed the second sack of Rome as God's vengeance for this slight. He phrased his account in the form of a prophecy:

> Yet there will however be in the first place and at no longer distance of time a second coming of the barbarian against Rome itself, during which also Leo . . . will deliver up with his own hands the divine vessels of the sanctuary into the hands of the barbarians, and will see with his own eyes the daughters of the emperor who is reigning at that time led into captivity.[59]

Yet Leo's prestige did not suffer from this failure: two miracles in such a short time was too much to hope for. To the contrary, he continued to exercise authority—primacy—over the church throughout the surviving Roman world, up until his death in 461. He left a stunning heritage, in terms of the reputation of the Roman church, and a series of precedents that the papacy would cite over the next millennium to establish its supremacy over other churches. Nor were Roman claims likely to be any less ambitious under Leo's successor,

Hilarius, or to be expressed more timidly. This was the same man who had vainly tried to silence the anti-Flavian lynch mob at Second Ephesus and who had been forced to escape in disguise. Even through the worst humiliations and scandals of Dark Ages Rome, the memory of Leo and Hilarius survived to lay a solid foundation for the future papacy.

Part 3

A World to Lose

No son of a Roman emperor will sit on the throne of his father, so long as the sect of the Chalcedonians bears sway in the world.
                                        Severus of Antioch

8

How the Church Lost Half the World

If any one of them says that the council of Chalcedon is true, let him go;
but drown in the sea those that say it is erroneous and false.
Emperor Heraclius, c. 635

In 653 the soldiers of Roman emperor Constans II stormed into
Rome's Lateran Palace. They arrested the current pope, Martin I,
together with Maximus, one of the great Christian scholars and
mystics of the age. Both men were carried off into exile and suffered the horrible abuses that the Romans inflicted on those who
spoke or wrote against the emperor. Torturers cut off Maximus's
right hand and tore out his tongue. Martin died two years later in
exile in the Crimea, Maximus a few years later in Georgia. On the
strength of their heroic defense of Christian truth at the cost of
their lives, the Orthodox/Catholic churches regard both men as
martyrs: Pope Martin is a saint, Maximus a confessor.[1]

The two men suffered because they opposed the emperor on
one of the most critical and most divisive issues of his reign, the
so-called Monothelete (One Will) position. *Two hundred years* after
Chalcedon, two hundred years after Marcian had demanded an end

to "profane wrangling," the empire was no closer to a settlement.[2] Church and court were grasping for some kind of solution that could conceivably satisfy both sides, the adherents of One Nature and Two Natures. In the 630s, a solution seemed at hand: whether Christ had one nature or two, he operated with one will. Surely that could provide some kind of basis of agreement, enough of a common ground to hold the loyalty of Egypt and Syria, Africa and the West? But it did not, as the imperial raid on the Lateran suggests. Martin and Maximus suffered because they held firm to Chalcedon.

The imperial violence is not too surprising, but what is really remarkable is the late date, which points to the limitations of Chalcedon and its achievement. Long after 451, it was not obvious that the Chalcedonian regime was going to triumph. Over the next 150 years, there were some periods when blue orthodoxy reigned at court, but there were long spells—several decades at a stretch—when regimes either tolerated Monophysites or were actively sympathetic. The bishops and patriarchs they supported made every effort to spread and enforce their views. People learned hopeful lessons from recent history. Chalcedon itself had been a countercoup against Second Ephesus, so why should it not be reversed in its turn? By 510 or so, in fact, Chalcedon looked as if it was on its way to becoming a dead letter. Not until well into the sixth century did the Chalcedonian cause decisively gain the upper hand.[3]

Even after Chalcedon achieved political victory, the same issues keep being debated over and over, endlessly erupting anew in new forms. Schisms between major regions and jurisdictions become normal and almost accepted, even between Rome and Constantinople. Depositions and purges were a regular fact of church life, while extreme violence and rioting split cities and provinces. And gradually, dissident jurisdictions took the once unthinkable step of establishing alternative parallel churches.[4] Table 8.1 suggests a rough chronology of the ups and downs of the Chalcedonian order.

TABLE 8.1
THE SHIFTING RELIGIOUS BALANCE
IN THE ROMAN EMPIRE C.470–650

470–518	Dominance of Monophysite or near-Monophysite imperial regimes
480–550	Emergence of separate Nestorian church
510–600	Emergence of separate Monophysite churches
518–630	Strong imperial enforcement of Chalcedonian order
630–50	Collapse of Roman Christian rule over Egypt and Near East

Although the imperial regime could never admit the fact, the Christian world was by 600 divided into several great transnational churches, each with its own claims to absolute truth. This was an ugly reality for those who idealized the church as the seamless, united body of Christ. As long as Roman and Christian rule lasted over Egypt and the East, the empire would never find a workable solution to the theological crisis. Two into one would never go.[5]

Chalcedon's Enemies

Chalcedon survived because it developed deep roots in a number of crucial and well-organized centers, which held both prestige and active political power. Chalcedonian beliefs were strong in Asia Minor and the Balkans, the core territories of empire, and in Constantinople itself. They also prevailed in the Western provinces. Rome, throughout, was a solid bastion of support. Monasteries housed some of the most devoted supporters of official orthodoxy.[6]

But Chalcedon continued to offend large sections of the Eastern empire. By the sixth century, anti-Chalcedonian views were already the norm in large sections of the Eastern Christian world, where debate raged between different factions of the One Nature cause, between Miaphysites and hard-core Eutychians. Chalcedonian bishops were likely to find themselves purged or hounded from office. Even when the bishops remained true to Chalcedon, dissident lower clergy and monks maintained their own faith, and some won supporters by their asceticism and holy lives and tales of their miracles. One Monophysite hero was the saintly monk and bishop Peter the Iberian, who traveled widely in Palestine and neighboring lands. He consecrated clergy and taught believers, "while others he enlightened and brought into the fold of the orthodox [anti-Chalcedonian] Church."[7]

Egypt, of course, showed not the slightest willingness to forgive or forget. The patriarchate remained badly divided, with overlapping and competing jurisdictions prevailing from 451 through 482. Although the detailed succession does not matter immensely, Table 8.2 suggests the degree of chaos in the city.

Timothy the Weasel had built a firm foundation for a Coptic church that could survive imperial hostility. From 477, the church was again divided between Coptic and Chalcedonian factions, with the Copts led by Peter Mongus, the Stammerer, Timothy's former deacon. Peter was utterly uncompromising, to the point of ordering the desecration of the tombs of his Chalcedonian predecessors.[8]

In the official *History of the Patriarchs of the Coptic Church of Alexandria*, complaints about Chalcedon become so frequent a part of the text that they become almost the obligatory introduction to the life of each new incumbent:

But the empire of the Romans remained established upon the ever-renewed memory of the impure council of Chalcedon; for it was not built upon the foundation of the firm Rock, which belongs to God the Word who is Jesus Christ.[9]

TABLE 8.2
THE PATRIARCHATE OF
ALEXANDRIA AFTER CHALCEDON

Proterius	Chalcedonian	451–57	murdered
Timothy Aelurus	anti-Chalcedon	454–60	expelled
Timothy II Salofakiolos	Chalcedonian	460–75	expelled
Timothy Aelurus, restored	anti-Chalcedon	475–77	died in office
Peter III Mongus	anti-Chalcedon	477	expelled
Timothy II, restored	Chalcedonian	477–82	died in office
John I	Chalcedonian	482	expelled
Peter III Mongus, restored	anti-Chalcedon	482–90	died in office

We read casually that one individual was "a Roman, and a blasphe-mous Chalcedonian."[10] By the mid-eighth century, with Egypt under the firm rule of Muslim Arabs, one would have thought that the church would have more urgent problems to confront, but ancient hatreds still rankled:

The patriarch, Abba Michael, assembled his bishops, and wrote a letter . . . giving an account of the foundation of the church of the martyr, Saint Mennas, and of the troubles and banishments endured by our fathers, the patriarchs, at the hands of the Chalcedonians, and of the taking of the churches from them by the hands of the princes of the Romans.[11]

In any theological struggle, the first thousand years are always the bitterest.

Egypt mattered immensely in its own right, but Egyptian beliefs also spread to the neighboring kingdoms that looked to Alexandria as their spiritual capital. The old-established churches of Nubia and Ethiopia were also Monophysite and long remained so—the Nubians until the death of that church in the late Middle Ages, and the Ethiopians up to the present day. The Ethiopian church still boasts the title of *Tawahedo*—Oneness.[12]

But One Nature views spread far beyond Egypt's cultural sphere. Although Syria had once been the heartland of Antiochene Two Nature theology, a strong Monophysite party emerged during the struggles following Chalcedon. In 469, one Peter the Fuller mobilized the urban crowd against the Chalcedonian patriarch of Antioch and successfully replaced him. As patriarch, he ruled as an aggressive Monophysite, who was spiritual godfather to generations of later clergy. He also devised what became a common litmus test of religious loyalty when he changed the Thrice Holy to declare that the one Holy God "was crucified for us" (*ho staurotheis di hemas*). Although twice ejected from his diocese, he left a permanent Monophysite stamp on Antioch. This change revolutionized the empire's political geography.[13]

The doctrinal shift became even stronger after 500 or so, and its effects endured for centuries. To be a Chalcedonian in Syria soon was to be stigmatized as a heretic, as much a deviant and traitor as one would be in Alexandria. Monophysite historian John of Ephesus tells how one Flavian was patriarch of Antioch in the early sixth century, but "being convicted of the heresy of the two natures"— that is, a Chalcedonian—he was deposed. A later anti-Monophysite incumbent "was proved to be a Nestorian, and was also ejected and expelled." The conversion of Antioch was so important because of the extraordinarily wide connections of that city. In the first century, Antioch was the chief base for Christian expansion in the east; four hundred years later, it reprised this role in the Monophysite cause.[14]

But even mapping the very large dissident areas of the Near East does not give a full picture of the degree of religious unrest. Constantinople itself was divided, and struggles between the Green and Blue circus factions were at their height in the early sixth century. Just how potentially deadly these Gangs of New Rome actually were became obvious in 532, when the two sides briefly made common cause in a riotous insurgency that threatened the survival of the regime. Thousands were killed before order was restored.[15]

Monophysite Empire

The continuing Jesus Wars gave nightmares to every succeeding emperor. Several incumbents tried to come up with compromise solutions to bring all sides together, and like the Monotheletes of the seventh century, all would fail. The basic problem was straightforward. The empire could suppress heresies and had done so effectively enough in the past. But matters became much more difficult when a heresy was so widespread as to be the normal Christian attitude in large areas of the empire and, moreover, in wealthy and populous areas essential to keeping the state going.[16]

The gravest threat to the new order followed a coup in 475. The general Basiliscus rose against Zeno, temporarily driving him into exile and establishing himself on the emperor's throne. As so often in this century, the political struggle was a family spat. By profession, Basiliscus was a brother-in-law, and not a shining example of the breed. He had no military talents to speak of, and his greatest achievement to date was losing most of a Roman fleet in a futile attack on Carthage. It is a matter of debate whether the disaster resulted from his epic incompetence or from the fact that he was taking bribes from his enemy, Gaiseric. But whatever the truth, he was the brother-in-law of the previous emperor Leo, and his niece was Zeno's queen, and that made him a player in the imperial succession. (See Table 8.3.)

TABLE 8.3
ROMAN EMPERORS IN THE EAST
(SOLE EMPERORS AFTER 476)

Leo I	457–74
Zeno	474–91
(Basiliscus	475–76, usurper)
Anastasius	491–518
Justin I	518–27
Justinian	527–65
Justin II	565–78
Tiberius II	578–82
Maurice	582–602
Phokas	602–10
Heraclius	610–41
Constans II	641–68
Constantine IV	668–85

NOTE: This table omits short-lived emperors, and most pretenders.

Basiliscus attempted a Monophysite counterrevolution. On Leo's death in 474, Alexandrian monks had rushed to Constantinople to demand a repudiation of Chalcedon, and they found sympathetic ears in the new usurper. Basiliscus restored Monophysite-inclined patriarchs, including Peter the Fuller and Timothy the Weasel, while Constantinople's patriarch Acacius was leaning toward their positions. Basiliscus then addressed to Timothy a sweeping general letter. This encyclical condemned "the proceedings that have disturbed the unity and order of the holy churches of God, and the peace of the whole world, that is to say, the so-called Tome of Leo, and all things said and done at Chalcedon in violation of the holy symbol of Nicea." These horrible documents were to be repudiated and anathematized, and all records of them burnt. Instead, the councils of Nicea and First Ephesus were to be regarded as the final and decisive statements of doctrine.[17]

Every bishop in the empire had to sign on to the encyclical, and a very large number did so. Possibly they were suffering from Vicar of Bray syndrome, the urge to keep their jobs at whatever cost. Most later claimed that they has subscribed "not designedly but of necessity, having agreed to these matters with letters and words, not with the heart." But the mass defection indicates just how fragile was the settlement achieved at Chalcedon. The patriarch of Jerusalem signed, and so did five hundred other bishops—rather more, in fact, than the number who had affirmed Chalcedon in 451. If Alexandria, Antioch, and Jerusalem were now all controlled by Monophysites, what exactly was the church's consensus position on the nature of Christ?[18]

Once again, the Egyptian empire threatened to extend its reach to the palace in Constantinople. The Weasel now acted as if he were the de facto religious head of the empire, consecrating and restoring like-minded believers. He unilaterally restored the patriarchate of Ephesus, appointing his own man to the post. He even presided over yet another council at Ephesus, at which Asian bishops offered full support to Basiliscus's declaration. They threatened that if anyone tried to change what he was proposing, "the whole world will be turned upside down, and the evils which have proceeded from the synod at Chalcedon will be found trifling in comparison, notwithstanding the innumerable slaughters which they have caused, and the blood of the orthodox which they have unjustly and lawlessly shed."[19]

But the religious reaction proved short-lived, as Timothy's arrogant behavior angered so many other bishops—had Egyptians learned nothing from 449? After some wavering, Constantinople's patriarch, Acacius, now became a strong voice for Chalcedonian orthodoxy. Preparing to confront the emperor, he gathered the most powerful ammunition he could find, in the form of the renowned spiritual athlete, Daniel the Stylite. As the events of 431 had shown, nothing intimidated a pious emperor more than a bona fide saint and miracle worker. Acacius induced Daniel to leave the pillar on which he had lived these many years, entering the world only to prophesy, heal, and exorcize, and persuaded him to oppose the new encyclical. Daniel's appearance before Basiliscus constituted a kind of religious terrorism that the emperor absolutely had to heed (en route to the palace, Daniel broke his journey just long enough to heal a leper). Basiliscus issued a fulsome apology, while the Constantinople mob rejoiced, shouting "The Emperor is orthodox! Burn alive the enemies of orthodoxy!" Meanwhile, Basiliscus and Acacius "lay prostrate on the ground at the holy man's [Daniel's] feet." Basiliscus now issued a new encyclical reversing the first, a kind of un-encyclical, but it was too late to soothe his enemies. Zeno seized power once again in 476, killing his rival. He kept his promise not to shed the blood of Basiliscus or his family, but that did not stop him from starving them to death.[20]

So lethally were Zeno and Basiliscus at each other's throats that neither could spare time to preserve the Western empire, notionally based in Rome, which quietly wound up in the ominous year of 476. And so fascinated were the contemporary historians with the religious struggles that they paid almost incidental attention to this event in the distant marches of empire. Defending or repealing Chalcedon was a matter of vital political significance, unlike the termination of an imperial tradition that dated to the time of Augustus. Historians have to know their priorities.

But, in fact, terminating the Western empire did have its religious consequences, as Roman power in the West now ceased to function outside parts of Italy. By 476, Gaiseric's Vandal regime still ruled North Africa, the Visigoths had created a mighty kingdom in Gaul and Spain, while other barbarians dominated Italy. All these regimes were proudly Arian and stood aloof from either the Roman state or the Catholic Church. Vandal Arians persecuted Catholics, forcibly rebaptizing them into that church.[21] Glancing at a map of shifting frontiers told any Roman emperor that the regions he had to appease in order to rule were overwhelmingly in the eastern Mediterranean. If Gaul, Africa, and Spain had slipped

off the political map, Egypt now mattered more than ever. Bringing Eastern Monophysites into the fold mattered far more than
keeping Western Catholics happy.

This new calculation gave a critical new priority to winning over
the Monophysites, especially in Egypt. In 482, Zeno tried to settle the
knotty dispute once and for all. His Henoticon, or act of union, reasserted the creed as laid out at Nicea and First Ephesus. It repeated
condemnations of both Nestorius and Eutyches, while reissuing
Cyril's Anathemas. More controversially, Zeno's document tried to
reach a christological statement that would offend neither side, avoiding the poisoned words *nature* and *person*. Its only reference to Chalcedon was in passing, and almost insulting:

> every one who has held or holds any other opinion, either at
> the present or another time, whether at Chalcedon or in any
> synod whatever, we anathematize; and specially the before-
> mentioned Nestorius and Eutyches, and those who maintain
> their doctrines.[22]

The Henoticon was a statesmanlike attempt at theological compromise, and it won early successes. Whatever they thought about
the One Nature or Two Natures, some were "caught by the artful
composition of that document; and others influenced by an inclination for peace." In 482, even Alexandrian diehard Monophysite
Peter Mongus agreed to compromise enough to sign the document.
Incredibly, given recent conflicts, Peter was now in communion
with Constantinople.[23]

Of course, the compromise did not satisfy everyone. Extreme
Monophysites who deserted the Coptic patriarchs became the anar-
chistic *acephali*, the "headless ones," who rejected both emperors
and bishops, and they remained a faction on the far fringes of belief
for centuries afterward. Much more serious were the effects of the
Henoticon on the followers of Chalcedon. When Peter Mongus
signed on, his Chalcedonian rival in Alexandria begged the Roman

pope to rescue orthodoxy in the East. The Pope responded by excommunicating not just Peter but also Acacius of Constantinople.
Ensuring maximum visibility, Chalcedonian monks actually pinned
the sentence to Acacius's robes while he was celebrating the Eucharist. This affair represented a degree of division among the churches
at least as bad as anything witnessed in the year or two between
Second Ephesus and Chalcedon, and the crisis lasted much longer.
From 484 to 519, this Acacian schism divided the Eastern and
Western churches, leaving the Roman popes out in the cold and
subject to the direct rule of the Arian Goths. When in the 490s another patriarch of Constantinople tried to patch up the quarrel and
reaffirm Chalcedon, the emperor first contemplated assassinating
him but settled for deposing him as a Nestorian.[24]

Isolated from all the major Eastern churches, the popes grew
ever more pessimistic about the chance of regaining influence. One
token of their desperation was the increasingly extreme claims they
made for their own powers, claims that they would scarcely have
dared make if they had been closer to political realities. In 494, Pope
Gelasius wrote an extraordinary letter expressing what would
become known as Two Sword theory. Christ had spoken of two
swords, which Gelasius read as two powers ruling the world, priestly
and royal. As the pope lectured the emperor, religious power always
took precedence over the secular, so that kings ruled at the pleasure
of priests and, specifically, popes. In later centuries, this letter would
gain immense weight as the charter of papal power over the secular
realm, suggesting once more how the fifth-century crisis served as
the foundation of the medieval Western church. Between 1070 and
1320, the doctrine would allow popes to depose several emperors
and kings and to force many more into groveling submission. In the
490s, though, the extraordinary nature of the political claims merely
indicated how far removed Rome was from any realistic prospect of
power or influence at the imperial court. Gelasian doctrine looked
not so much far-sighted as delusional.[25]

The empire remained in greenish hands for decades to come, as the Henoticon gave the Monophysites enough of what they demanded, while infuriating the Catholics. Zeno's successor Anastasius (491–518) was theologically sophisticated enough in his own right to have been a candidate for the patriarchate of Antioch. (The alternative career path points to the very thin line separating church from state in this era.) But while he personally held Monophysite opinions, he disliked persecution or unrest. Accordingly, he tried to operate a moderate policy balancing the two factions, purging or exiling only the egregious troublemakers who violated what we might call prevailing community standards. He only removed those bishops who were "promoters of change, wherever he detected any one either proclaiming or anathematizing the synod of Chalcedon in opposition to the practice of the neighborhood." In contemporary eyes, of course, moderation implied dangerous heretical leanings. Orthodox mythology claimed he was a secret Manichaean, one of those who denied Christ's material reality.[26]

Monophysite power reached its height around 511–12, with aggressively anti-Chalcedonian leaders appointed to key offices—Timotheus to the patriarchate of Constantinople, Severus to Antioch. Egypt's stubborn Copts now found that their views were becoming the church's mainstream. Severus himself wrote to Alexandria's patriarch, John, confirming that he, too, followed "the same faith of Pope Cyril and Pope Dioscorus." Alexandrian church scholars believed that God had "raised up royalty and priesthood together for the Church, in the persons of the prince Anastasius, the pious believer, and the patriarch Severus, the Excellent, clothed with light, occupant of the see of Antioch, who became a horn of salvation to the orthodox Church." In Antioch, crowds urged Severus to move further, to the outright condemnation of Chalcedon: "For a long time," they urged, "we have wanted to partake of the holy mysteries. Set our city free from the council of Chalcedon! Anathematize now this council that has turned the world upside down! The cursed Tome of Leo. . . . Whoever will not do so is a wolf and not a shepherd."[27]

Constantinople itself, though, was very difficult to control. When Anastasius tried to add the words "who was crucified for us" to the Thrice Holy, the move provoked a bloody riot in the capital, showing the popular support for Chalcedon. Leading the insurgents were the monks of the *Akoimetai*, the "unceasing" ones whose liturgies and prayers continued every day and night, without interruption. Not for the first time, protesters turned to a Theodosian woman for help, namely Anicia Juliana, a granddaughter of the Western emperor Valentinian III. Using the suicidally daring slogan "Another emperor for Rome!" anti-Monophysites tried to bring in her husband as the successor to Anastasius, but he wisely refused the offer. The repression that followed was unsurprisingly brutal, given the scale of the emergency and the narrowness of the regime's escape. "Many perished under torture and many were thrown into the sea."[28]

By 500 or so, the churches were in absolute doctrinal disarray, a state of chaos that might seem routine to a modern American denomination, but which in the context of the time seemed like satanic anarchy. This is the account of the church historian Evagrius:

the synod of Chalcedon was neither openly proclaimed in the most holy churches, nor yet was repudiated by all: but the bishops acted each according to his individual opinion. Thus, some very resolutely maintained what had been put forth by that synod, and would not yield to the extent of one word of its determinations, nor admit even the change of a single letter, but firmly declined all contact and communion with those who refused to admit the matters there set forth. Others, again, not only did not submit to the synod of Chalcedon and its determinations, but even anathematized both it and the Tome of Leo.[29]

Stern mutual acts of exclusion and excommunication divided the Christian world:

> the Eastern bishops had no friendly intercourse with those of the West and Africa, nor the latter with those of the East. The evil too became still more monstrous, for neither did the presidents of the eastern churches allow communion among themselves, nor yet those who held the sees of Europe and Africa, much less with those of remote parts.[30]

Religious violence could break out seemingly at any time and place. To suggest the tone of conflict in this era, we might take a story from Syria. Around 512, Antioch's patriarch, Flavian, came under heavy Monophysite pressure, which eventually forced Anastasius to depose and exile him. Decades later, some old eyewitnesses reported the horrors surrounding the conflict. One firebrand was the Monophysite bishop Philoxenus, an old disciple of Peter the Fuller. Philoxenus galvanized the monks from many miles around to storm Antioch. They "rushed into the city in a body with great noise and tumult, trying to compel Flavian to anathematize the synod of Chalcedon and the Tome of Leo." But the invasion appalled the city's people, whether out of loyalty to Flavian or simple disgust at these savage attackers. The citizens "made a great slaughter of [the monks], so that a very large number found a grave in the Orontes, where the waves performed their only funeral rites." We don't know what "a very large number" would mean in this context, but the phrase must at a minimum refer to some dozens of fatalities.[31]

Just as it seemed that nothing could save the settlement proclaimed at Chalcedon, once again, political accident came to the rescue. In 518, Anastasius died, to be succeeded as emperor by the illiterate general Justin. As Justin favored Chalcedon, the regime once again began its game of musical dioceses, purging bishops who refused to conform to the new order and appointing

or restoring loyal Chalcedonians. Justin also ended the schism between Rome and Constantinople. Monophysites remembered him
as Justin the Terrible.

Saving Chalcedon

At the time, the change of 518 looked like just another phase in a
game that really need have no ending. It seemed quite plausible that
Orthodox and Monophysite emperors might replace each other
randomly through the centuries to come, and any religious believer
who was temporarily out of sympathy with one regime knew that
the best response was patience, to await the rise of a new, friendlier
court. Only long after the event could it be seen that Justin's accession marked the beginning of a long-reigning dynasty, one friendly
to Chalcedon. From 518 through 602, this Justinianic dynasty ruled
long enough—and asserted the principles of Chalcedon strongly
enough—to create a sense of inevitable imperial support for that
particular version of orthodoxy.

Also different in scale was the repression that the new regime was
prepared to use to secure its position. Securing the armed forces was a
vital first step, and soldiers had to agree to Chalcedon as a precondition
of receiving rations. Then it was the church's turn. Over fifty bishops
were deposed or exiled in Syria and Asia Minor alone, including the
holders of some of the greatest sees. In Syria, anti-Chalcedonians were
persecuted in 519, 532, and 536, leaving an obvious sense that this pattern would recur. Monophysite writers noted grimly the appearance of
a comet in 519, a cosmic harbinger that accurately foretold the dreadful events to come. God's vengeance against the persecutors was still
more explicit in the great Antioch earthquake of 526, which reputedly
killed hundreds of thousands. Anyone who failed to read God's anger
in such tokens and wonders simply did not understand the principles
of scientific observation.[32]

Paul the Jew, who succeeded Severus as patriarch of Antioch, was
a notorious persecutor of Monophysites. One Nature believers

"had to leave their monasteries, were robbed, captured, put in irons, locked up in prisons, brought before courts and subjected to various tortures." They were forced to hide in the countryside, to take refuge on exposed hillsides and caves, always in danger of being hunted down.[33] Other bishops were even more savage, acting in ways that foreshadowed the pogroms and heresy hunts of the High Middle Ages. In the great eastern city of Amida, the new bishop, Abraham, burned and crucified those who defied him, using his soldiers to force communion bread into the mouths of the reluctant. One priest who resisted even these efforts was remembered ever after under the heroic name of Cyrus the Spitter—although Cyrus himself was burned alive shortly afterward.[34]

The Great Schisms

In the face of these persecutions, Monophysites acknowledged a sense of permanent exclusion, and restructured accordingly. By the mid-sixth century, vast sections of the once-united Christian church had seceded from the Great Church allied to the empire. The Christian world was now a patchwork of rival churches, each regarding itself as the only authentic body of Christ.

The first grouping to achieve independent status was the Church of the East, commonly known as the Nestorian church, which refused to accept the decisions of First Ephesus. The Church of the East maintained its loyalty to Nestorius, who it regarded as a maligned Father of learning and holiness. As one later disciple commemorated Nestorius,

So you undertook the labor of a long voyage from the East to the West to give light to the souls that were plunged in the darkness of the Egyptian error, and intent on the smoke of the blasphemy of Apollinarius. Men, however, loved the darkness more than the light, since the eyes of their minds were dimmed by personal prejudice.[35]

The church kept alive scholarly works that were suspect in the Roman Christian world.

What allowed the Nestorians so much freedom of action was that their most important centers were in the Eastern Syriac world, in eastern Syria, Mesopotamia, and Persia. These regions were either wholly independent from imperial control or at worst only occasionally under Roman influence. As the old Antiochene theology fell under ever greater suspicion within the Roman world, scholars and theologians retreated further east, particularly to Edessa, where Ibas had founded a prestigious school. In 489, though, the emperor Zeno tried to destroy the movement as part of his attempt to win Monophysite sympathy. The school now relocated from Edessa to Nisibis in Mesopotamia, an ancient Christian center. Its followers were thus under the power of the Persian Empire, the rival superpower of the day, and by the late fifth century the movement enjoyed a fair degree of toleration. In 498, the church's head was officially declared patriarch of Babylon, although his actual seat was at the Persian imperial capital of Seleucia/Ctesiphon. In the early seventh century, the great scholar and mystic Mar Babai was able to use this independence from Rome to undertake a systematic rethinking of Two Nature theology, while reorganizing church structures. Although scarcely known in the West, Babai the Great was intellectually on a par with any of the famous church fathers.[36]

Although they remained a minority within an empire that officially followed the Zoroastrian faith, this Persian context gave the church the potential for huge geographical expansion, with missions deep into Central Asia—into Kyrgyzstan, Turkmenistan, and Afghanistan. By the start of the seventh century, the Nestorians were pushing into China, and other missionaries followed sea routes to India and Sri Lanka.[37]

But the Nestorians were not the only church that evolved free from the power of Constantinople and Rome. Other open schisms followed, fulfilling the worst possible nightmares of the era of Ephesus and Chalcedon. Egypt was already operating in de facto independence, and the Western Syriac churches were not far behind, as Monophysite clergy appointed by Anastasius established lasting power bases. And although the long period of imperial sympathy for Monophysite thinking ended in 518, that theological school adapted to changed circumstances rather than simply fading away.[38]

By far the most important figure in the new movement was Severus, patriarch of Antioch from 512 to 518, who became the patron saint of the Monophysite cause. Historian W. H. C. Frend reasonably calls him "one of the great figures of the religious history of the eastern Mediterranean," which is quite a claim when we think of the people he is being compared with. We may recall him for his absolute rejection of any and all worldly comforts, including beds, or any food that might please the palate. Severus's career illustrates not just the extraordinary dedication of the Monophysite cause, but also the creation of whole alternative structures. Born in Pisidia, in Asia Minor, he become a monk near Gaza, in the heart of the territory dominated by Peter the Iberian. Severus joined a house founded and run by the most rigid followers of Eutyches and One Nature belief.[39] So extreme was Severus that he rejected the Henoticon and denounced Alexandria's Peter Mongus for accepting it. Bloodshed generally followed in Severus's wake, initially at Alexandria, where he stirred violence between Orthodox and Monophysites, and then similar events followed at Constantinople. As patriarch of Antioch, he systematically persuaded or forced his inferior clergy to follow his line. Severus created another precedent in his policy of strictness (*akribeia*), which meant prohibiting his followers from taking communion at the hands of Chalcedonian clergy.[40]

When Justin took power in 518, Severus fled Antioch rather than face arrest and worse: Justin ordered his tongue cut out for sedition. Significantly, his followers continued to regard him as the legitimate patriarch until his death in about 538, creating yet another schism in a great jurisdiction. So influential was he that the empire decreed that anyone possessing Severus's writings must burn them immediately, and those who did not would lose their right hands. In later years, Severus achieved a transnational position something like that of the pope among the Catholic churches. It is mainly due to him that by the 530s, the Monophysites in various lands and speaking different languages were beginning to act in concert. They were coming to look like an alternative global church.[41]

During the last years of Anastasius, Egypt, too, was becoming a liberated zone for One Nature dissidents, and it was the obvious place for Severus to seek exile. One watershed occurred in 516, when the Monophysite-leaning emperor appointed a like-minded patriarch of Alexandria—but the mob there still rejected him just on the grounds that he was the representative of the corrupt *archontes*, the rulers. In the context, the word refers to Roman imperial authorities, but there were precedents for reading it as the diabolical forces ruling the material world. Between the emperor and the devil, there did not seem to be too sharp a line drawn. The events of 516 amounted almost to an open declaration of independence by the Egyptian church, which adopted Monophysitism as a national religion.[42]

Justinian

In 527, Justin was succeeded by his nephew Justinian, who would rule for almost forty years. He began his reign anxious to soothe tensions between the pro- and anti-Chalcedonians and gave some favor to Monophysite clergy. From the mid-530s, though, he swung decisively toward the Chalcedonian side. Partly, this was because his great wars of reconquest were restoring Roman power over substantial areas of the old Western empire—Italy, North Africa, even southern Spain—so that the empire once again had to take account of Western sensibilities. Under pressure from the Roman pope, Justinian deposed the Monophysite-inclined patriarch of Constantinople, Anthimus. He followed up with a purge of the great sees "so that from that time forward, the synod at Chalcedon was openly proclaimed in all the churches; and no one dared to anathematize it; while those who dissented, were urged by innumerable methods to assent to it."[43]

Justinian's actions in Alexandria marked a historic break. Ever since Peter Mongus's time, the patriarchate had been united in a single office controlled by Monophysites, ruling over pro- and anti-Chalcedonians. The last person to hold this united post was Theodosius, but Justinian deposed him in 536, and the patriarch spent decades imprisoned in Constantinople. Thereafter, the Coptic and Chalcedonian patriarchates would never again be unified, and the two churches would have different, competing successions.[44]

But Justinian's position was rather more complicated than this account might suggest, and once again, court women played a pivotal role. If Justinian was committed to defending Chalcedon, his queen, Theodora, was just as sympathetic to the Monophysite cause. This split mattered so much because Theodora was such an extraordinarily powerful figure in her own right, virtually a coemperor. Personally brilliant, she was a very influential figure at court and a wonderful asset for dissident church leaders.

So balanced between the two positions was Justinian's court—so much was it, so to speak, a union between two distinct persons and two natures—that we might ask whether this division was a matter of accident or policy. Perhaps Theodora was just a strong figure in her own right, who refused to be cowed by her husband, but conceivably, the two agreed to maintain their differences for political reasons. While Justinian ruled as the most orthodox emperor, attracting the faithful support of all Chalcedonians, Theodora provided a useful safety valve, a friend at court to whom Monophysites knew they could turn. That reduced the need for dissidents to venture into rebellion or plotting coups. However unlikely such a calculation may seem, the historian Evagrius actually implies such a conscious policy choice.[45]

The Fifth Council

In other ways, too, Justinian tried to keep open avenues of communication with the Monophysites. In the 540s, the emperor was concerned about the continuing popularity of the radical and mystical theological ideas of the third-century Alexandrian father Origen, whose theories enjoyed a long afterlife. But attacking Origenism promised a political bonus for an emperor with his particular religious difficulties. Just suppose that Origen's ideas could be linked to some of the fifth-century theologians who had been the main exponents of Two Nature theory, to Theodore of Mopsuestia, Theodoret of Cyrrhus, and Ibas of Edessa. What better way to win over the believers in One Nature than to denounce their oldest and most loathed enemies?

Accordingly, in 543, Justinian proposed a statement denouncing the Three Chapters, a highly selective collection of texts that expressed the most daring and controversial ideas of these theologians. All three, of course,—Theodore, Theodoret, and Ibas—had been the recurring bugbears of the Cyrillians, who saw them as Nestorians. The appearance of Ibas and Theodoret at Chalcedon had incited a near riot. Finally, almost a century later, Justinian would strike at the memory of the long-dead trio, and particularly the writings in which they attacked the sainted Cyril. He would show the Monophysites once and for all that a strong wall of separation existed between Chalcedon and the Nestorians. Ideally, it would be a splendid gesture of reconciliation.[46]

But Justinian had failed to learn the most basic lesson of church politics in this era: let sleeping councils lie. When he tried to enlist the current pope Vigilius in this cause, he found the pope nervous about what amounted to a posthumous trial of men who could no longer defend themselves. Vigilius also knew that two of the three had been vindicated and restored by Chalcedon, and he had no wish to revive that argument. The popes saw the defense of Chalcedon as an absolute principle, fighting any attempt to weaken even its most marginal provisions, and most Western churches agreed with that position. The thoroughly unnecessary religious dispute rapidly evolved into a quarrel between emperor and pope. The battle included, in 547, the pope's forcible detention in Constantinople and his later exile.[47]

In 553, the emperor convened a gathering at Constantinople that was recognized as the Fifth General Council, the successor to Chalcedon. The gathering attracted some 160 bishops, overwhelmingly from the East, as Justinian's prolonged wars had devastated what remained of Roman society in Italy and Africa. Eventually, the council gave Justinian what he wanted and restated the hypostatic union in even more clearly Cyrilline terms. But the victory gained him next to nothing in the East, and even cost him a new schism of some Italian provinces.[48]

Remarkably, this affair did nothing to quench Justinian's thirst for religious quarrels. So bizarre did his behavior become, in fact, that it lends support to the contemporary view of the historian Procopius, who saw the emperor as a flaky megalomaniac who governed soundly only when he listened to his wife. Theodora died, however, in 548, and from that point onward Justinian became visibly older and crazier. In his last years, he adopted his own particular heresy, an extreme fringe of Monophysite belief that was too outrageous for most One Nature believers and even harked back to Eutyches. This was the school of the *Aphthartodocetae* or Incorruptibles, who held that Christ's body was always incorruptible. Fortunately, the emperor died just as he was on the point of trying to impose the weird doctrine on the whole church and of inciting further chaos.

The New Monophysite Church

Although Chalcedon triumphed under Justinian, Theodora's court became a refuge for Monophysites and a center for organization. She fostered monasteries and convents for the hundreds of religious expelled from religious houses across Syria and Asia Minor, establishments that survived untouched for decades. She was reputedly responsible for appointing Anthimus as patriarch of Constantinople in 535, although he was associated with the ultra-hard-line Severus. After Anthimus was deposed the following year, he took refuge in her palace for twelve years. She protected Severus himself, and she hosted Theodosius, the exiled patriarch of Alexandria, who made Constantinople the seat of a virtual government in exile well into the 560s.[49]

The religious division became more rigid and formalized from the 540s, partly because of the cumulative disasters striking the civilized world. The year 541 marked the onset of a wide-ranging plague comparable to the notorious Black Death of the fourteenth century. Reportedly, three hundred thousand died in Constantinople alone. Over the course of several decades the disease killed millions across Europe, Asia, and Africa, weakening empires already stretched to the breaking point by decades of warfare. This was a catastrophic moment in the history of the ancient world, one of the critical transition points to the much poorer and more localized world of the Middle Ages.[50] It also had its religious consequences in a society thoroughly used to reading divine signs. Each side, Chalcedonian and Monophysite, recognized how offended God was by any tokens of religious compromise. Further polarizing the two sides was Theodora's death, which destroyed the last hopes of the Monophysites. By this point, even optimists could no longer deny that the empire had abandoned what they saw as true Christianity.

The main activist was the Syrian Jacobus Baradaeus—Hobo Jake—who succeeded Severus as the builder of the Monophysite church in Syria and the East. Early in Justinian's reign, Jacobus and some colleagues had gone to Constantinople to plead with Theodora on behalf of Monophysite clergy exiled or imprisoned throughout the East. From the early 540s, he operated as a bishop based in Edessa, which he used as a missionary center.

He evangelized far and wide for what was in effect a new or reborn church, which is commonly known as Jacobite. By some accounts, he ordained literally thousands of clergy and created a new church hierarchy. When he consecrated a new patriarch of Antioch in 544, he ensured that that city, too, would have a permanent schism between rival hierarchies, favoring or opposing Chalcedon, just as had occurred at Alexandria. At Ephesus in 558, he appointed as alternative bishop, one John, whose fiercely partisan writings are a major source for the period. After Theodosius of Alexandria died in 566, John became effective head of the Monophysite party.[51]

By the end of that century, a Jacobite church extended its power over much of Syria and the East, besides the great church of Egypt. And besides the celebrities—the bishops and patriarchs— many lesser monks and clergy were forming what would become a thriving Monophysite culture, a whole world of alternative Christian writing and thought. This world cultivated such familiar expressions of devotion as the lives of saints and martyrs and a whole separate tradition of Christian history writing. They glorified heroes of the faith like Severus and Peter the Iberian. Just as the founding fathers of Christian historiography commemorated the sufferings of martyrs in the face of pagan power, so their successors told of the atrocities inflicted on the saints by the wicked pseudo-Christian empire. The new church also evolved new linguistic patterns. While Greek remained the core language of Christianity, Syrian Monophysites moved heavily to Syriac as the natural language of their church, just as Egyptian Monophysites relied ever more on Coptic.[52]

These organizations also freely extended their power beyond the notional frontiers of the Roman world. Just as Egyptian Christianity dominated neighboring African kingdoms, so Syrian believers had their own distinct sphere of influence in the East. In Armenia, two councils of Dvin (506 and 554) officially rejected Chalcedon and brought that church within the now vast Monophysite network.[53]

Repression

Given the theological views of the time, it would have been unthinkable for the Christian Roman Empire to tolerate separate denominations, but individual emperors varied greatly in how strictly to enforce Chalcedonian orthodoxy. Conditions for the Monophysites grew harsher under Justinian's successor, Justin II. He was a deeply troubled individual who fell ever deeper into insanity: reputedly, he sought to soothe his agonies by having the palace filled constantly with blaring organ music. Long before that stage, however, he tried to eliminate the Monophysite issue once and for all, using as his chief agent the patriarch of Constantinople, John Scholasticus. A learned man, John struggled to find a formula that would satisfy both sides. Briefly, he seemed to have squared the circle, and in 571 he actually achieved a kind of reunion and reconciliation. Tranquility lasted precisely a year, until the Monophysites condemned Chalcedon once more.[54]

According to Monophysite accounts, John then became a savage persecutor, and in that tradition his memory took on demonic form.

> In an angry decree, he commanded that all the places where the [Monophysite] believers assembled should be shut up, the altars in them razed, their priests and bishops seized and cast into prison, and all who met there for worship driven away and dispersed, and commanded never to enter them again.[55]

Monophysite historian John of Ephesus listed the persecutions inflicted upon his fellow believers in these years, the bishops deposed or forced to conform. In one incident, the patriarch demanded the conformity of Stephanos, bishop of Cyprus. The story may or may not be true—John had no interest in writing fair or objective history—but it gives an idea of what the different sides believed of their enemies. Somehow or other, Stephanos had to be forced to take the communion bread that would show his adherence to Chalcedon. Allegedly, the patriarch sent clergy and guards

> with orders to beat him with clubs, until he vomited blood, or consented to their communion. Twelve of them accordingly beat him until he fell down speechless in the midst, and lay apparently dead. But on seeing him lie motionless, and dying as it seemed, they ran, and brought four pails of water, which they dashed over him, and so after a long time his soul returned to him again, and he returned to life as from the dead. And thus by force he was compelled to submit to communion with them.[56]

Persecution reached the stage of invalidating the clerical orders of the Monophysites, who had to be reordained if they wished to continue in the priesthood. This was a serious step indeed, a frightening legal innovation that struck at the principle of apostolic succession. However wrong they might be theologically—or at least however far removed from the views of the establishment—Monophysite clergy clearly stemmed from the same church and looked back to the same sequences of venerated saints and clergy from whom they derived their authority. Was this now to be invalidated by imperial command? If so, that represented an irrevocable breach between the two sides. As Bishop Stephanos protested, "Woe! woe! Christianity is ruined! The regulations of the Christian church are overthrown. All the constitutions and canons of the church of God are confounded and trampled under foot, and are undone!"[57] Although Stephanos had been canonically ordained and had served as bishop for twenty years, he was now to be "deposed from the priesthood of the orthodox" and reordained. Ultimately the patriarch stepped back from this extreme measure, but the affair left a bitter legacy of ill-feeling.

Not all emperors ruled with anything like this degree of ferocity, and some were reluctant to treat Christians in ways that should only be confined to the church's enemies. When the patriarch tried to continue the persecutions under the new emperor, Tiberius II, he found a frosty reception. If they were Christians, said Tiberius, he would not act against them: "Why," he asked, "do you urge me to persecute Christians, as if I were a Diocletian, or one of those old heathen kings? Go, sit in your church, and be quiet, and do not trouble me again with such things." But Tiberius was exceptional. From the 560s onward, the "true orthodox Christians"—or the Monophysites, as their enemies called them—were the regular targets of persecution and discrimination.[58]

The Threat to the East

One hundred fifty years after Chalcedon, the Christian world seemed to be at an impasse. While the Monophysites knew that realistically they could never win over the empire, the Orthodox also knew that they could not eliminate the dissidents, who were not just going to wither away.

Religious divisions on this scale were deadly dangerous politically when dissidence was concentrated in eastern portions of the empire that served as heavily garrisoned military frontiers. Roman rivalry with Persia was not new. In 260 the Persians had captured the emperor Valerian, whose stuffed body long remained on exhibit as a trophy at the Persian court. Wars persisted over the following centuries, with the advantage swinging sometimes to Rome, sometimes to Persia. But the intensity of conflict escalated mightily during the sixth century, and so did the prizes at stake. Instead of just battling over debated border provinces like Armenia and Mesopotamia, the two empires were engaged in an epic struggle for survival. Throughout the sixth and early seventh centuries, the Persians pressed hard on the heart of the Eastern empire—on Syria and Palestine, Asia Minor and even Egypt. The wars had an explicitly religious quality, as the Persians grounded their claims for expansion in their Zoroastrian faith; each side fought for the greater glory of its God. Conquests were often accompanied by acts of destruction and massacre explicitly directed against the other side's faith, against (respectively) churches and Zoroastrian fire temples. Politically and religiously, this was an endgame.[59]

Bitter wars raged during 502–5, 527–32, and 540–45, and fighting was endemic from 572 through 591. Generally, the Persians did a superb job of maintaining and expanding their position. They fought as an advanced state with the best technology of the day, all the latest engineering and siege machines, and they had the advantages of discipline and strategy that Western barbarian forces generally lacked. Foreshadowing the knightly warfare of the Middle Ages, the Persians also made devastating use of their massed heavy cavalry, the riders, *cataphractarii*, clad in effective armor.[60]

Some Persian successes caused real panic around what was left of the Roman world. In 540, the Persians ravaged Syria, sacking and looting some of the greatest centers of early Christianity. They utterly destroyed Antioch, carrying off tens of thousands of its residents. This was only a few years after the city was crippled by a great earthquake. Although Justinian sought to rebuild Antioch after the Persian conquest, it never recovered fully. In ruining Syria's traditional outlet on the Mediterranean, the disaster also turned the area more toward the east, in terms of culture and economy. In so doing, it reoriented the Syrian church toward the harder-line Monophysite regions of the interior.[61]

The Roman situation all but collapsed early in the seventh century. When Heraclius took the throne in 610, he had to confront what looked like a near-terminal crisis, with the Persians pressing hard on the eastern frontier. Meanwhile, the barbarian Avars— kin to the Huns—were sweeping through the Balkans. In 614, the Persians captured Jerusalem, which was subject to a horrendous massacre: "the evil Persians, who had no pity in their hearts, raced to every place in the city and with one accord extirpated all the people." Men, women and children were mowed down "like cabbages."

Holy churches were burned with fire, other were demolished, majestic altars fell prone, sacred crosses were trampled underfoot, life-giving icons were spat upon by the unclean. Then their wrath fell upon priests and deacons; they slew them in their churches like dumb animals.[62]

Persians even carried off what was believed to be the True Cross itself, the most precious relic in all Christendom. They overran Syria and Asia Minor, reaching as far west as Chalcedon itself, and they invaded Egypt. At the height of the crisis, Constantinople was besieged by tens of thousands of Avars, supported by the Persian navy. The Persians were coming close to supplanting the Roman Empire.[63]

If not for the military genius of Heraclius, the Roman story would have ended at that point. As it was, he succeeded in decisively rolling back Persian power and restoring Roman rule over most of the Middle East by the late 620s. Heraclius was arguably the greatest Roman leader and general since the height of the united Empire. But just as he looked back to the most potent Roman values, so he behaved like a medieval crusader king, pledged to the service of the Mother of God.[64]

This was, then, a desperately dangerous time for Roman power in the East, and specifically for Christians. Apart from the impact of prolonged war and plague, the Christian world was entering a frighteningly bleak era of shrinking opportunities and intense strains. Although Persia was defeated, large portions of the Eastern world were economically devastated and depopulated, with a crushing tax burden on surviving communities. It was a very bad time indeed to have most of the population of Egypt, Syria, Palestine, and Mesopotamia in varying degrees of disaffection from the empire, verging on open revolt.[65]

Failure of the Will

In a last-ditch attempt to reunite the empire's factions, Heraclius sought a new solution to the ancient dispute over Christ's nature. No obvious answers presented themselves. Theologians had wrestled exhaustively with the question of persons and natures, and almost any formulation or compromise was guaranteed to infuriate somebody. All that remained was to sidestep the basic problem. Put in simple terms, the empire now proposed new grounds for agreement that ignored the issue of One Nature or Two Natures. But could not everyone agree that Christ had just one will? Or as Constantinople's patriarch Sergius declared, Chalcedon was right in defining the hypostatic union: the person of Christ really did unite two natures, one divine and one human. But after that, Christ had only one will, which was divine: one will, and one *energeia* or operation.[66]

About 626, Heraclius raised his new scheme with Bishop Cyrus, who would become a principal ally in the attempt to win back Monophysites. Hearing that the new theological compromise had Sergius's support, Cyrus offered his backing, and so did the Roman pope, Honorius. In 630, Cyrus was sent to Egypt as both patriarch and prefect, and he enjoyed remarkable success in winning over Coptic bishops and clergy. As later Coptic historians complained, "a countless number of them went astray, some of them through persecution, and some by bribes and honors, and some by persuasion and deceit." The Coptic patriarch Benjamin went into hiding.[67]

Monotheletism had staying power, backed as it was by two of the most powerful and ambitious late Roman emperors: Heraclius himself and his grandson and successor Constans II. Heraclius had saved the empire, and his prestige allowed him to declare the new doctrine formally in his *Ekthesis* (the "Exposition" of the Faith) of 638. Constans was another strong ruler, who in 663 became the first Eastern "Roman emperor" in two centuries actually to visit Rome.[68]

Soon, though, both Chalcedonians and Monophysites denounced the new doctrine as yet another unsavory new heresy. Mennas, brother of the Coptic patriarch Benjamin, led a revolt in Egypt, precipitating some of the worst persecutions in a long and bloody story and helping to ensure Chalcedon's place in the Coptic annals of infamy. Mennas was duly martyred. Imperial forces

> caused lighted torches to be held to his sides until the fat of his body oozed forth and flowed upon the ground, and knocked out his teeth because he confessed the faith; and finally commanded that a sack should be filled with sand, and the holy Mennas placed within it, and drowned in the sea.[69]

His death was suitably trinitarian, a kind of execution by baptism. Three times he was submerged and half-drowned, and each time he was asked if he would concede the truth of Chalcedon, until finally he perished. "Thus they were unable to vanquish this champion, Mennas, but he conquered them by his Christian patience."[70] Cyrus's regime seized many Coptic churches and gave them to loyal believers.

If the new synthesis failed to win over the Monophysites, it was sufficiently friendly to One Nature theory to appall the Orthodox. For one thing, the new school traced its origins to the work of Severus of Antioch, the ultimate Monophysite role model. From 633, the monk Sophronius campaigned against the Monotheletes, and he gained a powerful platform for his views the following year when he became patriarch of Jerusalem. Like the Henoticon before it, a policy designed to provide a platform for union proved only to create wholly new divisions. In 648, Constans's *Typus* tried to forbid further discussion of the natures of Christ. In modern American terms, the age-old war was to be ended by a simple policy of "Don't ask, don't tell."

The chief opponent of the new policy was Maximus, a former imperial official who had retired to a monastery. In 626, however, the Persian invasion drove him to seek refuge in North Africa, where he became a disciple of Sophronius and learned the evils of the Monothelete argument. How, he asked, can we possibly speak of any kind of human nature without a human will? Maximus now went into public opposition, debating the new patriarch of Constantinople so effectively that the patriarch recanted his position. Maximus then moved to Rome, where he mobilized support against One Will teachings. In 649, a council held in the Lateran condemned Monothelete beliefs, although that condemnation ran flat contrary to the wishes of the empire. That action, which the emperor saw as ecclesiastical mutiny, was what precipitated the attack of 653 and the deaths of Martin and Maximus.

And yet again, an imperial attempt to create harmony would collapse in ruin. Finally, in 680, a new emperor called yet another council—the sixth, held once more in Constantinople. This gathering rejected the Monothelete position and reasserted Chalcedonian orthodoxy. In the process, it also condemned a number of heretics who had advanced Monothelete positions, or given in to them, including Cyrus of Alexandria. Another of the names subjected to anathema was the Roman pope, Honorius, who had died in 638. This condemnation had lasting implications for future debates over papal power, as a clear example of a pope being not merely in error but in outright heresy, and moreover the Roman church acknowledged this fact. This precedent would cause real problems for nineteenth-century advocates of papal infallibility. But that was a debate for another millennium.[71]

Islam at the Gates

The year 681 marked an important anniversary, as it was exactly three hundred years since the Council of Constantinople, which had initiated the long series of debates over the natures of Christ. And after three long centuries of running arguments and mutual denunciations, all the schisms and defections, it might well have

seemed that such internal fights would never end, that the old debates would return endlessly in ever more intricate recycled forms.
But the cycle was, in fact, about to be broken decisively. The sixth
council gathered in Constantinople to debate natures and wills only
very shortly after the new force of Islam had literally been at the
gates. From 674 through 678, Constantinople had been subjected to
yet another siege, this time by Muslim forces.

While the empire was sunk in its religious feuds, other forces
were stirring in the Middle East, especially in the Arabian peninsula,
then an undesirable no-man's-land between Rome and Persia. About
610, a Meccan named Muhammad believed that he had received
prophetic visions demanding that all peoples acknowledge their
submission (*Islam*) to the one almighty God. Those people who accepted the creed of Islam were known as Muslims. Following his
divine mission, Muhammad sent proclamations to the world's most
powerful leaders, including Heraclius, who found the new faith
quite appealing—or so later Muslim legend claimed. Muhammad, in
turn, strongly sympathized with the Romans against the Persians,
whom he regarded as pagan enemies, and he was shocked when the
heathen Persians took Jerusalem.[72]

After Muhammad's death in 632, his followers launched a mighty
series of wars against the great empires of the day, which were, of
course, exhausted by decades of warfare. Within a spectacularly
short period of just twenty years, Arab Muslim forces had absorbed
Persia and Mesopotamia to the east, while in the west they had conquered Egypt, Syria, and Palestine. In itself, this firestorm did not
necessarily mark a radical new phase in history. Other states and
barbarian tribes had previously overrun large portions of the
Roman Empire, before being either defeated or themselves being
absorbed into Roman culture, religion, and society. Even direct
sieges of Constantinople were nothing new. But by the 680s, it was
obvious that this movement was indeed something different, a new
kind of religion and civilization that seemed set to rival the Roman
Empire, and quite likely to supplant it.[73]

The story of Islam's rise is familiar enough, but, in fact, it is difficult to understand except in the context of the Christian divisions of the time. For one thing, Islam developed in a society pervaded by Jewish and Christian influences, and "Christian" in this context was overwhelmingly likely to mean Monophysite or Nestorian. Early Muslim traditions recalled Muhammad's interaction with Christians and Christian clergy, while Christian propaganda against Islam presented Muhammad as a crude plagiarist who freely stole his ideas from the older religion. As it stands, such an idea is wildly oversimplified, but some curious Christian themes do appear in the Quran's treatment of Jesus. While absolutely denying the divinity of Christ, the Quran presents a Jesus who looks very much like the figure familiar in the Syriac-speaking churches. The Quran follows the Docetic view that the crucifixion of Jesus was an illusion: "They did not slay him, and neither did they crucify him, but it only seemed to them [as if it had been] so . . . God exalted [Jesus] unto Himself."[74]

Christian divisions also go far toward explaining the swift collapse of the Roman position in the Middle East, where popular sentiment leaned so heavily toward either the Monophysite and Nestorian churches. Repeatedly, writers from these traditions describe the relief with which local inhabitants greeted the Arab conquerors, who promised an end to the heavy-handed regime of the Roman Empire, and the Chalcedonian order. Even as they bemoaned the bloodshed associated with the conquest, most Egyptians were happy to see the back of the defeated governor, Cyrus, and the restoration of the exiled Coptic patriarch Benjamin.[75]

Some Christian writers—Monophysite and Nestorian—saw the Arabs as God's scourge, the weapon he chose in order to punish the empire for its theological blunders and its brutality toward its true-believing opponents. The *History of the Alexandrian Patriarchs* comments that "the Lord abandoned the army of the Romans before him, as a punishment for their corrupt faith, and because of the anathemas uttered against them, on account of the council of

Chalcedon, by the ancient fathers." John of Nikiu recorded the defeats suffered by "Heraclius, the emperor of the Chalcedonians."[76]

At least in the early decades of the new order, most Christians saw little reason to change their opinion. Muslims cared nothing for the sectarian divisions among their Christian subjects, provided they respected Muslim authority and paid their taxes on time. Moreover, the Muslims needed skilled Christians of every kind—scribes and notaries, architects and metalworkers. The first century or so after the conquest marked something like a golden age for the Christian communities, who were now free of Roman oppression.

Egypt's Coptic church now achieved everything it had been fighting for since the time of Cyril and Dioscuros. One great patriarch, Benjamin, reigned from 622 to 661. In his time, the Chalcedonian church collapsed, and its properties reverted to Coptic control. Remaining Chalcedonian believers faced a desperate dilemma, having either to accept Coptic authority or abandon Christianity altogether. Some at least took the second option, accepting Islam as the only way they had left of continuing the fight against their ancient Monophysite foes. Once they had "accepted the detestable doctrine of the Beast, that is, Mohammed," they "took arms in their hands and fought against the Christians. And one of them, named John, the Chalcedonian of the Convent of Sinai, embraced the faith of Islam, and quitting his monk's habit he took up the sword, and persecuted the Christians who were faithful to our Lord Jesus Christ."[77] The Copts triumphed—but at what a cost!

In Syria and Mesopotamia, Jacobite and Nestorian churches enjoyed peace and prestige. By the eighth century, the Jacobite church included perhaps 150 archbishops and bishops. Under Muslim rule, the different anti-Chalcedonian churches moved to create more formal alliances and mergers. In 728, a council formally established communion between the Armenian church and the Jacobites, who formed a solid anti-Chalcedonian front.[78]

But political salvation came at an exorbitant price. For centuries, Christians survived and even flourished in Muslim-dominated societies, but steadily, the Muslim share of the population grew, while Christian communities became ever smaller minorities, subject to harsher and more discriminatory laws. Christian Alexandria increasingly became Muslim Alexandria, until thoroughly Muslim Cairo appropriated much of its wealth and glory. From the thirteenth century, a series of political and military disasters combined with economic and climatic change to create an intolerable environment for minorities, some of which were eliminated altogether.[79]

By default, then, the future of Christianity lay elsewhere. It lay in those shrinking regions still subject to the Roman Empire, which no longer had any need to conciliate the opinions of an Egypt or a Syria that it no longer tried to control. In the long run, though, the Christian future would be in those regions of Western Europe that had never defied Chalcedon. Chalcedonian ideas triumphed not because of the force of their logic, but because the world that opposed them perished.

9

What Was Saved

We shall never cease to return to this formula [of Chalcedon], because whenever it is necessary to say briefly what it is that we encounter in the ineffable truth that is our salvation, we shall always have recourse to its modest, sober clarity. But we shall only really have recourse to it (and this is not at all the same thing as simply repeating it), if it is not only our end but also our beginning.

Karl Rahner

At the end of the sixth century, a Byzantine writer told the story of a holy monk named Cyriacus, who lived near the Jordan River. The pilgrim Theophanes visited him, seeking advice, and was so impressed that he would have stayed to study and learn. The obstacle was that in his home region, Theophanes was in communion with the Nestorians. Cyriacus was appalled. How could his visitor follow such a dreadful set of beliefs, which denied the Mother of God? Well, said the pilgrim, that's all very well, but all the different groups say the same thing: unless you are in communion with us, you'll be damned. How should I know which version of the truth is correct?

Cyriacus, fortunately, was in a position to help. Come and sit in my cave, he invited, and God will reveal his truth. After long prayer, Theophanes was granted a vision of "a dark and stinking place throwing up flames of fire, and in the flames he saw Nestorius, Eutyches,

Apollinarius, Dioscuros, Severus, Arius, Origen and others like them." An angelic guide warned him frankly that this was the place reserved for heretics, blasphemers, and those who followed them. If Theophanes hoped for a better, cooler eternity, he needed to return at once to the one true mother church, the holy Catholic and apostolic Church that followed the doctrines of Chalcedon. "For I tell you," said the angel, "even if a person practices all the virtues there are, unless he believes rightly he will be crucified in this place."[1]

Later generations of believers must envy Theophanes. However stern the warnings he was given, the choices he had to make were transparently clear. Not only did he live in a world in which theological right and wrong were starkly obvious, but he was given irrefutable evidence of which set of opinions was objectively correct. His angel, at least, did not bother to explain any of the intervening stages by which the church had reached its definitions. Why, for instance, were Dioscuros and Nestorius burning in hell, and not Flavian or Leo? In more recent centuries, in contrast, these issues of process look much more troubling—so troubling, in fact, that they must raise questions about why the churches believe what they do.

Looking at history, the process of establishing orthodoxy involved a huge amount of what we might call political accident—depending on the outcome of dynastic succession, on victory or defeat in battle, on the theological tastes of key royal figures. Throughout, we are always tempted to say: if only this event had worked out differently, or this, or this. It is a story of ifs, and matters might very easily have gone another way.

For later generations of Christians—and, by implication, for other religions—that conclusion is humbling. The Christian experience includes an immense variety of different strands, different interpretations, and most find at least some justification in Scripture or tradition. Over time, a great many of these alternative forms have been labeled as heretical or actively excluded from the Christian worldview altogether, but it is not obvious why one current triumphs over another. Try as they might to develop institutions or structures to determine truth, by trusting historical authority or by seeking consensus, churches have never found a path that avoids the powerful pressures of individual ambition and political interest. If nothing else, that experience argues strongly for being tolerant about the diversity of nonessential expressions of faith. Viewed historically, we know that other versions might have succeeded, and might yet do so in times to come.

At the same time, stressing these external forces is not a simple acceptance of cynicism, a crude assertion that "might makes faith." Try as they would, many powerful secular rulers struggled to enforce their wills on the churches, to little avail. Outsiders—even those as strong as Constantine—could never twist the church into their own image unless their wishes coincided with those of sizable factions within the Christian community. For all the political intrigue involved, the fifth-century churches settled their doctrinal issues by battles and compromises fought between fellow members of those churches, clerical and lay. Christians struggled with Christians until they established what they believed to be truth.

Also, from a Christian perspective—or for other faith traditions—chance is not a valid concept. Deeply embedded in Jewish and Christian Scriptures is the idea of Providence, of God's intervening in history, often through highly improbable agents. Chalcedon offers powerful ammunition for those who accept such an interpretation, if only because the outcome of the religious debate was, in worldly terms, so very unlikely. In the context of the time, the forces pushing to make Christ a purely divine figure seemed overpowering, not least because a god-man was such a familiar concept to a society in transition from paganism. Devotional practice and iconography supported such a move, with the glorification of Christ as divine all-ruler, and his goddesslike Mother. And belief in One Nature found its strongest advocates in the oldest and greatest centers of the faith, the sources of its finest scholarship. Looking at the world fifty years or so after Chalcedon, with an empire weighted ever more heavily toward the East, only a foolhardy prophet would have given Chalcedon any chance whatever of staging a political comeback. Despite all this, though, the memory of Chalcedon revived, and its definitions prevailed, after long decades in which they seemed destined to oblivion.

Somehow, amazingly, the church preserved its belief that Christ was human as well as God. And today, that belief is the standard, official doctrine for the vast majority of Christian institutions—all Catholic and Orthodox believers as well as virtually all Protestants.

Resurrections Without End

Despite this victory, the battles of Ephesus and Chalcedon continue to be refought among people who perhaps know nothing of those original events. That is typical of Christian history, in that ideas and beliefs continue to resurface long after they have supposedly been defeated or killed. Sometimes they might survive as clandestine underground traditions, or might be rediscovered through reading and scholarly research, as we see in the modern Western revival of Gnosticism. Or perhaps the same impulses that gave rise to these movements in ancient times, the same ways of reading Scripture, still survive in later communities. Long centuries after the Roman Empire thought it had destroyed the last Arians, similar ideas reappeared in the Western world in the form of Unitarianism. Any society in which Christian believers read the historic texts of the faith and study its history, however casually, will at some point rediscover most of the ancient views of Christ and his role. The history of Christian belief is a story of resurrections without end.

For whatever reason, then, ideas and beliefs never perish utterly, and that is certainly true of the strands of belief that dominated fifth-century debate. Even when no conceivable connection exists between ancient and modern thought, the same ideas resurface unbidden. To see an example of this, look at a work by the seventeenth-century poet John Donne, by common consent one of the greatest pieces of devotional writing in the English language. In his "Good Friday, 1613. Riding Westward," Donne imagines that the rising sun that stands behind him as he travels becomes a vision of the crucified Christ. But what must strike anyone who knows the ancient christological debates is how Monophysite Donne's poem sounds in thought and language. With a couple of doctrinal exceptions, it is the sort of language that Alexandria's Dioscuros and Severus of Antioch would have loved. Had they known the poem, they would probably have insisted that church members sign on to its doctrines before being admitted to communion.

> *But that Christ on His cross did rise and fall,*
> *Sin had eternally benighted all.*
> *Yet dare I almost be glad, I do not see*
> *That spectacle of too much weight for me.*
> *Who sees God's face, that is self-life, must die;*
> *What a death were it then to see God die? . . .*
> *Could I behold those hands, which span the poles*
> *And tune all spheres at once, pierced with those holes?*
> *Could I behold that endless height, which is*
> *Zenith to us and our antipodes,*
> *Humbled below us? or that blood, which is*
> *The seat of all our souls, if not of His,*
> *Made dirt of dust, or that flesh which was worn*
> *By God for His apparel, ragg'd and torn?*[2]

Nobody can look God in the face and live, says Donne, so what dreadful fate must befall me if I witness the crucifixion—that is, if I saw the death of the God who created the heavens and still sustains them? God died. What if I actually saw the damage inflicted on the human flesh that God wore as his costume, his "apparel," on this earth? This is all very close to the standard

Monophysite version of the Thrice Holy hymn: Holy God, Holy and Mighty, Holy Immortal, Who was Crucified for Us, have mercy on us! God the Word has died!

No one has suggested that John Donne was radically unorthodox in his belief or that he had any doubts about the Chalcedonian statements he was required to agree with as a faithful clergyman of the Church of England. No secret Monophysite cells operated underground in Jacobean London, no Coptic agents. Donne had, quite independently, pursued the logic of a quite common devotion, contemplating the sufferings of Christ, to the point where his ideas and images would have gladdened the heart of Eutyches—assuming that anything ever gladdened the stern Eutyches.

Long after the fifth century, other thinkers would pursue similar courses, leading them to extreme versions of One Nature or Two Nature thought. Through the Middle Ages and beyond, the old heresies of Adoptionism and Docetism continued to thrive across Europe and the Near East. At one extreme, Dualists constituted a whole alternative church complete with a separate hierarchy. At real risk to their lives, many ordinary Christians found they could no longer accept the church's teaching that Christ had a human nature, as matter was so evidently evil and soiled. Nor, obviously, could Mary have given birth to God. Christ had one nature, which was purely divine, and his human image was a mere semblance. At most, the power of Christ visited the man Jesus and left him when he had served the higher purpose.

During the religious turmoil of the sixteenth century, new controversies revived ancient christological feuds. Martin Luther and his successors leaned toward an Alexandrian interpretation of Christ's role. Luther taught that Christ's divine and human natures experienced an interchange of divine and human qualities, a "communication of attributes," which mingled the two natures in a way that Chalcedonians forbade. Calvin, in contrast, was much more Antiochene in insisting on the reality of both natures, human as well as divine. Even more extreme ideas flourished among the extreme wing of the so-called Radical Reformation. Early Anabaptists preached that Jesus did not inherit his human flesh from Mary, but represented a body custom built by the Logos.[3]

With greater religious diversity, thinkers again explored theological paths that might once have been closed to them in order to answer the central question of Christianity: who do you say that I am? And once again, they reached answers that would have been familiar long centuries before. As believers read the New Testament, they wrestled with the apparent contradictions. If Jesus was fully God, how could his knowledge of God be limited? How could he seem to draw such distinctions between himself and the Father? Particularly in the nineteenth century, some Protestant thinkers found an explanation for this in the letter to the Philippians, and their insights continued to find followers.

In Philippians, we may recall, an ancient hymn tells how Christ, being equal with God, voluntarily emptied himself to assume human form. Since the sixteenth century, theologians have explored that idea of emptying, *kenosis*, to suggest that the Son of God deliberately gave up many of his divine attributes in order to live among us. Jesus would thus have been divine from the moment of conception, but only in his later life would he fully realize the fact. A Christ limited in that way would truthfully admit to not knowing the time of the end of the world, knowledge available only to his Father. Such a kenotic approach might even mean, as early Two Nature thinkers held, that Jesus gradually realized his true divine identity, that in a sense his Godhood really did appear in him in stages. In that way, we could vindicate the arguments of early believers like Paul of Samosata, who were long condemned as heretics but who now edge back into the Christian mainstream. We might even speculate that Christ's full divine consciousness burst upon him at the moment of his baptism in the Jordan, which the Gospels present as such a turning point in his career. As a means of interpreting Christ's identity, ideas of kenosis remain controversial, as some churches regard them as a betrayal of Chalcedonian orthodoxy; but once again, they show the stubborn persistence of subterranean currents in Christian thought.[4]

Christ Today

In modern times, too, ancient debates and creeds are much in evidence, despite the official victory of Chalcedon. The most successful of these new-old theologies is technically called Theopaschitism, the idea that one of the Trinity suffered for us (*Unus ex Trinitate passus est*). This idea surfaced early in the sixth century, as a compromise attempt to bridge the gulf separating Chalcedonians and their enemies. The formula was vindicated at the fifth council, held at Constantinople in 553, but it long remained suspect because of its suggestion that God could or did suffer, that he was passible. In the twentieth century, though, the theory went from strength to strength. In the words of one modern commentator,

> The age-old dogma that God is impassible and immutable, incapable of suffering, is for many no longer tenable. The ancient Theopaschite heresy that God suffers has, in fact, become the new orthodoxy. A list of modern Theopaschite thinkers would include Barth, Berdyaev, Bonhoeffer, Brunner, Cobb, Cone and liberation theologians generally, Küng, Moltmann, Reinhold Niebuhr, Pannenberg, Ruether and feminist theologians generally, Temple, Teilhard and Unamuno.[5]

As Christian triumphalism has foundered, as visions of Christendom faded, so Christian scholars turned increasingly to a God who suffered alongside his creation. For liberation theologians and feminists, for Christian thinkers who identify Jesus as the brother of the oppressed, the idea of a God who really suffers alongside the poor and marginalized is fundamental.

Looking at popular versions of Christianity also induces a sense of *déjà vu*, or rather, *déjà cru*—already believed. Many ordinary Christians, and cultural Christians, pay little attention to Chalcedon's subtle distinctions. Near-Monophysite views are most strongly in evidence around Christmastime. The churches officially follow Chalcedon in preaching a Christ in two natures, without confusion, change, division, or separation; but popular devotion unabashedly worships God lying in the manger. If a sixth-century Chalcedonian bishop returned to the modern world, he would devote himself to searching through the hymnbooks of most churches and tearing out the many pages in which lyrics expressed overtly One Nature ideas. For many modern believers, Christ was obviously never human enough to doubt his own credentials or mission, to fear the cross, or to fantasize, however briefly, about pursuing a quiet existence with a wife and family.

In other ways, too, modern Christians take their own sides in those bygone debates. In the ancient world, the greatest difficulty lay in persuading ordinary believers that Christ might be anything less than purely divine. In contrast, many modern believers struggle with contemplating a Jesus who is more than human. They do their best to reconcile the moral insights of the wise teacher Jesus with what they see as the supernatural encumbrances that have over time been built upon his memory. For two centuries, after all, successive modern "quests" for Jesus have sought this human reality, trying to place the figure of the Gospels ever more firmly in the historical context of Jesus' time and, by implication, with all its constraints and limitations. If Christ was divine, many feel, then this was through the man Jesus progressively developing a divine consciousness. And that process might be available to human beings who follow Christ in their own moral struggles. The One Nature principles of Eutyches and Apollinarius survive today, through the beliefs of millions who never heard their names; and so do the views of a human Jesus proposed by the Ebionites and by Paul of Samosata.

Creed or Chaos

But if the same problems recur endlessly through history, so, in theory, should the same solutions. However much we may think that modern controversies are new and unprecedented, they rarely are, and that means that looking back to past debates might well provide a mine of useful insights for the present day.[6]

This point may seem strange when past theological debates seem so abstruse that their memory can be embarrassing to modern churches. Did churches in the distant past really tear themselves apart over what today seem such verbal minutiae? We live in an age when the term *theological* has implications of irrelevant hairsplitting: "It's just a theological quibble." Still more poisonous is a word like *dogma*. Such objections to theological enterprise are not new. Do churches today fall into internecine conflict over issues of biblical authority and sexual regulations while millions of Christians starve? In the 1930s, some Anglican thinkers urged that the churches should put aside matters of technical theology, as of interest only to cloistered academics. And their proposal received a devastating answer from Dorothy Sayers, one of the great lay theologians of the age.

In her 1940 essay *Creed or Chaos*, Sayers tried to explain just why such theological debates and questioning should not be set aside, but rather should remain central to what the church did. For one thing, she argued, the fact that we today regard all these great issues of Christology as trivial or technical means that all these questions have been settled through the strivings of earlier generations. We live on the accumulated cultural and intellectual capital of those earlier thinkers—of Athanasius, Cyril, Leo and the rest—without whom the church would have fallen into moral and spiritual chaos far worse than anything recorded in historical times. The orthodoxy they established is the firm foundation of all modern churches, which we ignore at our peril.[7]

But Sayers also pointed out that, however much moderns might despise theology, ordinary people actually devoted a great deal of effort to theological speculation, and the conclusions they reached usually reproduced the very ideas that had been confronted in the fifth and sixth centuries. Far from sidelining theology, modern churches needed constantly to reexamine and restate the grounds of their belief.

Christology was central to Sayers' argument. The church proclaimed Christ as God and man, but what did that mean to many ordinary believers "except that God the Creator (the irritable old gentleman with the beard) in some mysterious manner fathered upon the Virgin Mary something amphibious, neither one thing nor t'other, like a merman?"[8] Sayers cites several popular views of Christ's nature and shows how faithfully they reproduce ideas like Nestorianism or Eutychianism. For the latter case, she plausibly imagines a modern Everyman objecting that "it can't have mattered very much to Him if he was God. A god can't really suffer like you and me. Besides the parson says we are to try and be like Christ; but that's all nonsense—we can't be God, and it's silly to ask us to try."[9]

Or modern believers might easily adopt Apollinarian views. If Christ was God, they might object, then he knew everything that was going to happen, so that his sufferings were really no more than a kind of playacting. And if he was God, he couldn't actually be tempted in any real sense, could he? What kind of example can an ordinary Christian find in stories like that? As Sayers says, this view makes it all but impossible to speak of "Christian principles" as vaguely practical or achievable. The debates continue until, "Complicated as the theology is, the average man has walked straight into the heart of the Athanasian Creed, and we are bound to follow."[10] For Sayers, a different Christology leads to a different approach to ethics, to Christian behavior, and to the possibility of "following Christ."

Sayers was not of course suggesting any kind of suppression of these ancient/modern heresies, even if such a thing were vaguely conceivable in a twentieth-century context. Rather, she made a profound observation about the development of Christian thought over time. Theophanes might be granted absolute certainty about the truth of doctrine, but he was in a tiny and miraculous minority. Whatever councils achieved, however successfully churches defeated rival interpretations of faith, those alternative ideas were and are structural parts of the Christian faith and are perhaps integral to human religious psychology. Such beliefs always would reappear and would always need to be engaged and confronted. In an ideal world, free of the power struggles of antiquity, that dialogue can itself be a positive thing, a way in which Christian thought develops its own self-understanding. A religion that is not constantly spawning alternatives and heresies has ceased to think and has achieved only the peace of the grave.

Appendix:
The Main Figures in the Story

Acacius: patriarch of Constantinople (471–89). In 482, Acacius persuaded the emperor to issue the Henoticon, a document aimed at winning over both supporters and opponents of the Council of Chalcedon. The ensuing controversy resulted in a decades-long split between the churches of Rome and Alexandria.

Aelia Eudoxia (died 404): empress, wife of the emperor Arcadius, and deadly enemy of John Chrysostom.

Aetius (396–454): Flavius Aetius, Roman general who dominated the Western Roman Empire (c.433–54) and defeated Attila the Hun. He was murdered by the emperor Valentinian III in a court intrigue.

Ambrose (c.340–97): born in Gaul, bishop of Milan from 374, and a dominant voice in the Western church. He established the prestige and independence of the church in the face of Roman imperial authority.

Anastasius (430–518): born in what is now Albania, Roman emperor (491–518), he supported the Monophysite party and was out of communion with the Roman papacy.

Anatolius: representative of Dioscuros of Alexandria in the imperial capital, Constantinople. Following the murder of Flavian of Constantinople in 449, Dioscuros helped place Anatolius in the patriarchate. Despite his early connections, Anatolius turned against the Alexandrian party and allied with the Roman pope. He died violently, probably at the hands of Dioscuros's followers.

Anthimus: patriarch of Constantinople (535–36). The Roman pope forced his deposition, and he spent years in hiding, protected by the empress Theodora.

Aspar (c.400–471): from the barbarian people of the Alans, Aspar was the leading military figure in the Eastern Roman Empire (c.430–70). The emperor Leo eventually murdered him.

Athanasius of Alexandria (293–373): as secretary to Bishop Alexander of Alexandria, he became a leading spokesman for the Trinitarian position at the Council of Nicea (325). He became bishop himself in 328, but his repeated political battles meant that he would spend much of his time in office in exile.

Babai the Great (551–628): leading scholar and reformer of the Church of the East, the "Nestorian" Church. He gave a sound systematic basis to Two Nature Christology.

Barsaumas: leading Syrian monk and an aggressive supporter of One Nature teachings. His monks provided a frightening armed force that supported Dioscuros at the Second Council of Ephesus.

Basiliscus: Roman emperor (475–76), Basiliscus was the brother-in-law of the emperor Leo. After Leo died, Basiliscus organized a coup d'état against the new emperor, Zeno, and ruled briefly. He tried to place the Monophysite party in power throughout the church.

Benjamin of Alexandria (590–661): a Monophysite, whose brother Mennas was martyred by the Byzantine government,

Benjamin served as pope of the Coptic church from 622 until his death in 661.

Candidian: imperial count (senior official) charged to maintain order at the Council of Ephesus in 431. The enemies of Nestorius criticized him as being too favorable to the accused heretic.

Celestine I: Roman pope (422–32), and an important player at the First Council of Ephesus (431).

Chrysaphius: eunuch official who held power at the court of Theodosius II through the 440s; a strong supporter of One Nature theories of Christ and a supporter of Eutyches. He was executed or lynched when the regime changed in 450.

Constans II (630–668): Roman emperor (641–68), Constans tried to settle the continuing debate over the natures of Christ by creating a common position on which they could unite, the idea of the One Will, Monotheletism.

Cyril of Alexandria (378–444): nephew of Theophilus, bishop of Alexandria, Cyril succeeded him as bishop in 412. He was an aggressive critic of Nestorius of Constantinople, whom he confronted and defeated at the First Council of Ephesus (431).

Damasus (305–384): born in Spain, he became Roman pope in 366 and greatly expanded the prestige and self-confidence of the papacy.

Diodore of Tarsus: founder of the great Christian school of Antioch, who died around 390.

Dioscuros of Alexandria: personal secretary to Cyril of Alexandria, who in 444 succeeded Cyril as patriarch. Dioscuros was the leading figure at the Second Council of Ephesus (449), the "Gangster Synod," and he was deposed at the Council of Chalcedon (451). He died in 454.

Domnus of Antioch: nephew of John, patriarch of Antioch, Domnus succeeded him in that office in 441. He tried to defend other bishops who were under attack for being too sympathetic to Two Nature views, so that he himself was deposed at the Second Council of Ephesus (449). He retired to a monastery and made no further claim to his see.

Eudocia (Aelia Eudocia) (401–60): wife of the emperor Theodosius II and a scholar and philosopher in her own right. She long remained a rival at court to her sister-in-law Pulcheria. She was sympathetic to the Monophysites.

Eudoxia (Licinia Eudoxia) (422–62): daughter of Emperor Theodosius II, she married Emperor Valentinian III. She reportedly invited the Vandal king Gaiseric to sack Rome in 455.

Eusebius: as bishop of Dorylaeum, Eusebius attacked christological views that he thought veered too far toward overstressing either One Nature or Two Nature approaches: he thus became a major enemy both of Nestorius in the 430s and of Eutyches in the 440s. The Second Council of Ephesus (449) deposed him, but he took refuge with Pope Leo in Rome. The Council of Chalcedon (451) restored him to favor. Not to be confused with the great church historian of the same name.

Eutyches (380–456): a Constantinople monk who held the senior rank of archimandrite. His Monophysite views provoked a religious struggle within Constantinople in the 440s, which in turn led directly to the Second Council of Ephesus (449).

Flavian: patriarch of Constantinople (446–49), he attempted to discipline the monk Eutyches for his views on Christ's nature, but the controversy led to Flavian himself facing opposition at the Second Council of Ephesus. At that council, a mob maltreated Flavian so badly that he died shortly afterward.

Galla Placidia (392–450): Roman princess who was abducted by Visigoths when Rome fell in 410. She married the Western Roman emperor Constantius III and bore his son Valentinian III. Galla Placidia was the virtual ruler of the Western empire for many years as the regent for her son. She was a strong supporter of papal and Chalcedonian Christianity.

Gregory Nazianzus (c.330–90): great Christian theologian and church father, one of the so-called Cappadocian Fathers and one of the prime enemies of Arians and of various theologies that detracted from the godhood of the Holy Spirit.

Heraclius (575–641): Roman emperor from 610, he saved the empire from destruction by the Persians and was long remembered in Monophysite history as a severe persecutor.

Hilarius: Roman archdeacon who attended the Second Council of Ephesus (449), where he tried unsuccessfully to curb the illegal proceedings. He reigned as pope (461–68).

Ibas: Syrian theologian who served as bishop of Edessa (435–57). At the First Council of Ephesus, he criticized both Nestorius and Cyril of Alexandria. Supporters of Cyril tried to have Ibas's ideas condemned, and he was tried (448–49). The Council of Chalcedon restored him to office.

Irenaeus: imperial count who tried to maintain order at the First Council of Ephesus (431), his attempts at maintaining fairness led to his being denounced as a supporter of Nestorius. Irenaeus later became bishop of Tyre, where he was himself attacked for alleged Nestorianism.

Jacobus Baradaeus (c.500–578): Monophysite monk whom Bishop John of Ephesus ordained as bishop in 541 with authority over the Monophysite churches of the East. Jacobus became the founder and organizer of a whole alternative Eastern church that became known as Jacobite.

John of Antioch: patriarch of Antioch (429–41), John was the leader among the Eastern bishops in the controversies surrounding Nestorius. John's late arrival at the First Council of Ephesus (431) was critical in shaping the events of that gathering. He eventually patched up a reconciliation with his archrival Cyril of Alexandria.

John of Ephesus (507–86): one of the most important figures in the Monophysite church in the East, but the Orthodox emperor Justinian also entrusted him with campaigns against paganism. John was a leading historian of church affairs in his time, particularly from a Monophysite point of view.

John Chrysostom (347–407): born in Antioch and studied under Diodore of Tarsus. In 398, he became archbishop of Constantinople, but a feud with Theophilus of Alexandria and the empress Aelia Eudoxia led to his being deposed and banished. John is famous as one of the greatest Christian preachers.

Justa Grata Honoria: Roman princess, sister of the Western Roman emperor Valentinian III. While confined in a convent for plotting against her brother, she tried to call on the aid of Attila the Hun, which gave the Huns a legal justification for their assaults on the empire.

Justinian (483–565): nephew of the Roman emperor Justin I, whom he succeeded in office in 527. Justinian reconquered large sections of the old Western empire. Although he favored Orthodox and Chalcedonian Christianity, his wife, Theodora, ensured that some Monophysite clergy enjoyed protection. In 553, Justinian called the Second Council of Constantinople as a means of drawing together Chalcedonians and Monophysites.

Juvenal: bishop of Jerusalem (422–58), Juvenal was heavily engaged in most of the ecclesiastical wars of his time, his main motive being to establish the patriarchal authority of his see of Jerusalem.

He supported Dioscuros of Alexandria at the Second Council of Ephesus in 449 and opposed him at Chalcedon in 451.

Leo I (401–74): born in Thrace and ruled as Eastern Roman emperor from 457 to 474.

Marcian (396–457): a prominent Roman soldier who became Eastern Roman emperor in 450 and married the princess Pulcheria. Marcian and Pulcheria called the Council of Chalcedon in 451 and enforced its decisions.

Maximus the Confessor (c.580–662): theologian and mystic who opposed the Roman Empire's policy of insisting that Christ had only One Will: critics called this view the Monothelete heresy. His opposition led to his trial and condemnation. He was tortured and mutilated, and died in exile.

Memnon of Ephesus: bishop of Ephesus at the time of the great council held in that city in 431. Memnon cooperated closely with Cyril of Alexandria against Nestorius.

Nestorius (386–c.451): born in Syria and trained in Antioch, Nestorius became archbishop of Constantinople in 428, but his views attracted much opposition. Following the First Council of Ephesus (431), he was deposed and exiled.

Peter the Fuller: patriarch of Antioch (471–88), Peter was a strong Monophysite, who did much to spread those views in Syria.

Peter the Iberian (411–91): born in Georgia, Peter was a celebrated monk and a leader in the Monophysite cause. He helped organize the Monophysite church in Palestine.

Peter Mongus, the Stammerer: deacon to Timothy Aelurus, patriarch of Alexandria, Peter became patriarch himself in 477 and was a leader in the Monophysite cause until his death in 490.

Proclus: an associate of John Chrysostom, Proclus became bishop of Cyzicus. He was passed over as archbishop of Constantinople, and when Nestorius took the post in 428, Proclus attacked him for his views on the Virgin Mary. Proclus preached influential sermons and homilies on the Virgin and the Incarnation. He was archbishop of Constantinople from 434 to 446.

Proterius: chosen to replace Dioscuros as patriarch of Alexandria after the Council of Chalcedon in 451, he was murdered by an insurgent Alexandrian mob in 457.

Pulcheria (399–453): daughter of the Roman emperor Arcadius and sister of Theodosius II, she was probably the most powerful person within the Eastern Roman Empire for some decades. She was a critical force in shaping church orthodoxy. In 450 she married Marcian, who became emperor, and together they called and supported the Council of Chalcedon.

Severus of Antioch (465-c.540): monk and organizer of Monophysite churches. Severus was bishop of Antioch from 512 to 518 but was deposed when the imperial regime changed. He continued to be the main spiritual force behind the Monophysite movement throughout Egypt and the East.

Shenoute (died 466): abbot of Egypt's great White Monastery, in fact a vast monastic complex. Like the patriarch Cyril, Shenoute held the One Nature teachings of the Coptic church.

Theodora (c.500–548): wife of the emperor Justinian and a supporter of the Monophysite cause in the church and the empire.

Theodore of Mopsuestia (c.350–428): born in Antioch, where he was associated with John Chrysostom and Diodore. In 392, he became bishop of Mopsuestia. Theodore wrote widely and daringly on theological matters, although the mainstream church later condemned some of his ideas as heretical.

Theodoret of Cyrrhus (393–457): born at Antioch and became bishop of Cyrrhus in 423. He became a leading activist in the debates surrounding Nestorius and was a principal adviser to the bishops of Antioch in their conflicts with Alexandria. The second Council of Ephesus (449) condemned and excommunicated him, but he was restored by the Council of Chalcedon (451). Theodoret was also a significant historical source in his own right.

Theodosius I (347–95): born in Spain, emperor of both Eastern and Western Roman Empires from 379 to 395. He called the First Council of Constantinople in 381.

Theodosius II (401–50): Eastern Roman emperor from 408 through 450. He was strongly influenced through much of his reign by his sister Pulcheria. Theodosius was responsible for calling both the First and Second Councils of Ephesus.

Theodosius of Alexandria: patriarch of Alexandria from 535 to 567 and a Monophysite leader. In 536, the Orthodox/Chalcedonian church ceased to recognize his authority, beginning a formal schism in Alexandria that lasted for centuries.

Theophilus of Alexandria: bishop of Alexandria (385–412). He suppressed pagan temples in Alexandria. He engaged in a political feud with John Chrysostom, in which John was deposed from his see of Constantinople.

Timothy Aelurus: patriarch of Alexandria (454–77), although he spent much of that time in exile or in hiding from imperial authorities. He was a Monophysite and a deadly enemy of the Chalcedonian cause.

Timothy Salofakiolos: in 460, the emperor chose Timothy as patriarch of Alexandria in the Chalcedonian cause. The local Monophysites opposed him so strongly that his power seemed shaky, giving him his nickname of "Wobbly Cap." He was deposed in 475 but returned to office from 477 to 481.

Valentinian III (419–55): Western Roman emperor (425–55).

Zeno (425–91): Eastern Roman emperor from 474. He issued the Henoticon in 482, which was an unsuccessful attempt to end debate between One Nature and Two Nature believers.

Notes

INTRODUCTION: WHO DO YOU SAY THAT I AM?

1. Matt. 16:13–15.
2. Frances M. Young, "Monotheism and Christology," in Margaret M. Mitchell and Frances M. Young, eds., *The Cambridge History of Christianity: Origins to Constantine* (New York: Cambridge Univ. Press, 2006), 452–69; Brian E. Daley, "Christ and Christologies," in Susan Ashbrook Harvey and David Hunter, eds., *The Oxford Handbook of Early Christian Studies* (New York: Oxford Univ. Press, 2008), 886–905.
3. "I and the Father are one" is from John 10:29–30. "Anyone who has seen me has seen the Father" is from John 14:8–9.
4. "You are from beneath" is John 8:23. "Before Abraham was" is John 8:58.
5. "The Father is greater than I" is from John 14:28. "No man knows the hour" is from Mark 13:32.
6. John 1:1–14: "The Word was made flesh" is John 1:14.
7. Col. 2:9.
8. John 11:31–36: "Jesus wept" is John 11:35.
9. For the "blood of God" see Ignatius, Ephesians 1.1, in Bart Ehrman, ed. and trans., *The Apostolic Fathers,* (Cambridge, MA: Harvard Univ. Press, 2003), 1:219; Allen Brent, *Ignatius of Antioch* (London: T & T Clark, 2007).
10. Alois Grillmeier, *Christ in Christian Tradition*, vol. 1, *From the Apostolic Age to Chalcedon (451),* rev. ed., trans. John Bowden (Louisville, KY: Westminster John Knox, 1975).
11. Jaroslav Pelikan and Valerie Hotchkiss, eds., *Creeds and Confessions of Faith in the Christian Tradition*, 4 vols. (New Haven: Yale Univ. Press, 2003); Richard Price and Mary Whitby, eds., *Chalcedon in Context* (Liverpool: Liverpool Univ. Press, 2009).
12. Edward Gibbon, *The History of the Decline and Fall of the Roman Empire* (London: Henry G. Bohn, 1854), 5:235.
13. Witold Witakowski, trans., *The Chronicle of Pseudo-Dionysius of Tell-Mahre* (Liverpool: Liverpool Univ. Press, 1996), 35–36.

14. Quoted from R. Payne Smith, ed., *The Third Part of the Ecclesiastical History of John Bishop of Ephesus* (Oxford: Oxford Univ. Press, 1860), 7–8.

CHAPTER ONE: THE HEART OF THE MATTER

1. Richard Price and Michael Gaddis, eds., *The Acts of the Council of Chalcedon* (Liverpool: Liverpool Univ. Press, 2007), 2:156 for "Slaughter him!" For the "Gangster Synod," see William Bright, *The Age of the Fathers* (London: Longmans, Green, 1903), 2:479–94; John Chapman, "Robber Council of Ephesus," *Catholic Encyclopedia* (1909), vol. 5, at http://www.newadvent.org/cathen/05495a.htm.

2. W. H. C. Frend, *The Rise of the Monophysite Movement* (Cambridge: Cambridge Univ. Press, 1972); W. H. C. Frend. *The Rise of Christianity* (Philadelphia: Fortress, 1984).

3. For long-term religious and cultural trends in this era, see Peter Brown, *The Rise of Western Christendom,* rev. ed. (Oxford: Blackwell, 2003). Gerald O'Collins, *Christology* (New York: Oxford Univ. Press, 1995). I have throughout this book used Henry Chadwick, *The Church in Ancient Society* (New York: Oxford Univ. Press, 2001).

4. Thomas R. Lindlof, *Hollywood Under Siege* (Univ. Press of Kentucky, 2008).

5. Averil Cameron, "The Cult of the Virgin in Late Antiquity," in R. N. Swanson, ed., *The Church and Mary* (Woodbridge, UK: Boydell, 2004), 1–21; Miri Rubin, *Mother of God* (New Haven: Yale Univ. Press, 2009).

6. Stephen W. Need, *Truly Divine and Truly Human* (Peabody, MA: Hendrickson 2008).

7. Pauline Allen, "The Definition and Enforcement of Orthodoxy," in Averil Cameron, Bryan Ward-Perkins, and Michael Whitby, eds., *The Cambridge Ancient History: Late Antiquity and Successors A.D. 425–600* (Cambridge: Cambridge Univ. Press, 2000), 811–34; Mark Edwards, "Synods and Councils," in Augustine Casiday and Frederick W. Norris, eds., *The Cambridge History of Christianity: Constantine to c.600* (New York: Cambridge Univ. Press, 2007), 367–85; and Karl-Heinz Uthemann, "History of Christology to the Seventh Century," in the same volume, 460–500.

8. Grillmeier, *Apostolic Age to Chalcedon*, 520–42; Robert Victor Sellers, *The Council of Chalcedon* (London: S.P.C.K., 1953); Price and Gaddis, eds., *Acts of the Council of Chalcedon,* 1:1–75. As late as 1951, the Catholic Church still felt the council important enough to celebrate its 1500th anniversary: Alois Grillmeier, ed., *Das Konzil von Chalkedon*, 3 vols. (Würzburg, Germany: Echter-Verl, 1951).

9. J. N. D. Kelly, *The Athanasian Creed* (New York: Harper and Row, 1964).

10. The quotes are from Leo the Great, "Letters and Sermons," in Philip Schaff and H. Wace, eds. *A Select Library of Nicene and Post-Nicene Fathers of the Christian Church* (New York: Christian Literature Company, 1895), series 2, vol. 12, 39–43; p. 41 for Lazarus; Alois Grillmeier, *Christ in Christian Tradition*, vol. 2, *From the Council of Chalcedon (451) to Gregory the Great (590–604)* (London: Mowbray, 1996); Bernard Green, *The Soteriology of Leo the Great* (New York: Oxford Univ. Press, 2008).

11. "Their blindness leads them" is from Leo the Great, "Letters and Sermons," in Schaff and Wace, *Fathers of the Christian Church*, 58, altered.

12. "If anyone has put his trust in Christ" is quoted from J. Stevenson, *Creeds, Councils and Controversies* (London: S.P.C.K., 1966), 98. "We should not now be able to overcome" is from Leo the Great, "Letters and Sermons," in Schaff and Wace, *Fathers of the Christian Church*, 39. Donald Fairbairn, *Grace and Christology in the Early Church* (New York: Oxford Univ. Press, 2003).

13. Norman Russell, *The Doctrine of Deification in the Greek Patristic Tradition*, rev. ed. (New York: Oxford Univ. Press, 2006).

14. Frend, *Rise of Christianity*.

15. Paul B. Clayton, *The Christology of Theodoret of Cyrus* (New York: Oxford Univ. Press, 2007). In the modern world, I am thinking of the controversy surrounding Jesuit theologian Jon Sobrino, whose christological views encountered such ferocious criticism from the Vatican. See for instance his *Christology at the Crossroads* (Maryknoll, NY: Orbis Books, 1978).

16. Brown, *Rise of Western Christendom,* 113–22. Jaroslav Pelikan, *Jesus through the Centuries* (New Haven: Yale Univ. Press, 1999).

17. Clayton, *Christology of Theodoret of Cyrus*.

18. Elizabeth S. Bolman, ed., *Monastic Visions* (New Haven: Yale Univ. Press, 2002); Robert S. Nelson and Kristen M. Collins, eds., *Holy Image, Hallowed Ground* (Los Angeles: J. Paul Getty Museum, 2006). For Christ as infant, see Evagrius, "History of the Church," in Edward Walford, ed., *A History of the Church* (London: Henry G. Bohn, 1854), 258; Nestorius, *The Bazaar of Heracleides*, ed., G. R. Driver and Leonard Hodgson (Oxford: Clarendon, 1925), 137–38.

19. Euan Cameron, *Interpreting Christian History* (Oxford: Blackwell, 2005).

20. Ramsay MacMullen, *Christianizing the Roman Empire A.D. 100–400* (New Haven: Yale Univ. Press, 1986), 93.

21. Philip Jenkins, *The Lost History of Christianity* (San Francisco: HarperOne, 2008).

22. Eugène Hyvernat, "Coptic Persecutions," *Catholic Encyclopedia* (1911), vol. 11, at http://www.newadvent.org/cathen/11707a.htm. Birger A. Pearson and James E. Goehring, eds., *The Roots of Egyptian Christianity* (Philadelphia: Fortress, 1986); Stephen J. Davis, *The Early Coptic Papacy* (Cairo: American Univ. in Cairo Press, 2005); Roger S. Bagnall, ed., *Egypt in the Byzantine World, 300–700* (Cambridge: Cambridge Univ. Press, 2007); James E. Goehring and Janet A. Timbie, eds., *The World of Early Egyptian Christianity* (Washington, DC: Catholic Univ. of America Press, 2007).

23. Frend, *Rise of the Monophysite Movement*; Brown, *Rise of Western Christendom*.

24. Chris Wickham, *Framing the Early Middle Ages* (New York: Oxford Univ. Press, 2005); Chris Wickham, *The Inheritance of Rome* (London: Allen Lane, 2009); Julia M. H. Smith, *Europe after Rome* (New York: Oxford Univ. Press, 2005).

25. Brown, *Rise of Western Christendom*. Leslie Webster and Michelle Brown, eds., *The Transformation of the Roman World A.D. 400–900* (Berkeley: Univ. of California Press, 1997).

26. Jenkins, *Lost History of Christianity*.

27. Fergus Millar, *A Greek Roman Empire* (Berkeley: Univ. of California Press, 2006); Henry Chadwick, *East and West* (New York: Oxford Univ. Press, 2003).

28. J. M. Wallace-Hadrill, *The Barbarian West, 400–1000* revised ed. (Oxford: Blackwell, 1996). For the prevailing languages of the fifth century, see Millar, *Greek Roman Empire*, 84–129.

29. James Carroll, *Constantine's Sword* (New York: Houghton Mifflin, 2001); Elaine Pagels, *Beyond Belief* (New York: Random House, 2003); Karen King, *What Is Gnosticism?* (Cambridge, MA: Belknap of Harvard Univ. Press, 2003); Bart D. Ehrman, *Lost Christianities* (New York: Oxford Univ. Press, 2003); David L. Dungan, *Constantine's Bible* (Minneapolis: Fortress, 2007). A similar story of fall and decline is told by Rita Nakashima Brock and Rebecca Ann Parker, *Saving Paradise* (Boston: Beacon, 2008), although they place the transition much later.

30. Richard E. Rubenstein, *When Jesus Became God* (New York: Harcourt Brace, 1999).

31. For other rituals of inclusion, see Michael Philip Penn, *Kissing Christians* (Philadelphia: Univ. of Pennsylvania Press, 2005).

32. Ramsay MacMullen, *Voting About God in Early Church Councils* (New Haven: Yale Univ. Press, 2006). Norman P. Tanner, ed., *Decrees of the Ecumenical Councils* (Washington, DC: Georgetown Univ. Press, 1990).

33. Michael Gaddis, *There Is No Crime for Those Who Have Christ* (Berkeley: Univ. of California Press, 2005).

34. MacMullen, *Voting About God*.

35. Millar, *Greek Roman Empire*.

36. Gaddis, *No Crime for Those Who Have Christ*.

37. Guy G. Stroumsa, "Religious Dynamics Between Christians and Jews in Late Antiquity (312–640)," in Casiday and Norris, *Cambridge History of Christianity*, 151–72.

38. H. A. Drake, "The Church, Society and Political Power," in Casiday and Norris, *Cambridge History of Christianity*, 403–28.

39. Gaddis, *No Crime for Those Who Have Christ*. For the world of the monks, see Susan Ashbrook Harvey, *Asceticism and Society in Crisis* (Berkeley: Univ. of California Press, 1990); Daniel Caner, *Wandering, Begging Monks* (Berkeley: Univ. of California Press, 2002); Jennifer L. Hevelone-Harper, *Disciples of the Desert* (Baltimore: Johns Hopkins Univ. Press, 2005).

40. Gustaf Aulén, *Christus Victor* (New York: Macmillan, 1972); Sandra Visser and Thomas Williams, *Anselm* (New York: Oxford Univ. Press, 2009).

41. Alan Cameron, *Circus Factions* (New York: Oxford Univ. Press, 1976).

42. Evagrius, "History of the Church," in Walford, *History of the Church*, 386, altered.

43. Thomas Sizgorich, *Violence and Belief in Late Antiquity* (Philadelphia: Univ. of Pennsylvania Press, 2008); Patrick Cockburn, *Muqtada Al-Sadr* (New York: Scribner, 2008).

CHAPTER TWO: THE WAR OF TWO NATURES

1. Frend, *Rise of Christianity*. For a still very readable discussion of the theological issues and debates, see Edward Gibbon, *Decline and Fall of the Roman Empire*, 5:197–284; Anthony Maas, "Christology," *Catholic Encyclopedia* (1912), vol. 14, at http://www.newadvent.org/cathen/14597a.htm; J. Levison and P. Pope-Levison, "Christology," in William A. Dyrness and Veli-Matti Kärkkäinen, eds., *Global Dictionary of Theology* (Downers Grove, IL: IVP Academic, 2008), 167–86; Giusto Traina, *428 AD* (Princeton: Princeton Univ. Press, 2009).

2. Raymond E. Brown, *An Introduction to New Testament Christology* (New York: Paulist, 1994); Gregory Riley, *One Jesus, Many Christs* (San Francisco: HarperSanFrancisco, 1997); Richard Bauckham, *God Crucified* (Carlisle, UK: Paternoster, 1998); Jaroslav Pelikan, *The Emergence of the Catholic Tradition (100–600)*, vol. 1, *The Christian Tradition* (Chicago: Univ. of Chicago Press, 1971).

3. Ignatius is quoted from his letter to the Ephesians 7, in Bart Ehrman, ed., *Apostolic Fathers*, 2 vols. (Boston: Harvard Univ. Press, 2003), vol. 1, 227; Henry Bettenson, ed. *The Early Christian Fathers* (Oxford: Oxford Univ. Press, 1969); J. N. D. Kelly, *Early Christian Doctrines*, 5th rev. ed. (New York: Harper & Row, 1978); James H. Charlesworth and James R. Mueller, *The New Testament Apocrypha and Pseudepigrapha* (Metuchen, NJ: Scarecrow, 1987); Helmut Koester, *Ancient Christian Gospels* (Philadelphia: Trinity Press International, 1990). For the complex interaction between "heretical" thought and what became orthodoxy, see Mark Edwards, *Catholicity and Heresy in the Early Church* (Farnham, UK: Ashgate, 2009).

4. For the Ebionites, see Eusebius of Caesarea, *The Ecclesiastical History*, 2 vols. ed. and trans. Kirsopp Lake, Loeb Classical Library (London: Heinemann, 1926–32), Book 3, 26–28; Antti Marjanen and Petri Luomanen, eds., *A Companion to Second-Century Christian "Heretics"* (Leiden: Brill, 2005); Matt Jackson-McCabe, ed., *Jewish Christianity Reconsidered* (Minneapolis: Fortress, 2007).

5. Ehrman, *Lost Christianities*; Bart D. Ehrman, *The Orthodox Corruption of Scripture* (New York: Oxford Univ. Press, 1993).

6. The gospel of Peter is quoted from Wilhelm Schneemelcher, ed., *New Testament Apocrypha* rev. ed. (London: SCM, 1963), 1:184. For Cerinthus, see Eusebius, *Ecclesiastical History*, Book 3, 28. "Represented Jesus" is quoted from Irenaeus writing c.180: Alexander Roberts and James Donaldson, eds., *The Apostolic Fathers, Justin Martyr, Irenaeus*, in *Ante-Nicene Fathers* (New York: Scribner, 1926), 1:352; "This Christ passed through Mary" is quoted from Roberts and Donaldson, *Apostolic Fathers, Justin Martyr, Irenaeus*, in *Ante-Nicene Fathers*, 1:325. For the stress on Christ's resurrection as the moment of "declaring," see Rom. 1:3–4.

7. C. C. Martindale, "Epiphany," *Catholic Encyclopedia* (1909), vol. 5, at http://www .newadvent.org/cathen/05504c.htm; Everett Ferguson, *Baptism in the Early Church* (Grand Rapids: Eerdmans, 2009).

8. For Paul of Samosata, see Eusebius, *Ecclesiastical History*, Book 7, 27–30; Paul's views are quoted from Frederick C. Conybeare, "Paul of Samosata," *Encyclopedia Britannica* (New York: Encyclopedia Britannica, 1911), 20:958; Epiphanius, *The Panarion of Epiphanius of Salamis*, 2 vols., trans. Frank Williams (Leiden: Brill, 1987–94), 2:209–18; Virginia Burrus, *"Begotten, Not Made"* (Stanford: Stanford Univ. Press, 2000), 22–25.

9. See 2 John 1:7; Phil. 2:7. "Atheists and infidels" is adapted from Ignatius *Trallians* 10, in Ehrman, *Apostolic Fathers*, 1:264–65. Mani is quoted from Epiphanius, *Panarion of Epiphanius*, 2:227; Tertullian's *De Carne Christi* is from Allan Menzies, ed., *Latin Christianity: Its Founder, Tertullian*, in *Ante-Nicene Fathers* (New York: Scribner, 1926), 3:911–51.

10. Epiphanius, *Panarion of Epiphanius*, 2:121–27; Young, "Monotheism and Christology," in Mitchell and Young, *Cambridge History of Christianity*, 452–69.

11. Henry Bettenson, ed., *The Later Christian Fathers* (Oxford: Oxford Univ. Press, 1969); Trevor Hart, "Creeds, Councils and Doctrinal Development," in Philip F. Esler, ed., *The Early Christian World* (New York: Routledge, 2000), 1:636–59.

12. "There never was" is from John Bowden, "Christology" in John Bowden, ed., *Encyclopedia of Christianity* (New York: Oxford Univ. Press, 2005), 220; Rowan Williams, *Arius*, rev. ed. (Grand Rapids: Eerdmans, 2002); Thomas C. Ferguson, *The Past Is Prologue* (Leiden: Brill, 2005); J. Rebecca Lyman, "Arius and Arians," in Harvey and Hunter, *Oxford Handbook of Early Christian Studies*, 237–57.

13. J. N. D. Kelly, *Early Christian Creeds*, 3rd ed. (New York: Longman, 1981, originally published 1972). For the Council of Nicea, see Timothy D. Barnes, *Constantine and Eusebius* (Cambridge, MA: Harvard Univ. Press, 1981); Timothy D. Barnes, *Athanasius and Constantius* (Cambridge, MA: Harvard Univ. Press, 1993); John Behr, *The Way to Nicaea* (Crestwood, NY: St. Vladimir's Seminary Press, 2001); Mark Edwards, "The First Council of Nicaea," in Mitchell and Young, *Cambridge History of Christianity*, 552–67; Lewis Ayres, *Nicaea and Its Legacy* (New York: Oxford Univ. Press, 2006).

14. Karl-Heinz Uthemann, "History of Christology to the Seventh Century," in Casiday and Norris, *Cambridge History of Christianity*, 460–500.

15. Grillmeier, *Apostolic Age to Chalcedon*.

16. J. Stevenson, ed., *A New Eusebius* (London: S.P.C.K., 1957), 279–80. MacMullen, *Voting About God*, 26–27.

17. Gibbon, *Decline and Fall of the Roman Empire*, 5:207.

18. Apollinarius is quoted from Frend, *Rise of the Monophysite Movement*, 116.

19. "The Word of God has not descended" is from Stevenson, *Creeds, Councils and Controversies*, 96. "There is no distinction" is from Frend, *Rise of the Monophysite Movement*, 115.

20. Schaff is quoted from Philip Schaff, *The Creeds of Christendom* (Grand Rapids: Baker, 1993 printing), 2:64. Damasus is quoted from Theodoret, "Ecclesiastical History," in Schaff and Wace, *Fathers of the Christian Church*, 3:139. For the First Council of Constantinople, see Henry R. Percival, "The Seven Ecumenical Councils of the Undivided Church," in Schaff and Wace, *Fathers of the Christian Church*, 12:161–90. Rubenstein, *When Jesus Became God*, 211–31; Charles Freeman, *A.D. 381* (London: Pimlico, 2008).

21. These anathemas are from Theodoret, "Ecclesiastical History," in Schaff and Wace, *Fathers of the Christian Church*, 139–40.

22. Frend, *Rise of Christianity*, 629–42. Andrew Louth, "Later Theologians of the Greek East," in Esler, *Early Christian World*, 1:580–600; Edward Rochie Hardy, ed., *Christology of the Later Fathers* (Philadelphia: Westminster, 1954).

23. Stevenson, *Creeds, Councils and Controversies*, 115; Frend, *Rise of the Monophysite Movement*; Rubenstein, *When Jesus Became God*, 204–8.

24. Susan Wessel, *Cyril of Alexandria and the Nestorian Controversy* (New York: Oxford Univ. Press, 2004).

25. Lionel R. Wickham, ed., *Cyril of Alexandria: Select Letters* (Oxford: Clarendon, 1983); Norman Russell, *Cyril of Alexandria* (New York: Routledge, 2000); John A. McGuckin, *St Cyril of Alexandria: The Christological Controversy* (Crestwood, NY: St Vladimir's Seminary Press, 2004); Wessel, *Cyril of Alexandria*. For a partisan pro-Cyril account, see B. T. A. Evetts, ed., *History of the Patriarchs of the Coptic Church of Alexandria*, (Paris: Firmin-Didot, 1948–59), 2:403–23.

26. The quotes are from Cyril's Second Letter to Nestorius, in Price and Gaddis, *Acts of the Council of Chalcedon*, 1:175–77. John A. McGuckin, ed., *St. Cyril of Alexandria: On the Unity of Christ* (Crestwood, NY: St. Vladimir's Seminary Press, 1995); Steven A. McKinion, *Words, Imagery, and the Mystery of Christ* (Leiden: Brill, 2000).

27. Cyril's third letter is quoted from Stevenson, *Creeds, Councils and Controversies*, 284.

28. For the forgeries, see Frend, *Rise of the Monophysite Movement*, 121.

29. Brent, *Ignatius of Antioch*; Susan Ashbrook Harvey, "Syria and Mesopotamia," in Mitchell and Young, *Cambridge History of Christianity*, 331–50.

30. Frances M. Young, *From Nicaea to Chalcedon* (Philadelphia: Fortress, 1983); Robert C. Hill, *Reading the Old Testament in Antioch* (Leiden: Brill, 2005); Raffaella Cribiore, *The School of Libanius in Late Antique Antioch* (Princeton: Princeton Univ. Press, 2007); Isabella Sandwell, *Religious Identity in Late Antiquity* (New York: Cambridge Univ. Press, 2007).

31. Frederick G. McLeod, *The Image of God in the Antiochene Tradition* (Washington, DC: Catholic Univ. of America Press, 1999); Robert C. Hill, *Diodore of Tarsus: Commentary on Psalms 1–51* (Leiden: Brill, 2005); Clayton, *Christology of Theodoret*, 53–74.

32. Theresa Urbainczyk, *Theodoret of Cyrrhus* (Ann Arbor: Univ. of Michigan Press, 2002); Frederick G. McLeod, *The Roles of Christ's Humanity in Salvation* (Washington, DC: Catholic Univ. of America Press, 2005); István Pásztori-Kupán, *Theodoret of Cyrus* (New York: Routledge, 2006).

33. Frend, *Rise of Christianity.*

34. Richard Lim, *Public Disputation, Power and Social Order in Late Antiquity* (Berkeley: Univ. of California Press, 1995), 149.

35. MacMullen, *Voting About God*, 28–29. Cyril's Third Letter is found in Percival, "Seven Ecumenical Councils," in Schaff and Wace, *Fathers of the Christian Church*, 9:201–5: this passage is from 204.

36. Edward Pace, "Hypostatic Union," *Catholic Encyclopedia* (1910), vol. 7, at http://www.newadvent.org/cathen/07610b.htm. Stevenson, *Creeds, Councils and Controversies*, 36.

37. Green, *Soteriology of Leo the Great*; Susan Wessel, *Leo the Great and the Spiritual Rebuilding of a Universal Rome* (Leiden: Brill, 2008), 209–57.

38. Cameron, *Circus Factions*; MacMullen, *Voting About God*, 13.

39. Patrick T. R. Gray, *The Defense of Chalcedon in the East (451–553)* (Leiden: Brill, 1979), 18; Cornelia B. Horn, *Asceticism and Christological Controversy in Fifth-Century Palestine* (New York: Oxford Univ. Press, 2006); Hagith Sivan, *Palestine in Late Antiquity* (New York: Oxford Univ. Press, 2008).

CHAPTER THREE: FOUR HORSEMEN: THE CHURCH'S PATRIARCHS

1. Brown, *Rise of Western Christendom*, 93–122; Chadwick, *Church in Ancient Society;* Claudia Rapp, *Holy Bishops in Late Antiquity* (Berkeley: Univ. of California Press, 2005).

2. For Athanasius and Alexander, see Khaled Anatolios, *Athanasius* (New York: Routledge, 2004), 3. David Brakke, "Athanasius," in Esler, *Early Christian World*, 2:1102–27; Davis, *Early Coptic Papacy*. Evetts, *Patriarchs of the Coptic Church of Alexandria*, 2:425–43.

3. Leo the Great, "Letters and Sermons," in Schaff and Wace, *Fathers of the Christian Church*, 21:5–15.

4. "Peter has spoken thus through Leo" is from Price and Gaddis, *Acts of the Council of Chalcedon*, 2:24.

5. "And which is now professed" is from Henry Bettenson, ed., *Documents of the Christian Church* (London: Oxford Univ. Press, 1943), 31.

6. For the state of the African episcopate, see Erika Hermanowicz, *Possidius of Calama* (New York: Oxford Univ. Press, 2008); for the patriarch of the East, see Jenkins, *Lost History of Christianity.*

7. Raymond Van Dam, *The Roman Revolution of Constantine* (New York: Cambridge Univ. Press, 2007). For the First Council of Constantinople, see Percival, "Seven Ecumenical Councils," in Schaff and Wace, *Fathers of the Christian Church*, 12:161–90.

8. J. N. D. Kelly, *Golden Mouth* (Ithaca, NY: Cornell Univ. Press, 1995); Helmut Koester, ed., *Ephesos, Metropolis of Asia* (Valley Forge, PA: Trinity Press International, 1995). For John Chrysostom and Ephesus, see Sozomen, "Ecclesiastical History," in Schaff and Wace, *Fathers of the Christian Church*, 2:403.

9. E. A. J. Honigmann, "Juvenal of Jerusalem," in *Dumbarton Oaks Papers*, no. 5 (Cambridge, MA: Harvard Univ. Press, 1950), 209–79.

10. "Never abided by one opinion" is from Evagrius, "History of the Church," in Walford, *History of the Church*, 356.

11. For the development of the papacy, see Jeffrey Richards, *The Popes and the Papacy in the Early Middle Ages* (New York: Routledge, 1979); Eamon Duffy, *Saints and Sinners* (New Haven: Yale Univ. Press, 1997); Philippe Levillain, ed., *The Papacy: An Encyclopedia* (New York: Routledge, 2002); Wessel, *Leo the Great*; Roger Collins, *Keepers of the Keys of Heaven* (New York: Basic Books, 2009).

12. John R. Curran, *Pagan City and Christian Capital* (New York: Oxford Univ. Press, 1999); Dennis Trout, "Saints, Identity and the City," in Virginia Burrus, ed., *Late Ancient Christianity* (Minneapolis: Fortress, 2005), 164–87; for the emergence of papal and pilgrim Rome, see Éamonn Ó Carragáin and Carol L. Neuman de Vegvar, eds., *Roma Felix* (Burlington, VT: Ashgate, 2007).

13. "We bear the burdens" is from Klaus Schatz, *Papal Primacy* (Collegeville, MN: Liturgical Press, 1996), 30.

14. Leo the Great, "Letters and Sermons," in Schaff and Wace, *Fathers of the Christian Church*, 7. Wessel, *Leo the Great*, 285–321.

15. Smith, *Europe after Rome*; Stephen Mitchell, *A History of the Later Roman Empire, A.D. 284–641* (Oxford: Blackwell, 2007); John F. Drinkwater, *The Alamanni and Rome 213–496* (Oxford: Oxford Univ. Press, 2007); Michael Kulikowski, *Rome's Gothic Wars from the Third Century to Alaric* (New York: Cambridge Univ. Press, 2007); Traina, *428 AD*.

16. Leo the Great, "Letters and Sermons" in Schaff and Wace, *Fathers of the Christian Church*: for "dictatorial" attitudes, 6; for Gaul, 8–12; for Leo and Illyricum, 6. Johann Peter Kirsch, "Pope St. Leo I (the Great)," *Catholic Encyclopedia* (1910), vol. 9, at http://www.newadvent.org/cathen/09154b.htm. Wessel, *Leo the Great*, 53–136; Paul-André Jacob, ed., *La Vie d'Hilaire d'Arles* (Paris: Editions du Cerf, 1995).

17. Alan Cameron and Jacqueline Long, *Barbarians and Politics at the Court of Arcadius* (Berkeley: Univ. of California Press, 1993); Bryan Ward-Perkins, *The Fall of Rome and the End of Civilization* (Oxford: Oxford Univ. Press 2005); Peter Heather, *The Fall of the Roman Empire* (New York: Oxford Univ. Press, 2006). For Rome's shrinking population, see Barry Cunliffe, *Europe Between the Oceans* (New Haven: Yale Univ. Press, 2008), 426.

18. "We have no very clear information" is from Leo the Great, "Letters and Sermons," in Schaff and Wace, *Fathers of the Christian Church*, 83; Millar, *A Greek Roman Empire*, 1–38, 84–129.

19. John Drinkwater and Hugh Elton, eds., *Fifth-Century Gaul* (New York: Cambridge Univ. Press, 1992). For the growing confidence of Western Christianity in this age, see R. A. Markus, *The End of Ancient Christianity* (Cambridge: Cambridge

Univ. Press, 1991); Ivor Davidson, "Later Theologians of the West," in Esler, *Early Christian World*, 1:602–34.

20. Davis, *Early Coptic Papacy*; Roger S. Bagnall, *Egypt in Late Antiquity* (Princeton: Princeton Univ. Press, 1993). See the essays in Bagnall, *Egypt in the Byzantine World, 300–700*, especially Zsolt Kiss, "Alexandria in the Fourth to Seventh Centuries," 187–206.

21. Evetts, *Patriarchs of the Coptic Church of Alexandria*, 1. Walther Bauer, *Orthodoxy and Heresy in Earliest Christianity* (London: SCM, 1972); Pearson and Goehring, *Roots of Egyptian Christianity*; Birger A. Pearson, *Gnosticism and Roman and Coptic Egypt* (New York: T & T Clark, 2004); Birger A. Pearson, "Egypt," in Mitchell and Young, *Cambridge History of Christianity*, 351–65.

22. Colin H. Roberts, *Manuscript, Society, and Belief in Early Christian Egypt* (London: published for the British Academy by Oxford Univ. Press, 1979). C. Wilfred Griggs, *Early Egyptian Christianity* (Leiden: Brill, 1990).

23. Christopher Haas, *Alexandria in Late Antiquity* (Baltimore: Johns Hopkins Univ. Press, 1997). Goehring and Timbie, *World of Early Egyptian Christianity*.

24. Socrates, "Ecclesiastical History," in Schaff and Wace, *Fathers of the Christian Church*, 2:126–27; Sozomen, "Ecclesiastical History," in Schaff and Wace, *Fathers of the Christian Church*, 2:385–86. Norman Russell, *Theophilus of Alexandria* (New York: Routledge, 2007); David Frankfurter "Christianity and Paganism I: Egypt," in Casiday and Norris, *Cambridge History of Christianity*, 173–88.

25. "The Alexandrian public" is from Socrates, "Ecclesiastical History," in Schaff and Wace, *Fathers of the Christian Church*, 159–60. In fact, Alexandria was notorious for faction and confrontational dissidence long before the triumph of Christianity: see Andrew Harker, *Loyalty and Dissidence in Roman Egypt* (New York: Cambridge Univ. Press, 2008). For the lynching, see Stevenson, *Creeds, Councils and Controversies*, 60–61.

26. Frend, *Rise of the Monophysite Movement*, 72; Rebecca Krawiec, *Shenoute and the Women of the White Monastery* (New York: Oxford Univ. Press, 2002); Caroline T. Schroeder, *Monastic Bodies* (Philadelphia: Univ. of Pennsylvania Press, 2007). For Egyptian trends, see Alois Grillmeier, *Christ in Christian Tradition*, vol. 2, *From the Council of Chalcedon (451) to Gregory the Great (590–604)*, part 4, *The Church of Alexandria with Nubia and Ethiopia after 451* (Louisville, KY: Westminster John Knox, 1996), 167–228; David Frankfurter, ed., *Pilgrimage and Holy Space in Late Antique Egypt* (Leiden: Brill, 1998).

27. Patrick Healy, "Parabolani," *Catholic Encyclopedia* (1911), vol. 11, at http://www.newadvent.org/cathen/11467a.htm. Stevenson, *Creeds, Councils and Controversies*, 158–59, 191–92.

28. Socrates, "Ecclesiastical History," in Schaff and Wace, *Fathers of the Christian Church*, 159–61. Evetts, *Patriarchs of the Coptic Church of Alexandria*, 2:430–43.

29. This account is drawn from Socrates, "Ecclesiastical History," in Schaff and Wace, *Fathers of the Christian Church*, 159–61.

30. All quotes are from Socrates, "Ecclesiastical History," in Schaff and Wace, *Fathers of the Christian Church*, 159–60.

31. Socrates, "Ecclesiastical History," in Schaff and Wace, *Fathers of the Christian Church*, 160.

32. All quotes are from Socrates, "Ecclesiastical History," in Schaff and Wace, *Fathers of the Christian Church*, 160; R. H. Charles, ed., *The Chronicle of John, Bishop of Nikiu* (London: Williams & Norgate, 1916), 100–102; Michael A. B. Deakin, *Hypatia of Alexandria* (Amherst, NY: Prometheus, 2007).

33. Harold G. Marcus, *A History of Ethiopia*, rev. ed., (Berkeley: Univ. of California Press, 2002).

34. Frend, *Rise of Christianity*.

35. Vasiliki Limberis, *Divine Heiress* (New York: Routledge, 1994).

36. Brian Croke, "Justinian's Constantinople" in Michael Maas, ed., *The Cambridge Companion to the Age of Justinian* (Cambridge: Cambridge Univ. Press, 2005), 60–86.

37. Socrates, "Ecclesiastical History," in Schaff and Wace, *Fathers of the Christian Church*, 138–39; Sozomen, "Ecclesiastical History," in Schaff and Wace, *Fathers of the Christian Church*, 399–401; Kelly, *Golden Mouth*; Chadwick, *Church in Ancient Society*, 479–98; Jaclyn L. Maxwell, *Christianization and Communication in Late Antiquity* (Cambridge: Cambridge Univ. Press, 2006).

38. Socrates, "Ecclesiastical History," in Schaff and Wace, *Fathers of the Christian Church*, 138–52; Sozomen, "Ecclesiastical History," in Schaff and Wace, *Fathers of the Christian Church*, 402–18; Theodoret, "Ecclesiastical History," in Schaff and Wace, *Fathers of the Christian Church*, 151–56; J. N. D. Kelly, *Jerome: His Life, Writings, and Controversies* (New York: Harper & Row, 1975); Limberis, *Divine Heiress*; Russell, *Theophilus of Alexandria*.

39. J. W. H. G. Liebeschuetz, *Barbarians and Bishops* (Oxford: Clarendon, 1990).

CHAPTER FOUR: QUEENS, GENERALS, AND EMPERORS

1. Averil Cameron. *The Mediteranean World in Late Antiquity, A.D. 395–600* (New York: Routledge, 1993); Chadwick, *Church in Ancient Society*; Webster and Brown, *Transformation of the Roman World A.D. 400–900*.

2. Liebeschuetz, *Barbarians and Bishops*; Averil Cameron, *The Later Roman Empire* (Cambridge, MA: Harvard Univ. Press, 1993).

3. Timothy D. Barnes, *The New Empire of Diocletian and Constantine* (Cambridge, MA: Harvard Univ. Press, 1982); Matthew P. Canepa, *The Two Eyes of the Earth* (Berkeley: Univ. of California Press, 2009).

4. Kate Cooper and Julia Hillner, eds., *Religion, Dynasty and Patronage in Early Christian Rome, 300–900* (New York: Cambridge Univ. Press, 2007); Wessel, *Leo the Great*, 10–16.

5. Cameron and Long, *Barbarians and Politics*; Penny MacGeorge, *Late Roman Warlords* (Oxford: Oxford Univ. Press, 2003).

6. Millar, *Greek Roman Empire*, 39–83; Drinkwater and Elton, *Fifth-Century Gaul.*

7. Christopher Kelly, *Ruling the Later Roman Empire* (Cambridge, MA: Harvard Univ. Press, 2004); Adrian Goldsworthy, *The Fall of the West* (London: Weidenfeld and Nicolson, 2009). Shaun Tougher, *The Eunuch in Byzantine History and Society* (New York: Routledge, 2008).

8. Quoted from C. D. Gordon, ed., *The Age of Attila* (Ann Arbor: Univ. of Michigan Press, 1960), 27–28.

9. Millar, *Greek Roman Empire*, 130–67; Derek Krueger, "Christian Piety and Practice in the Sixth Century," in Maas, *Cambridge Companion to the Age of Justinian*, 291–315.

10. Jaroslav Pelikan, *The Excellent Empire* (San Francisco: Harper & Row, 1987); Ward-Perkins, *Fall of Rome and the End of Civilization*; Heather, *Fall of the Roman Empire*; Goldsworthy, *Fall of the West.*

11. "The exaction of the taxes" is quoted from J. B. Bury, *A History of the Later Roman Empire from Arcadius to Irene* (London: Macmillan, 1889), 219. Salvian is quoted from his *On the Government of God*, ed., by Eva M. Sanford (New York: Columbia Univ. Press, 1930), 109. Goldsworthy, *Fall of the West.*

12. Raymond Van Dam, "Bishops and Society," in Casiday and Norris, *Cambridge History of Christianity*, 343–66; Rapp, *Holy Bishops in Late Antiquity*; Peter Brown, *Authority and the Sacred* (Cambridge: Cambridge Univ. Press, 1997).

13. Susan R. Holman, *The Hungry Are Dying* (New York: Oxford Univ. Press, 2001); Peter Brown, *Poverty and Leadership in the Later Roman Empire* (Hanover, NH: Univ. Press of New England, 2002); Andrew T. Crislip, *From Monastery to Hospital* (Ann Arbor: Univ. of Michigan Press, 2005); Wessel, *Leo the Great*, 179–207.

14. The charges against Ibas are listed in Price and Gaddis, *Acts of the Council of Chalcedon*, 2:285.

15. "Spirit of ambitious rivalry" is from Socrates, "Ecclesiastical History," in Schaff and Wace, *Fathers of the Christian Church*, 169. For "to prevent the disturbances," see Socrates, "Ecclesiastical History," in Schaff and Wace, *Fathers of the Christian Church*, 175.

16. James E. Goehring, *Ascetics, Society, and the Desert* (Harrisburg, PA: Trinity Press International, 1999); Columba Stewart, "Monasticism," in Esler, *Early Christian World*, 1:344–68; Philip Rousseau, "Monasticism," in Cameron, Ward-Perkins, and Whitby, *Cambridge Ancient History*, 14:745–80; David Brakke, *Demons and the Making of the Monk* (Cambridge, MA: Harvard Univ. Press, 2006).

17. Claudia Rapp, "Saints and Holy Men," in Casiday and Norris, *Cambridge History of Christianity*, 548–66; Evagrius, "History of the Church," in Walford, *History of the Church*, 272–75.

18. For "tombless corpses," see Evagrius, "History of the Church," in Walford, *History of the Church*, 284–87. Peter Brown, *Body and Society* (New York: Columbia Univ. Press, 1988); Peter Brown, *Society and the Holy in Late Antiquity* (Berkeley: Univ. of California Press, 1989); Susanna Elm, *Virgins of God* (New York: Oxford

Univ. Press, 1994); Teresa M. Shaw, *The Burden of the Flesh* (Minneapolis: Fortress, 1998); Dale B. Martin and Patricia Cox Miller eds., *The Cultural Turn in Late Ancient Studies* (Durham, NC: Duke Univ. Press, 2005). David G. Hunter, "Sexuality, Marriage and the Family," in Casiday and Norris, *Cambridge History of Christianity*, 585–600; also in the same volume, see Samuel Rubenson "Asceticism And Monasticism," 637–68.

19. The account of Severus is from Witakowski, *Pseudo-Dionysius of Tell-Mahre*, 14–15; Pauline Allen and Robert Hayward, *Severus of Antioch* (New York: Routledge 2004).

20. Peter Brown, *The World of Late Antiquity* (London: Thames and Hudson, 1971).

21. Peter Brown, *Power and Persuasion in Late Antiquity* (Madison: Univ. of Wisconsin Press, 1992).

22. Kenneth Holum, *Theodosian Empresses* (Berkeley: Univ. of California Press, 1982).

23. Stewart Irvin Oost, *Galla Placidia Augusta* (Chicago: Univ. of Chicago Press, 1968).

24. Socrates, "Ecclesiastical History," in Schaff and Wace, *Fathers of the Christian Church*, 164.

25. Christopher Kelly, *Attila the Hun* (Oxford: Bodley Head, 2008).

26. Evagrius, "History of the Church," in Walford, *History of the Church*, 304–5.

27. Sozomen, "Ecclesiastical History," in Schaff and Wace, *Fathers of the Christian Church*, 419–21. Ada B. Teetgen, *The Life and Times of the Empress Pulcheria, A.D. 339–A.D. 452* (London: Swan Sonnenschein, 1907).

28. "She first devoted her virginity" is from Sozomen, "Ecclesiastical History," in Schaff and Wace, *Fathers of the Christian Church*, 419. See also Horn, *Asceticism and Christological Controversy*. For women's piety in Christian antiquity, see Lynda L. Coon, *Sacred Fictions* (Philadelphia: Univ. of Pennsylvania Press, 1997); Krawiec, *Shenoute and the Women of the White Monastery*; Nicola Frances Denzey, *The Bone Gatherers* (Boston: Beacon, 2007).

29. Kate Cooper, "Empress and Theotokos," in Swanson, *Church and Mary*, 39–51; Limberis, *Divine Heiress*.

30. Sozomen, "Ecclesiastical History," in Schaff and Wace, *Fathers of the Christian Church*, 419.

31. Sozomen, "Ecclesiastical History," in Schaff and Wace, *Fathers of the Christian Church*, 419.

32. "He rendered his palace" is from Socrates, "Ecclesiastical History," in Schaff and Wace, *Fathers of the Christian Church*, 164–65. The story of his celibacy is from Charles, *Chronicle of John, Bishop of Nikiu*, 105.

33. For Spain, see Michael Kulikowski, *Late Roman Spain and Its Cities* (Baltimore: Johns Hopkins Univ. Press, 2004). For Christianity in Persia, see Elizabeth Key Fowden, *The Barbarian Plain* (Berkeley: Univ. of California Press, 1999); Joel Thomas Walker, *The Legend of Mar Qardagh* (Berkeley: Univ. of California Press, 2006).

34. Robert Louis Wilken, *John Chrysostom and the Jews* (Berkeley: Univ. of California Press, 1983); Charlotte Elisheva Fonrobert, "Jewish Christians, Judaizers, and Christian anti-Judaism," in Burrus, *Late Ancient Christianity*, 234–54. For the Callinicum case, see Stevenson, *Creeds, Councils and Controversies*, 137–38, 158. For a critique of the new intolerance, see Paula Frederiksen, *Augustine and the Jews* (New York: Doubleday, 2008).

35. Compare Scott Bradbury, *Severus of Minorca* (New York: Oxford Univ. Press, 1996).

36. For anti-Jewish laws, see Jacob Rader Marcus, ed., *The Jew in the Medieval World* (Cincinnati, OH: Hebrew Union College Press, 1999), 5–6. Millar, *Greek Roman Empire*, 84–129. For the mock crucifixion, see Socrates, "Ecclesiastical History," 161; Elliott Horowitz, *Reckless Rites* (Princeton: Princeton Univ. Press, 2006), 215–17; Charles, *Chronicle of John, Bishop of Nikiu,* 102–3. For the Antioch riot, see Witakowski, *Pseudo-Dionysius of Tell-Mahre*, 2–3; Walter de Lange, "Jews in the Age of Justinian," in Maas, *Cambridge Companion to the Age of Justinian*, 510–34.

37. Evagrius, "History of the Church," in Walford, *History of the Church*, 282–83; M. D. Usher, *Homeric Stitchings* (Lanham, MD: Rowman & Littlefield, 1998).

38. Stuart George Hall, "Ecclesiology Forged in the Wake of Persecution," in Mitchell and Young, *Cambridge History of Christianity*, 470–84.

39. Stephen Williams and Gerard Friell, *Theodosius* (New Haven: Yale Univ. Press, 1994); Neil B. McLynn, *Ambrose of Milan* (Berkeley: Univ. of California Press, 1994); Bill Leadbetter, "From Constantine to Theodosius," in Esler, *Early Christian World*, 1:258–92.

40. Freeman, *A.D. 381*; R. P. C. Hanson, *The Search for the Christian Doctrine of God* (Edinburgh: T. & T. Clark, 1988); Ferguson, *Past Is Prologue*. For earlier anti-Manichaean laws, see Stevenson, *Creeds, Councils and Controversies*, 95. For Theodosius and the Apollinarians, see Stevenson, *Creeds, Councils and Controversies*, 95–96.

41. Rubenstein, *When Jesus Became God*, 211–31; Freeman, *A.D. 381*; Chadwick, *Church in Ancient Society, 415–32*.

42. Virginia Burrus, *The Making of a Heretic* (Berkeley: Univ. of California Press, 1995); Stevenson, *Creeds, Councils and Controversies*, 151–55. For the Priscillianists in the fifth century, see Leo the Great, "Letters and Sermons," in Schaff and Wace, *Fathers of the Christian Church*, 12:20–26.

43. For Ambrose, see Theodoret, "Ecclesiastical History," in Schaff and Wace, *Fathers of the Christian Church*, 3:143; Stevenson, *Creeds, Councils and Controversies*, 140–42; McLynn, *Ambrose of Milan*. For the destruction of temples, see Stevenson, *Creeds, Councils and Controversies*, 261; Sozomen, "Ecclesiastical History," in Schaff and Wace, *Fathers of the Christian Church*, 393–94; John Moorhead, *Ambrose* (New York: Longman, 1999); Freeman, *A.D. 381*.

44. J. Rebecca Lyman, "Heresiology," in Casiday and Norris, *Cambridge History of Christianity*, 296–314; W. H. C. Frend, *The Donatist Church* (Oxford: Clarendon, 1985).

45. Socrates, "Ecclesiastical History," in Schaff and Wace, *Fathers of the Christian Church*, 158.

46. Freeman, *A.D. 381*.

47. W. H. C. Frend, "Martyrdom and Political Oppression." in Esler, *Early Christian World*, 2:815–39; Elizabeth A. Castelli, *Martyrdom and Memory* (New York: Columbia Univ. Press, 2004); Virginia Burrus, *Saving Shame* (Philadelphia: Univ. of Pennsylvania Press, 2007).

48. For John of Ephesus, see Witakowski, *Pseudo-Dionysius of Tell-Mahre*, 72. For the survival of paganism, see MacMullen, *Christianizing the Roman Empire A.D. 100–400*, 83; Ramsay MacMullen, *Christianity and Paganism in the Fourth to Eighth Centuries* (New Haven: Yale Univ. Press, 1999). Raymond Van Dam, *Becoming Christian* (Philadelphia: Univ. of Pennsylvania Press, 2003). For the slowness of the mass conversion process, see Ramsay MacMullen, *The Second Church* (Atlanta, GA: Society of Biblical Literature, 2009).

49. "The demon who is the originator" is from Price and Gaddis, *Acts of the Council of Chalcedon*, 2:150, my emphasis. Nestorius is paraphrased from Socrates, "Ecclesiastical History," in Schaff and Wace, *Fathers of the Christian Church*, 169.

CHAPTER FIVE: NOT THE MOTHER OF GOD?

1. Ian Gillman and Hans-Joachim Klimkeit, *Christians in Asia before 1500* (Ann Arbor: Univ. of Michigan Press, 1999); Jenkins, *Lost History of Christianity*.

2. Millar, *Greek Roman Empire*, 157–67; Traina, *428 AD*.

3. E. B. Pusey, preface to E. B. Pusey and P. E. Pusey, eds., *St. Cyril of Alexandria: Five Tomes Against Nestorius* (Oxford: James Parker, 1881), xl–xliv; John Chapman, "Nestorius and Nestorianism," *Catholic Encyclopedia* (1911), vol. 10, at http://www.newadvent.org/cathen/10755a.htm; Friedrich Loofs, *Nestorius and his Place in the History of Christian Doctrine* (Cambridge: Cambridge Univ. Press, 1914).

4. Socrates, "Ecclesiastical History," in Schaff and Wace, *Fathers of the Christian Church*, 169–70; Traina, *428 AD*, 7–9, 34–38.

5. For Proclus, see Socrates, "Ecclesiastical History," in Schaff and Wace, *Fathers of the Christian Church*, 169; D. F. Wright, "From 'God-Bearer' to 'Mother of God' in the Later Fathers," in Swanson, *Church and Mary*, 22–30. For Pulcheria, see Holum, *Theodosian Empresses*.

6. Young, *Nicaea to Chalcedon*; Wessel, *Cyril of Alexandria*.

7. Anastasius is quoted from Socrates, "Ecclesiastical History," in Schaff and Wace, *Fathers of the Christian Church*, 170–71; "Anathema, if any call" is from Pusey and Pusey, preface to *St. Cyril of Alexandria: Five Tomes* (hereafter referred to as Pusey, "Preface"), li; for the withdrawal from communion, lvi; Evagrius, "History of the Church," in Walford, *History of the Church*, 258.

8. "Akin to the putrid sore of Apollinarius" is from Pusey, "Preface," xx, liv–lv.

9. "Has God a Mother?" is from Pusey, "Preface," li.

10. Price, "Marian Piety and the Nestorian Controversy," in Swanson, *Church and Mary*, 31–38; Jaroslav Pelikan, *Mary through the Centuries* (New Haven: Yale Univ. Press, 1996); Luigi Gambero, *Mary and the Fathers of the Church* (San Francisco: Ignatius, 1999); Stephen J. Shoemaker, *The Ancient Traditions of the Virgin Mary's Dormition and Assumption* (New York: Oxford Univ. Press, 2006); Rubin, *Mother of God.*

11. Frend, *Rise of the Monophysite Movement*, 141; Douglas Burton-Christie, *The Word in the Desert* (New York: Oxford Univ. Press, 1993).

12. Evagrius, "History of the Church," in Walford, *History of the Church*, 257–58.

13. For the debate over Christotokos, see Pusey, "Preface," xlix; lv–lvi for Eusebius; xxi.

14. Socrates, "Ecclesiastical History," in Schaff and Wace, *Fathers of the Christian Church*, 170–71.

15. Proclus's sermon is quoted in Maurice Wiles and Mark Santer, eds., *Documents in Early Christian Thought* (New York: Cambridge Univ. Press, 1975), 61–63. For Proclus's other works, see Limberis, *Divine Heiress*; Nicholas Constas, *Proclus of Constantinople and the Cult of the Virgin in Late Antiquity* (Leiden: Brill, 2003).

16. Pusey, "Preface," liii; for Dalmatius, lxxxviii.

17. The accounts of Nestorius's maltreatment of his enemies are from Pusey, "Preface," lii–liv. "Immediately he had us seized" is from Pusey, "Preface," lii; "oppressed, famished" is from Pusey, "Preface," liii.

18. Limberis, *Divine Heiress*, 59.

19. Nestorius, *Bazaar of Heracleides*, 96.

20. Cyril's response to the sermons is from Pusey, "Preface," lxiv; see also lviii. *St. Cyril of Alexandria: Letters,* trans., John I. McEnerney, 2 vols. (Washington, DC: Catholic Univ. of America Press, 1987). For the Alexandrian view of Cyril, see Evetts, *Patriarchs of the Coptic Church of Alexandria*, 2:432–34.

21. Percival, "Seven Ecumenical Councils," in Schaff and Wace, *Fathers of the Christian Church*, 12:197–98.

22. Grillmeier, *Apostolic Age to Chalcedon*, 451–88.

23. Nestorius, *Bazaar of Heracleides*, 100, 349–51, paraphrased.

24. Pusey, "Preface," lviii–lx.

25. Percival, "Seven Ecumenical Councils," in Schaff and Wace, *Fathers of the Christian Church*, 12:197–98.

26. "Full of blasphemies" is quoted from Evetts, *Patriarchs of the Coptic Church of Alexandria*, 2:433–34; Nestorius's letter to Cyril can be found at http://www .monachos.net/library/Nestorius_of_Constantinople,_Second_Epistle_to_ Cyril_of_Alexandria

27. "speaks of the birth and suffering" is from Nestorius's second letter, at http:// www.tertullian.org/fathers/cyril_against_nestorius_00_intro.htm.

28. Nestorius, *Bazaar of Heracleides*, 92.

29. Pusey, "Preface," xxi–xxii.

30. "He who has seen me" is John 14:9; "I and my Father" is John 10:30. Quoted from Cyril's Third Letter, in Percival, "Seven Ecumenical Councils," in Schaff and Wace, *Fathers of the Christian Church*, 201–5. The passage about the ark is from P. E. Pusey, ed., *Cyril of Alexandria: Scholia on the Incarnation of the Only-Begotten* (Oxford: James Parker, 1881), 196.

31. Pusey, *Cyril of Alexandria: Scholia*, 194.

32. Frend, *Rise of the Monophysite Movement*, 125.

33. Price and Gaddis, *Acts of the Council of Chalcedon*, 2:295–96.

34. "Mary, my friends," is from Pusey, "Preface," xxii.

35. "Cyril availed himself" is quoted from Evetts, *Patriarchs of the Coptic Church of Alexandria*, 2:437; "For Arius and his followers," is from Evetts, *Patriarchs of the Coptic Church of Alexandria*, 2:433.

36. Pusey, "Preface," xxi.

37. Pusey, "Preface," lxvi; Wessel, *Leo the Great*, 209–57.

38. Percival, "Seven Ecumenical Councils," in Schaff and Wace, *Fathers of the Christian Church*, 201–5, paraphrased.

39. For a detailed commentary on the anathemas, see Percival, "Seven Ecumenical Councils," in Schaff and Wace, *Fathers of the Christian Church*, 206–18.

40. Millar, *Greek Roman Empire*.

41. Paraphrased from Pusey, "Preface," lxix–lxxi.

42. For John's caution, see Pusey, "Preface," xlvii–xlviii, lxvii; For Celestine's reactions, see Pusey, "Preface," lxix

43. Millar, *Greek Roman Empire*, 235–48; Socrates, "Ecclesiastical History," in Schaff and Wace, *Fathers of the Christian Church*, 172. John Chapman, "Council of Ephesus," *Catholic Encyclopedia* (1909), vol. 5 at http://www.newadvent.org/cathen/05491a.htm.

44. Stefan Karwiese, "The Church of Mary and the Temple of Hadrian Olympios" in Koester, *Ephesos, Metropolis of Asia*, 311–20; Vasiliki Limberis, "The Council of Ephesos" in Koester, *Ephesos, Metropolis of Asia*, 321–40.

45. For recent accounts of the council, see Wessel, *Cyril of Alexandria*, 138–90; McGuckin, *St. Cyril of Alexandria: The Christological Controversy*, 1–107. Leo Donald Davis, *The First Seven Ecumenical Councils* (Wilmington, DE: Glazier, 1983).

46. "The bishops are many" is from Evetts, *Patriarchs of the Coptic Church of Alexandria*, 2:438. Janet A. Timbie, "Reading and Rereading Shenoute's 'I Am Amazed'," in Goehring and Timbie, *World of Early Egyptian Christianity*.

47. Millar, *Greek Roman Empire*, 168–91; Pusey, "Preface," lxxiii; Nestorius, *Bazaar of Heracleides*, 106. For the Egyptian view of Candidian, see Evetts, *Patriarchs of the Coptic Church of Alexandria*, 2:438–39. "A great crowd" is from Socrates, "Ecclesiastical History," in Schaff and Wace, *Fathers of the Christian Church*, 172.

48. Evagrius, "History of the Church," in Walford, *History of the Church*, 259–61; Pusey, "Preface," lxxix; Nestorius, *Bazaar of Heracleides*, 113–16.

49. Nestorius, *Bazaar of Heracleides*, 350.

50. Wessel, *Cyril of Alexandria*.

51. Paraphrased from Nestorius, *Bazaar of Heracleides*, 135. For the proceedings of the council, see Percival, "Seven Ecumenical Councils," in Schaff and Wace, *Fathers of the Christian Church*, 191–242.

52. "Is it not evident" is from Nestorius, *Bazaar of Heracleides*, 133.

53. This account is summarized from Nestorius, *Bazaar of Heracleides*, 135–40.

54. "Nor to receive" is quoted from Percival, " Seven Ecumenical Councils," in Schaff and Wace, *Fathers of the Christian Church*, 237–39; Evagrius, "History of the Church," in Walford, *History of the Church*, 261; Chapman, "Council of Ephesus," *Catholic Encyclopedia*.

55. Pusey, "Preface," lxxx, lxxxi–lxxxiv; Percival, "Seven Ecumenical Councils," in Schaff and Wace, *Fathers of the Christian Church*, 226–29; Evagrius, "History of the Church," in Walford, *History of the Church*, 261. For the unrest in Ephesus, see Nestorius, *Bazaar of Heracleides*, 266–68. For Ibas on the anathemas ("packed with every form of impiety"), see Price and Gaddis, *Acts of the Council of Chalcedon,* 2:296–97: this also contains Ibas's remark about "no one dared to travel." We still have several lengthy letters that Theodoret wrote on these affairs: Theodoret, "Letters," in Schaff and Wace, *Fathers of the Christian Church*, 3:323–42; Clayton, *Christology of Theodoret*, 135–66.

56. Pusey, "Preface," xxix.

57. Chapman, "Council of Ephesus," *Catholic Encyclopedia*.

58. Evetts, *Patriarchs of the Coptic Church of Alexndria*, 2:438–39; Pusey, "Preface," lxxxv.

59. Evetts, *Patriarchs of the Coptic Church of Alexndria*, 2:440; Pusey, "Preface," lxxxvii–lxxxviii.

60. Quoted in Pusey, "Preface," lxxxviii.

61. All quotes are from Nestorius, *Bazaar of Heracleides*, 272–73, paraphrased.

62. All quotes are from Nestorius, *Bazaar of Heracleides*, 273–77.

63. All quotes are from Nestorius, *Bazaar of Heracleides*, 277–78, paraphrased.

64. Price and Gaddis, *Acts of the Council of Chalcedon,* 2:298; Evagrius, "History of the Church," in Walford, *History of the Church*, 262.

65. Price and Gaddis, *Acts of the Council of Chalcedon,* 1:178–83.

66. Evagrius, "History of the Church," in Walford, *History of the Church*, 271–72; Pusey, "Preface," lxxviii–lxxix.

67. Evagrius, "History of the Church," in Walford, *History of the Church*, 257.

68. All quotes are from Evagrius, "History of the Church," in Walford, *History of the Church*, 263–67. The letter is quoted at 266.

69. Paraphrased from Evetts, *Patriarchs of the Coptic Church of Alexandria*, 2:441.

CHAPTER SIX: THE DEATH OF GOD

1. Chadwick, *Church in Ancient Society*, 515–91; Price and Gaddis, *Acts of the Council of Chalcedon,* 3 vols. (Liverpool: Liverpool Univ. Press, 2007).

2. For Eudocia, see Evagrius, "History of the Church," in Walford, *History of the Church*, 284; Socrates, "Ecclesiastical History," in Schaff and Wace, *Fathers of the Christian Church*, 178; Holum, *Theodosian Empresses*. For Pulcheria's exile, see Charles, *Chronicle of John, Bishop of Nikiu* (London: Williams & Norgate, 1916), 106–8.

3. Ward-Perkins, *Fall of Rome and the End of Civilization*; Heather, *Fall of the Roman Empire*.

4. For social collapse as the result of official oppression, see Salvian, *On the Government of God*, 143–46. Wickham, *Framing the Early Middle Ages*; Wickham, *Inheritance of Rome*.

5. A. H. Merrills, ed., *Vandals, Romans and Berbers* (Burlington, VT: Ashgate, 2004).

6. Kelly, *Attila the Hun*; Millar, *Greek Roman Empire*, 39–83.

7. Brian Croke, *Count Marcellinus and His Chronicle* (New York: Oxford Univ. Press, 2001).

8. Priscus, quoted in Brian Croke, "The Context and Date of Priscus," *Classical Philology* 78, no. 4 (1983): 297–308.

9. Nestorius, *Bazaar of Heracleides*, 363, paraphrased.

10. Nestorius, *Bazaar of Heracleides*, 364.

11. Quoted from Nestorius, *Bazaar of Heracleides*, 339; Evagrius, "History of the Church," in Walford, *History of the Church*, 267; John Chapman, "Monophysites and Monophysitism," *Catholic Encyclopedia* (1911), vol. 10, at http://www.newadvent.org/cathen/10489b.htm; John Chapman, "Eutychianism." *Catholic Encyclopedia* (1909), vol. 5, at http://www.newadvent.org/cathen/05633a.htm.

12. Millar, *Greek Roman Empire*.

13. Nestorius, *Bazaar of Heracleides*, 336–41; Evagrius, "History of the Church," in Walford, *History of the Church*, 290.

14. Nestorius, *Bazaar of Heracleides*, 337–38. "all hypocrites ought to be extirpated!" is from Nestorius, *Bazaar of Heracleides*, 339. For Eutyches, see Price and Gaddis, *Acts of the Council of Chalcedon*, 1:23–30.

15. Nestorius, *Bazaar of Heracleides*, 336–37.

16. Nestorius, *Bazaar of Heracleides*, 352.

17. Nestorius, *Bazaar of Heracleides*, 336.

18. Clayton, *Christology of Theodoret*.

19. For Proclus, see Socrates, "Ecclesiastical History," in Schaff and Wace, *Fathers of the Christian Church*, 175–76. For Edessa, see Robert Doran, *Stewards of the Poor* (Collegeville, MN: Liturgical Press, 2006); and for the deep roots of Christianity in this area, see Judah B. Segal, *Edessa 'The Blessed City'* (Oxford: Clarendon, 1970); Steven K. Ross, *Roman Edessa* (London: Routledge, 2001).

20. Davis, *First Seven Ecumenical Councils*, 170–205.

21. "At last, and with difficulty" is from Theodoret, "Letters," in Schaff and Wace, *Fathers of the Christian Church*, 3:346; Grillmeier, *Apostolic Age to Chalcedon*, 488–520.

22. Theodoret, "Dialogues," in Schaff and Wace, *Fathers of the Christian Church*, 3:160–244; "God the Word" is from Theodoret, "Dialogues," in Schaff and Wace, *Fathers of the Christian Church*, 160. Compare Clayton, *Christology of Theodoret of Cyrus*, 215–82.

23. Bright, *Age of the Fathers*, 2:427–30.

24. Leo the Great, "Letters and Sermons," in Schaff and Wace, *Fathers of the Christian Church*, 12:32 (my emphasis).

25. Price and Gaddis, *Acts of the Council of Chalcedon*, 1:24–30.

26. Price and Gaddis, *Acts of the Council of Chalcedon*, 1:224.

27. Leo the Great, "Letters and Sermons," in Schaff and Wace, *Fathers of the Christian Church*, 32–34.

28. "Prelates were openly seized" and "the assaults of hunger" are from Nestorius, *Bazaar of Heracleides*, 341; "Ephesus . . . is appointed" is from Nestorius, *Bazaar of Heracleides*, 345. For Flavian and the emperor, see Nestorius, *Bazaar of Heracleides*, 341–42.

29. Stephen J. Davis, *The Early Coptic Papacy* (Cairo: American Univ. in Cairo Press, 2005).

30. Nestorius, *Bazaar of Heracleides*, 351.

31. Leo the Great, "Letters and Sermons," in Schaff and Wace, *Fathers of the Christian Church*, 32–38.

32. For the Tome, see Leo the Great, "Letters and Sermons," in Schaff and Wace, *Fathers of the Christian Church*, 39–43; Henry Chadwick, *The Early Church* (London: Penguin, 1967), 201n.

33. The Tome is also quoted in Price and Gaddis, *Acts of the Council of Chalcedon*, 2:14–24.

34. Leo the Great, "Letters and Sermons," in Schaff and Wace, *Fathers of the Christian Church*, 39.

35. Leo the Great, "Letters and Sermons," in Schaff and Wace, *Fathers of the Christian Church*, 40.

36. For the Manichaean comparison, see Leo the Great, "Letters and Sermons," in Schaff and Wace, *Fathers of the Christian Church*, 58. For Leo's hard-line toward the Manichaeans, see Leo the Great, "Letters and Sermons," in Schaff and Wace, *Fathers of the Christian Church*, 6–7; "crosses over into the mad view," is from Leo the Great, "Letters and Sermons," in Schaff and Wace, *Fathers of the Christian Church*, 92. Samuel N. C. Lieu, "Christianity and Manichaeism," in Casiday and Norris, *Cambridge History of Christianity*, 279–94.

37. Nestorius, *Bazaar of Heracleides*, 340.

38. Price and Gaddis, *Acts of the Council of Chalcedon*, vol. 1; Evagrius, "History of the Church," in Walford, *History of the Church*, 268–69, 290.

39. Price and Gaddis, *Acts of the Council of Chalcedon*, 1:144; Nestorius, *Bazaar of Heracleides*, 345–49.

40. Price and Gaddis, *Acts of the Council of Chalcedon*, 2:156; "destroyed all Syria" is from the same page.

41. Price and Gaddis, *Acts of the Council of Chalcedon*, vol. 1.

42. Nestorius, *Bazaar of Heracleides*, 354.

43. All quotes are from Price and Gaddis, *Acts of the Council of Chalcedon*, 1:152–53.

44. Price and Gaddis, *Acts of the Council of Chalcedon*, 1:155.

45. Price and Gaddis, *Acts of the Council of Chalcedon*, 1:134, 141.

46. Price and Gaddis, *Acts of the Council of Chalcedon*, 1:153–54.

47. All quotes are from Nestorius, *Bazaar of Heracleides*, 355–57.

48. Price and Gaddis, *Acts of the Council of Chalcedon*, 2:156.

49. Nestorius, *Bazaar of Heracleides*, 361–62.

50. Price and Gaddis, *Acts of the Council of Chalcedon*, 1:344.

51. Theodoret, "Letters," in Schaff and Wace, *Fathers of the Christian Church*, 323–24.

52. Honigmann, "Juvenal of Jerusalem," 209–79.

53. Leo the Great, "Letters and Sermons," in Schaff and Wace, *Fathers of the Christian Church*, 55–57; Theodoret, "Letters," in Schaff and Wace, Fathers of the Christian Church, 312–16, 323–24.

54. Price and Gaddis, *Acts of the Council of Chalcedon*, 2:272–99.

55. Chapman, "Robber Council of Ephesus."

56. See Leo the Great, "Letters and Sermons," in Schaff and Wace, *Fathers of the Christian Church*, 52–58 for Leo's response to the council. "Knowing they would suffer harm" is from Leo the Great, "Letters and Sermons," in Schaff and Wace, *Fathers of the Christian Church*, 53; "The violence of the bishop of Alexandria" is from Leo the Great, "Letters and Sermons," in Schaff and Wace, *Fathers of the Christian Church*, 54.

57. Leo the Great, "Letters and Sermons," in Schaff and Wace, *Fathers of the Christian Church*, 70–71. For Leo and Pulcheria, see also 44, 64–65.

58. Leo the Great, "Letters and Sermons," in Schaff and Wace, *Fathers of the Christian Church*, 71. Wessel, *Leo the Great*, 259–83.

59. Leo the Great, "Letters and Sermons," in Schaff and Wace, *Fathers of the Christian Church*, 52–58.

CHAPTER SEVEN: CHALCEDON

1. Evagrius, "History of the Church, in Walford, *History of the Church*, 287–90; Holum, *Theodosian Empresses*; Millar, *Greek Roman Empire*.

2. Francis Schaefer, "Council of Chalcedon," *Catholic Encyclopedia* (1908), vol. 3, at http://www.newadvent.org/cathen/03555a.htm; Sellers, *Council of Chalcedon*; M. Whitby, "The Church Historians and Chalcedon," in *Greek and Roman Historiography in Late Antiquity*, ed. Gabriele Marasco (Leiden: Brill, 2003).

3. Cameron, *Circus Factions*.

4. Charles, *Chronicle of John, Bishop of Nikiu*, 108.

5. John Robert Martindale, *The Prosopography of the Later Roman Empire* (Cambridge: Cambridge Univ. Press, 1971) 2:295–96.

6. Leo the Great, "Letters and Sermons," in Schaff and Wace, *Fathers of the Christian Church*, 64–71; Evagrius, "History of the Church," in Walford, *History of the Church*, 290–91; Wessel, *Leo the Great*, 259–83.

7. All quotes are from Evagrius, "History of the Church," in Walford, *History of the Church*, 291–93.

8. Price and Gaddis, *Acts of the Council of Chalcedon*, vol. 1; Price and Whitby, *Chalcedon in Context*; Evagrius, "History of the Church," in Walford, *History of the Church*, 290–301, 317–38.

9. Evagrius, "History of the Church," in Walford, *History of the Church*, 294.

10. Evagrius, "History of the Church," in Walford, *History of the Church*, 318. Compare Price and Gaddis, *Acts of the Council of Chalcedon*, 1:131.

11. "The adversary would" is from Leo the Great, "Letters and Sermons," in Schaff and Wace, *Fathers of the Christian Church*, 72.

12. Price and Gaddis, *Acts of the Council of Chalcedon*, 2:55.

13. Price and Gaddis, *Acts of the Council of Chalcedon*, 2:111.

14. Price and Gaddis, *Acts of the Council of Chalcedon*, 1:364.

15. Gray, *Defense of Chalcedon in the East*.

16. Price and Gaddis, *Acts of the Council of Chalcedon*, 1:134–35.

17. Price and Gaddis, *Acts of the Council of Chalcedon*, 2:149–51.

18. Price and Gaddis, *Acts of the Council of Chalcedon*, 2:149–51.

19. Price and Gaddis, *Acts of the Council of Chalcedon*, 2:117–63.

20. Price and Gaddis, *Acts of the Council of Chalcedon*, 2:183–205.

21. Price and Gaddis, *Acts of the Council of Chalcedon*, 2:198–200; Frend, *Rise of the Monophysite Movement*, 3.

22. Price and Gaddis, *Acts of the Council of Chalcedon*, 2:182–99.

23. Price and Gaddis, *Acts of the Council of Chalcedon*, 2:217–33.

24. Percival, "Seven Ecumenical Councils," in Schaff and Wace, *Fathers of the Christian Church*, 263.

25. Percival, "Seven Ecumenical Councils," in Schaff and Wace, *Fathers of the Christian Church*, 264.

26. Percival, "Seven Ecumenical Councils," in Schaff and Wace, *Fathers of the Christian Church*, 264; compare Price and Gaddis, *Acts of the Council of Chalcedon*, 2:203–4.

27. Percival, "Seven Ecumenical Councils," in Schaff and Wace, *Fathers of the Christian Church*, 264; compare Price and Gaddis, *Acts of the Council of Chalcedon*, 2:204; Kelly, *Early Christian Creeds*; John H. Leith, *Creeds of the Churches*, 3rd ed. (Atlanta: John Knox, 1982); Pelikan and Hotchkiss, *Creeds and Confessions of Faith*.

28. Leo the Great, "Letters and Sermons," in Schaff and Wace, *Fathers of the Christian Church*, 72–73.

29. Schaff, *Creeds of Christendom*, 2:62–63.

30. Schaff, *Creeds of Christendom*, 2:62–63.

31. Grillmeier, *Apostolic Age to Chalcedon,* 543–58.

32. Price and Gaddis, *Acts of the Council of Chalcedon,* 2:310–12.

33. Honigmann, "Juvenal of Jerusalem," 209–79.

34. Price and Gaddis, *Acts of the Council of Chalcedon,* 3:75–76; Percival, "Seven Ecumenical Councils," in Schaff and Wace, *Fathers of the Christian Church,* 287–90.

35. Leo the Great, "Letters and Sermons," in Schaff and Wace, *Fathers of the Christian Church,* 74–79; "the See of Alexandria may not lose" is from Leo the Great, "Letters and Sermons," in Schaff and Wace, *Fathers of the Christian Church,* 79.

36. "Let him realize" is from Leo the Great, "Letters and Sermons," in Schaff and Wace, *Fathers of the Christian Church,* 77; Wessel, *Leo the Great,* 323–44.

37. Price and Gaddis, *Acts of the Council of Chalcedon,* 3:111–20.

38. Charles, *Chronicle of John, Bishop of Nikiu,* 108–9.

39. For the response to Chalcedon, see Grillmeier, *Chalcedon from 451 to the Beginning of the Reign of Justinian.*

40. "It was then that the apostasy " is from D. M. Lang, ed., "Biography of the Holy Peter the Iberian," at http://www.angelfire.com/ga/Georgian/iber.html. See also Cornelia B. Horn and Robert R. Phenix Jr., *John Rufus: The Lives of Peter the Iberian, Theodosius of Jerusalem, and the Monk Romanus* (Leiden: Brill, 2008). For Leo and Juvenal, see Leo the Great, "Letters and Sermons," in Schaff and Wace, *Fathers of the Christian Church,* 97–98.

41. Evagrius, "History of the Church," in Walford, *History of the Church,* 302–303. For Leo's response to the Palestinian crisis, see Leo the Great, "Letters and Sermons," in Schaff and Wace, *Fathers of the Christian Church,* 81–82, 91–95. Jan-Eric Steppa, *John Rufus and the World Vision of Anti-Chalcedonian Culture* (Piscataway, NJ: Gorgias, 2002); Cornelia B. Horn, *Asceticism and Christological Controversy In Fifth-Century Palestine* (New York: Oxford Univ. Press, 2006); Brouria Bitton-Ashkelony and Aryeh Kofsky, *The Monastic School of Gaza* (Leiden: Brill, 2006); Sivan, *Palestine in Late Antiquity.*

42. Lang, "Holy Peter the Iberian."

43. Evetts, *Patriarchs of the Coptic Church of Alexandria,* 2:443–44.

44. Evagrius, "History of the Church," in Walford, *History of the Church,* 301.

45. Lang, "Holy Peter the Iberian."

46. Evagrius, "History of the Church," in Walford, *History of the Church,* 301.

47. Evagrius, "History of the Church," in Walford, *History of the Church,* 301–303.

48. Alois Grillmeier, *Christ in Christian Tradition,* vol. 2, *From the Council of Chalcedon (451) to Gregory the Great (590–604),* part 4, *The Church of Alexandria with Nubia and Ethiopia after 451* (Louisville, KY: Westminster John Knox, 1996), 7–35.

49. Lang, "Holy Peter the Iberian."

50. "Some of the Alexandrians" is from Evagrius, "History of the Church," in Walford, *History of the Church,* 306–7, alt.; "they left him lying" is from Lang, "Holy Peter the Iberian."

51. Evagrius, "History of the Church," in Walford, *History of the Church*, 306–7. For Leo's response, see Grillmeier, *Alexandria with Nubia and Ethiopia after 451*, 10–12; Leo the Great, "Letters and Sermons," in Schaff and Wace, *Fathers of the Christian Church*, 101; Wessel, *Leo the Great*, 323–44.

52. "Was eaten of worms" is from Charles, ed., *The Chronicle of John, Bishop of Nikiu*, 111.

53. Thomas Campbell, "St. Anatolius," *Catholic Encyclopedia*, vol. 1.

54. Evagrius, "History of the Church," in Walford, *History of the Church*, 312. Grillmeier, *Alexandria with Nubia and Ethiopia after 451*, 36–52.

55. Christopher Kelly, *Attila the Hun* (Oxford: Bodley Head, 2008).

56. "Was so impressed" is from Prosper of Aquitaine, quoted in J. H. Robinson, ed., *Readings in European History* (Boston: Ginn, 1905), 49–51.

57. Quoted in C. D. Gordon, ed., *The Age of Attila* (Ann Arbor: Univ. of Michigan Press, 1960), 52.

58. Evagrius, "History of the Church," in Walford, *History of the Church*, 304–5.

59. Nestorius, *Bazaar of Heracleides*, 379.

CHAPTER EIGHT: HOW THE CHURCH LOST HALF THE WORLD

1. Pauline Allen and Bronwen Neil, eds., *Maximus the Confessor and his Companions* (New York: Oxford Univ. Press, 2003); Demetrios Bathrellos, *The Byzantine Christ* (New York: Oxford Univ. Press, 2004); Melchisedec Toronen, *Union and Distinction in the Thought of St. Maximus the Confessor* (New York: Oxford Univ. Press, 2007); Andrew J. Ekonomou, *Byzantine Rome and the Greek Popes* (Lanham, MD: Lexington Books, 2007); Cyril Hovorun, *Will, Action and Freedom* (Leiden: Brill, 2008).

2. "Profane wrangling" is quoted from Stevenson, *Creeds, Councils and Controversies*, 341.

3. Frend, *Rise of the Monophysite Movement*; Johannes Oort and Johannes Roldanus, eds., *Chalkedon: Geschichte und Aktualität* (Leuven, Belgium: Peeters, 1997); Chadwick, *Church in Ancient Society*, 592–627; Stephen Mitchell, *A History of the Later Roman Empire, A.D. 284–641* (Oxford: Blackwell, 2007).

4. Gray, *Defense of Chalcedon in the East*.

5. Lamin Sanneh, *Disciples of All Nations* (New York: Oxford Univ. Press, 2007).

6. Gray, *Defense of Chalcedon in the East*.

7. "While others he enlightened" is from Lang, "Holy Peter the Iberian."

8. Grillmeier, *Alexandria with Nubia and Ethiopia after 451*, 37–45, 60–88; Aziz S. Atiya, ed., *The Coptic Encyclopedia*, 8 vols. (New York: Macmillan, 1991).

9. Evetts, *Patriarchs of the Coptic Church of Alexandria*, 2:445–46.

10. Evetts, *Patriarchs of the Coptic Church of Alexandria*, 3:66.

11. Evetts, *Patriarchs of the Coptic Church of Alexandria*, 3:121.

12. Grillmeier, *Alexandria with Nubia and Ethiopia after 451*, 263–389; Sir Laurence Kirwin, *Studies on the History of Late Antique and Christian Nubia* (Burlington, VT: Ashgate Variorum, 2002).

13. Gray, *Defense of Chalcedon in the East.*

14. "Being convicted of the heresy of the two natures" and "was proved to be a Nestorian" are from Smith, *John Bishop of Ephesus,* 78; John Chapman, "Monophysites and Monophysitism," *Catholic Encyclopedia,* vol. 10. Ernst Honigmann, *Évêques et Évêchés Monophysites d'Asie Antérieure au VIe Siècle* (Louvain, Belgium: L. Durbecq, 1951).

15. Procopius, *History of the Wars,* I, xxiv, trans. H. B. Dewing (New York: Macmillan, 1914), 219–30.

16. For the response to Chalcedon, see Grillmeier, *Chalcedon from 451 to the Beginning of the Reign of Justinian.*

17. The Encyclical is quoted from Evagrius, "History of the Church," in Walford, *History of the Church,* 340–48; Charles, *Chronicle of John, Bishop of Nikiu,* 111–14. For Basiliscus and his background, see Priscus quoted in R. C. Blockley, ed., *The Fragmentary Classicizing Historians of the Later Roman Empire* (Liverpool: Cairns, 1983), 2:361–69; and Malchus, quoted in 417–19.

18. "Not designedly but of necessity" is from Evagrius, "History of the Church," in Walford, *History of the Church,* 349.

19. Evagrius, "History of the Church," in Walford, *History of the Church,* 345.

20. For Daniel the Stylite, see Norman H. Baynes, ed., *Three Byzantine Saints* (Oxford: Blackwell, 1948): the quotes are from 52–59. Evagrius, "History of the Church," in Walford, *History of the Church,* 346–48.

21. Yitzhak Hen, *Roman Barbarians* (New York: Palgrave Macmillan, 2007); Peter S. Wells, *Barbarians to Angels* (New York: Norton, 2008). Evagrius, "History of the Church," in Walford, *History of the Church,* 397–98.

22. Quoted from Evagrius, "History of the Church," in Walford, *History of the Church,* 350–54.

23. "Caught by the artful composition" is from Evagrius, "History of the Church," in Walford, *History of the Church,* 367. For the success of the Henoticon, see Gray, *Defense of Chalcedon in the East,* 29–31. For the correspondence of Peter Mongus with Acacius of Constantinople, see Frederick C. Conybeare, "*Anecdota Monophysitarum,*" *American Journal of Theology* 9, no. 4 (1905): 719–40.

24. Cornelius Clifford, "Acacius," in *Catholic Encyclopedia* (1907), vol. 1, at http://www.newadvent.org/cathen/01457d.htm.

25. Gelasius is quoted from J. H. Robinson, ed., *Readings in European History* (Boston: Ginn, 1905), 72–73. Richards, *Popes and the Papacy.*

26. "Promoters of change" is quoted from Evagrius, "History of the Church," in Walford, *History of the Church,* 367. For Anastasius's reign, see Charles, *Chronicle of John, Bishop of Nikiu,* 121–32; A. D. Lee, "The Eastern Empire," in Cameron, Ward-Perkins, and Whitby, *Cambridge Ancient History,* 34–62; Grillmeier, *Christ in Christian Tradition,* vol. 2, *From the Council of Chalcedon (451) to Gregory the Great (590–604),* part 2, *The Church of Constantinople in the Sixth Century* (Louisville, KY: Westminster John Knox, 1995).

27. "Raised up royalty and priesthood" is from Evetts, *Patriarchs of the Coptic Church of Alexandria*, 2:449; "For a long time," is paraphrased from Witakowski, *Pseudo-Dionysius of Tell-Mahre*, 13–14; Grillmeier, *Constantinople in the Sixth Century*; Honigmann, *Évêques et Évêchés Monophysites d'Asie Antérieure au VIe Siècle.*

28. "Another emperor for Rome!" is from Witakowski, *Pseudo-Dionysius of Tell-Mahre*, 9; Evagrius, "History of the Church," in Walford, *History of the Church*, 386; Charles, *Chronicle of John, Bishop of Nikiu*, 126–28.

29. Evagrius, "History of the Church," in Walford, *History of the Church*, 367.

30. Evagrius, "History of the Church," in Walford, *History of the Church*, 367.

31. "Rushed into the city" is from Evagrius, "History of the Church," in Walford, *History of the Church*, 371. Roberta C. Chesnut, *Three Monophysite Christologies* (Oxford: Oxford Univ. Press, 1976); Sebastian Brock, M. A. Mathai Remban, et al., *Philoxenus of Mabbug* (Kottayam, India: St. Ephrem Ecumenical Research Institute, 1989); A. A. Vaschalde, *Three Letters of Philoxenus Bishop of Mabbôgh (485–519)* (Rome: Tip. della R. Accademia dei Lincei, 1902) at http://www.tertullian.org/fathers/philoxenus_three_02_part1.htm.

32. Witakowski, *Pseudo-Dionysius of Tell-Mahre*; Evagrius, "History of the Church," in Walford, *History of the Church*, 390–391; Charles, *Chronicle of John, Bishop of Nikiu*, 135–36.

33. Witakowski, *Pseudo-Dionysius of Tell-Mahre*, 22–24.

34. Witakowski, *Pseudo-Dionysius of Tell-Mahre*, 35–36. See also Harvey, *Asceticism and Society.*

35. Nestorius, *Bazaar of Heracleides*, 3.

36. Stephen Gero, *Bar·sauma of Nisibis and Persian Christianity in the Fifth Century* (Louvain: Peeters, 1981); G. J. Reinink, *Syriac Christianity under Late Sasanian and Early Islamic Rule* (Aldershot, UK: Ashgate, 2005); Adam H. Becker, *Fear of God and the Beginning of Wisdom* (Philadelphia: Univ. of Pennsylvania Press, 2006); Sebastian Brock, *Fire from Heaven* (Farnham, UK: Ashgate, 2006).

37. Adrian Fortescue, *The Lesser Eastern Churches* (London: Catholic Truth Society, 1913); Donald Attwater, *The Christian Churches of the East* 2 vols. (Milwaukee: Bruce Publishing, 1947–1948).

38. Grillmeier, *Constantinople in the Sixth Century.*

39. "one of the great figures" is from Frend, *Rise of the Monophysite Movement*, 201. Evagrius, "History of the Church," in Walford, *History of the Church*, 372–74. For Severus, see Iain R. Torrance, *Christology after Chalcedon* (Norwich, UK: Canterbury, 1988); E. W. Brooks, ed., *A Collection of Letters of Severus of Antioch* 2 vols. (Turnhout, Belgium: Brepols, 1985–2003); Allen and Hayward, *Severus of Antioch*; Youhanna Nessim Youssef, ed., *The Arabic Life of Severus of Antioch Attributed to Athanasius of Antioch* (Turnhout, Belgium: Brepols, 2004). For Gaza, see Brouria Bitton-Ashkelony and Aryeh Kofsky, eds., *Christian Gaza in Late Antiquity* (Leiden: Brill, 2004).

40. Frend, *Rise of the Monophysite Movement,* 62. For the Chalcedonian counterattack on Severus, see Patrick T. R. Gray, ed., *Leontius of Jerusalem* (New York: Oxford Univ. Press, 2006).

41. Evagrius, "History of the Church," in Walford, *History of the Church,* 389. For Justin and Severus, see Charles, *Chronicle of John, Bishop of Nikiu,* 133–34. Lucas van Rompay "Society and Community in the Christian East," in Maas, *Cambridge Companion to the Age of Justinian,* 239–66.

42. Frend, *Rise of the Monophysite Movement,* 72–74.

43. "From that time forward" is from Evagrius, "History of the Church," in Walford, *History of the Church,* 395. Averil Cameron, "Justin I and Justinian," in Cameron, Ward-Perkins, and Whitby, *Cambridge Ancient History,* 63–84; T. R. Gray "The Legacy of Chalcedon," in Maas, *Cambridge Companion to the Age of Justinian,* 215–38. For the disastrous effects of Justinian's policies, see James J. O'Donnell, *The Ruin of the Roman Empire* (London: Ecco, 2008).

44. For the growing sense of crisis in the 530s, see Gray, *Leontius of Jerusalem.* Grillmeier, *Alexandria with Nubia and Ethiopia after 451,* 53–59.

45. Evagrius, "History of the Church," in Walford, *History of the Church,* 394.

46. Gray, "Legacy of Chalcedon."

47. Claire Sotinel, "Emperors and Popes in the Sixth Century," in Maas, *Cambridge Companion to the Age of Justinian,* 267–90.

48. Richard Price, ed., *The Acts of the Council of Constantinople of 553,* 2 vols. (Liverpool: Liverpool Univ. Press, 2009). Evagrius, "History of the Church," in Walford, *History of the Church,* 419–23. Percival, "Seven Ecumenical Councils," in Schaff and Wace, *Fathers of the Christian Church,* 297–324. For Justinian's last years, see Charles, *Chronicle of John, Bishop of Nikiu,* 148–150.

49. Frend, *Rise of the Monophysite Movement.*

50. Evagrius, "History of the Church," in Walford, *History of the Church,* 409–12; Witakowski, *Pseudo-Dionysius of Tell-Mahre,* 87. Peregrine Hordern, "Mediterranean Plague in the Age of Justinian," in Maas, *Cambridge Companion to the Age of Justinian,* 134–60; William Rosen, *Justinian's Flea* (New York: Viking, 2007); Lester K. Little, ed., *Plague and the End of Antiquity* (Cambridge: Cambridge Univ. Press, 2007).

51. Harvey, *Asceticism and Society.* Honigmann, *Évêques et Évêchés Monophysites d'Asie Antérieure au VIe Siècle,* 168–77.

52. Jean-Baptiste Chabot, "Syriac Language and Literature," in *Catholic Encyclopedia* (1912), vol. 14, http://www.newadvent.org/cathen/14408a.htm; Samuel H. Moffett, *A History of Christianity in Asia,* 2nd rev. ed. (Maryknoll, NY: Orbis, 1998); Ignatius Aphram I. Barsoum, *The Scattered Pearls,* rev. ed. (Piscataway, NJ: Gorgias, 2003); Grillmeier, *Alexandria with Nubia and Ethiopia after 451,* 60–88.

53. Nina G. Garsoïan, *Church and Culture in Early Medieval Armenia* (Brookfield, VT: Ashgate, 1999); Nina G. Garsoïan, Thomas F. Mathews, and Robert W. Thomson,

eds., *East of Byzantium* (Washington, DC: Dumbarton Oaks, Center for Byzantine Studies, Trustees for Harvard University, 1982).

54. Evagrius, "History of the Church," in Walford, *History of the Church*, 426–30; and 436 for Justin's insanity.

55. Smith, *John Bishop of Ephesus*, 4–5.

56. Smith, *John Bishop of Ephesus*, 18–19.

57. Smith, *John Bishop of Ephesus*, 19–20.

58. Smith, *John Bishop of Ephesus*, 72–73.

59. Geoffrey Greatrex, "Byzantium and the East in the Sixth Century," in Maas, *Cambridge Companion to the Age of Justinian*, 477–509; Peter M. Edwell, *Between Rome and Persia* (London: Routledge, 2008); Zeev Rubin, "Persia and the Sasanian Monarchy," in Jonathan Shepard, ed., *The Cambridge History of the Byzantine Empire c.500-1492* (New York: Cambridge Univ. Press, 2009), 130–55; also R. W. Thompson, "Armenia," in Shepard, *Cambridge History*, 156–72.

60. Michael Whitby, *The Emperor Maurice and His Historian* (New York: Oxford Univ. Press, 1988). Evagrius, "History of the Church," in Walford, *History of the Church*, 433–44.

61. Greatrex, "Byzantium and the East," in Maas, *Cambridge Companion to the Age of Justinian*.

62. Frederick C. Conybeare, "Antiochus Strategos: The Capture of Jerusalem by the Persians in 614 A.D.," *English Historical Review* 25 (1910): 502–17, at 507.

63. Evetts, *Patriarchs of the Coptic Church of Alexandria*, 2:484–89; David M. Olster, *Roman Defeat, Christian Response, and the Literary Construction of the Jew* (Philadelphia: Univ. of Pennsylvania Press, 1994).

64. John F. Haldon, *Byzantium in the Seventh Century* (Cambridge: Cambridge Univ. Press, 1990); Webster and Brown, *Transformation of the Roman World*; Geoffrey Regan, *First Crusader* (New York: Palgrave Macmillan, 2001); Walter E. Kaegi, *Heraclius: Emperor of Byzantium* (Cambridge: Cambridge Univ. Press, 2003).

65. Peter Sarris, "The Eastern Empire from Constantine to Heraclius," in Cyril Mango, ed., *The Oxford History of Byzantium* (Oxford: Oxford Univ. Press, 2002), 19–59; Judith Herrin, *Byzantium* (Princeton: Princeton Univ. Press, 2008).

66. Andrew Louth, "The Emergence of Byzantine Orthodoxy," in Noble and Smith, *Cambridge History of Christianity*, vol. 3, *Early Medieval Christianities, c.600–c.1100*, 46–64; See the section on "The Church" in Elizabeth Jeffreys, John Haldon, and Robin Cormack, eds., *The Oxford Handbook of Byzantine Studies* (New York: Oxford Univ. Press, 2009), 571–630.

67. "A countless number" is from Evetts, *Patriarchs of the Coptic Church of Alexandria*, 2:491.

68. Cyril Hovorun, *Will, Action and Freedom* (Leiden: Brill, 2008); Peter Llewellyn, *Rome in the Dark Ages* (New York: Praeger, 1971).

69. Evetts, *Patriarchs of the Coptic Church of Alexandria*, 2:491–92.

70. Evetts, *Patriarchs of the Coptic Church of Alexandria*, 2:491–92.

71. Percival, "Seven Ecumenical Councils," in Schaff and Wace, *Fathers of the Christian Church*, 325–54.

72. Fred Donner, "The Background to Islam," in Maas, *Cambridge Companion to the Age of Justinian*, 510–34; Walter E. Kaegi, *Byzantium and the Early Islamic Conquests* (Cambridge: Cambridge Univ. Press, 1992).

73. Jenkins, *Lost History of Christianity*.

74. Jenkins, *Lost History of Christianity*. Quran 4:157–58.

75. Evetts, *Patriarchs of the Coptic Church of Alexandria*, 2:492–98; Charles, *Chronicle of John, Bishop of Nikiu*, 178–201.

76. "The Lord abandoned" is from Evetts, *Patriarchs of the Coptic Church of Alexandria*, 2:492–93; "Heraclius the emperor of the Chalcedonians" is from Charles, *Chronicle of John, Bishop of Nikiu*, 198.

77. The account of "John the Chalcedonian" is from Charles, *Chronicle of John, Bishop of Nikiu*, 201; also, "accepted the detestable doctrine." For Benjamin, see Evetts, *Patriarchs of the Coptic Church of Alexandria*, 2:487–518.

78. Reinink, *Syriac Christianity*.

79. Sidney H. Griffith, "Christians under Muslim rule," in Noble and Smith, *Cambridge History of Christianity*, vol. 3, *Early Medieval Christianities, c.600–c.1100*, 197–212; William Dalrymple, *From the Holy Mountain* (New York: Henry Holt, 1997).

CHAPTER NINE: WHAT WAS SAVED

1. John Moschus, *De Vitis Patrum*, chapter 26, at http://www.vitae-patrum.org.uk/page142.html.

2. John Hayward, ed., *John Donne: A Selection of His Poetry* (London: Penguin, 1950), 174–75.

3. Thomas N. Finger, *A Contemporary Anabaptist Theology* (Downers Grove, IL: InterVarsity, 2004), 365–420.

4. C. Stephen Evans, ed., *Exploring Kenotic Christology* (New York: Oxford Univ. Press, 2006).

5. Quoted from Ronald Goetz, "The Suffering God," *Christian Century*, April 16, 1986, 385; John Bowden, "Christology," in John Bowden, ed., *Encyclopedia of Christianity* (New York: Oxford Univ. Press, 2005). Gerald O'Collins, *Christology* (New York: Oxford Univ. Press, 1995).

6. Ben Quash and Michael Ward, eds., *Heresies and How to Avoid Them* (Peabody, MA: Hendrickson, 2007).

7. Dorothy Sayers, *Creed or Chaos* (London: Methuen, 1947), 25–46.

8. Sayers, *Creed or Chaos*, 33.

9. Sayers, *Creed or Chaos,* 33–34.

10. Sayers, *Creed or Chaos,* 35.

Index